Brazilian Upstream Oil and Gas

A Practical Guide to the Law and Regulation

Consulting Editor **Eduardo Pereira**

Consulting editor
Eduardo Pereira

Publisher
Sian O'Neill

Editor
Carolyn Boyle

Marketing manager
Alan Mowat

Production
Natalie Clarke

Publishing directors
Guy Davis, Tony Harriss, Mark Lamb

Brazilian Upstream Oil and Gas: A Practical Guide to the Law and Regulation
is published by
Globe Law and Business
Globe Business Publishing Ltd
New Hibernia House
Winchester Walk
London SE1 9AG
United Kingdom
Tel +44 20 7234 0606
Fax +44 20 7234 0808
Web www.globelawandbusiness.com

Printed and bound by CPI Group (UK) Ltd, Croydon, CR0 4YY

ISBN 978-1-905783-70-0

Table of contents

Introduction

Eduardo Pereira
Petra Energia

The petroleum industry in Brazil began operations in the early 1800s. Several individuals became involved in upstream activities throughout the 19th century and the early 20th century. However, little information about this period is available, mostly because there was no successful exploration until 1939. In 1941 the first commercial discovery was found and oil production began.

A couple of years later the Brazilian government faced intense public pressure to nationalise its oil reserves, fuelled by a campaign called "The oil is ours". After several years of debate, President Getulio Vargas proposed to Congress a new law to nationalise Brazilian oil and gas reserves. In 1953 Petrobras was established, with the exclusive right to explore for, develop and produce oil and gas. In other words, Petrobras received a 'grant' equivalent to the whole territory of Brazil – the fifth largest country in the world.

Over 50 years later, the state monopoly ended with the implementation of a constitutional amendment allowing private parties to participate in the upstream sector. However, it took another two years before the Petroleum Law was implemented and a licence regime was introduced.

At that time, Brazil was not seen as a candidate for upstream investment. The previous monopoly meant that only Petrobras knew Brazil's true situation, except for a few companies that had signed risk service agreements with Petrobras in the 1970s and 1980s. As a consequence, the first bid rounds in the late 1990s and in early 2000s were dominated by Petrobras and a few major companies. In the following bid rounds, independents and more foreign companies saw the opportunity to invest in Brazil. Some companies managed to hold large onshore acreage following strategic analysis of the history of Brazil and its neighbours.

Up until 2005, the Brazilian licence regime worked reasonably well. Several international companies and local companies were engaged in upstream activities. However, in 2005 Petrobras announced huge discoveries off the coast of Rio de Janeiro and Sao Paulo (the Campos and Santos basins). The oil was located below the salt layer (ie, pre-salt), around 7,000 metres below sea level; it emerged that under that salt layer could be trapped over 120 billion barrels of oil. Such discoveries could open a vast new market, as Brazil – for the first time in its history – could become a significant oil exporter.

The discovery aroused intense public and government interest. No pre-salt areas have as yet been awarded to private parties, as the government decided to analyse the petroleum regime as a whole. After several years of studies and debates, the government decide to change the petroleum regime to a model based on production sharing agreements. This was a radical change from the concession regime which had operated successfully for the past 10 years. However, the petroleum industry is quite familiar with the production sharing model, as this is the favoured structure in most African and many Asian counties. The most significant change in the Brazilian regime was the obligation to nominate Petrobras as the sole operator for any blocks operating under this regime.

The new petroleum regime did not replace the old regime in its entirety. Rather, the new regime modified a few terms of the existing petroleum law and both regimes now co-exist. In other words, Brazil implemented, for the first time in its history, a hybrid regime: at the same time, the law recognises the validity of both concession agreements and production sharing agreements. However, these regimes do not conflict with one other. The production sharing regime applies only for the pre-salt areas, as defined and delimited in the Production Sharing Agreement Law, and strategic areas which may be determined in the future. Everything else remains under the licence regime.

Several investors were confused by the new structure approved by Congress in 2010. Few English-language publications provide clear guidance on how the new petroleum regime works and how new players can get involved. Thus, an understanding of Brazil's upstream legal regime is crucial for international investors, as well as for foreign lawyers who may be asked to advise on upstream operations in Brazil.

This book does not analyse the history of the petroleum industry in Brazil. It is not the objective of this book to explain what was happening prior to the end of the state monopoly or why the Brazilian government decided to change its legal regime. Instead, it focuses on the current petroleum regime in Brazil in order to provide clear and general guidance for international players interested in understanding the main issues in the Brazilian upstream sector.

The first chapter deals with Brazilian general law. It is important for international investors to understand the types of legal structure that will affect its investment. For example, Brazil has federal laws, just like the United States or Australia. However, the Brazilian petroleum legal system is more similar to the Indian regime, as the petroleum law is a federal law and applies to both onshore and offshore areas. In contrast, federal law in the United States and Australia has far more limitations, and the regional provinces have far more discretion to regulate the upstream sector.

The second chapter analyses the most relevant regulatory bodies in the petroleum industry: the Ministry of Energy and the National Petroleum Agency. It is important to understand how they cooperate and how they regulate the licence and PSA regime.

The third chapter analyses the relevant players in the upstream sector and how they interact. This is a highly relevant chapter, as most foreign companies are confused as to whom they need to get involved with in order to operate in the Brazilian upstream sector, after the creation of a full national oil company and a production sharing regime.

The fourth chapter explains the current licence regime, while the fifth chapter explains the new petroleum regime and how concession agreements will co-exist alongside production sharing contracts.

The sixth chapter explores the key issues involving joint ventures in the upstream sector. It is important to understand how the government could interfere in M&A activities and the alternatives available in the upstream sector in Brazil.

The seventh chapter deals with a critical factor for the success of most upstream projects: access to infrastructure and related matters. The ongoing conflict between Sudan and South Sudan is a good example of how relevant access to infrastructure can be. Chapter eight outlines environmental concerns, which are likewise crucial the success of any project.

The ninth chapter deals with corporate tax applicable in the upstream sector. Without a sufficient understanding of these figures, it is difficult to make a decision on any major investment.

The tenth chapter explores a topical question for the petroleum industry. At some point, the installations used in exploration and production activities will no longer be needed and must be removed. It is therefore important to understand the current regime in Brazil, in order to evaluate whether a good system is in place or rather whether the Brazilian industry should learn from international experience how to avoid painful measures to avoid decommissioning obligations at the end of the project's life.

The eleventh and twelfth chapters analyse the key elements of upstream finance in Brazil. The former is tailored for international investors, while the latter is tailored for both international and Brazilian players, as RBL could play a major rule in the future of Brazilian hydrocarbon activities.

Finally, the last chapter deals with a highly relevant topic for any investor: dispute resolution. If something goes wrong, it is important to understand what can be done.

Industry collaboration is another key feature of this book. The chapters are written by highly respected Brazilian professionals, including experts from Campos Mello, Machado Meyer, Pinheiro Neto and Viera Rezende, as well as international experts from Ernst & Young and Merrill Lynch. This approach was the best solution to gather the opinions of leading experts from across the industry in a single publication. Their insights serve as reliable guidance for international investors and the lawyers assisting them, particularly for those who are not yet familiar with the country's legal system.

Although this book is tailored for international players, it may also benefit the Brazilian sector, as some relevant experts in the international arena share best practices from other regions which could assist in the future development of the petroleum industry in Brazil.

In conclusion, this book should provide guidance for parties who are interested in investing in Brazil, or who are at least interested in understanding the peculiarities and complexities of its petroleum regime.

Eduardo Pereira has been active in the oil and gas industry for over five years, and is an expert on joint operating agreements. His experience in this area – both academic and practical – is extensive. Dr Pereira is corporate director of Petra Energia and chief legal officer and vice president of Petra BV. He has played a key role in assisting Petra Energia in becoming Brazil's leading onshore oil and gas company. He concluded his doctoral thesis on oil and gas joint ventures at the University of Aberdeen. Currently he is also a research fellow at the Oxford Institute for Energy Studies.

The general principles of Brazilian law

Marcelo Viveiros de Moura
Décio Pio Borges de Castro
Pinheiro Neto Advogados

1. General overview of civil law

The main feature of the civil law system is the codification of laws. This is opposed to common law systems, which give greater importance to case law and preceding court decisions. Brazilian law is based upon a system of civil law; law therefore principally derives from legislation. However, whenever legislation is silent on a matter, the Brazilian courts can turn to indirect sources, such as legal doctrine and case law, as well as custom, analogy and the general principles of law and equity.

Interpreting the legislation involves analysing the applicable statutes, laws and regulations, with a view to determining their exact meaning and scope. The criteria used for such an analysis may be classified as literal, historical and systematic.

The codes and statutes on which the Brazilian civil law system is based may be amended, complemented or superseded by further statutes enacted in compliance with the legislative procedure established by the Federal Constitution of Brazil enacted on October 5 1988. In general, the Brazilian fields of civil and commercial law have enjoyed considerable stability.

2. The law in Brazil

2.1 The Federal Republic of Brazil

Brazil is a federal republic with a codified legal system. It is politically stable and organised under a democratic system in which the government is granted broad powers. Brazil's Constitution establishes a presidential system with three separate branches: executive, legislative and judicial.

The president is elected by direct vote for a term of four years; re-election is permissible. He or she has a broad range of powers, including the right to appoint ministers of state and key executives to selected administrative, political and higher court posts.

The legislative arm of the government comprises Congress (the Senate and the House of Representatives), the members of which are elected on a proportional representation basis weighted in favour of the less populated states. The judicial branch comprises the Federal Supreme Court, the Superior Court of Justice and various lower federal and state courts. These are described further below.

Brazil is divided administratively into 26 states and the federal district, Brasília. Each state is in turn divided into several municipalities. The authority, jurisdiction and autonomy of the states, municipalities and the federal district are determined by the Constitution.

Officials at every level are elected for four-year terms, with the possibility of re-election. At the state level, the executive branch comprises governors, the legislative branch comprises state representatives, and at the municipal level, the executive branch comprises mayors. City councillors are also elected for a four-year term of office.

Although the Constitution establishes a certain hierarchy between the federal government, the states and the municipalities, including the federal district, none of them – even the federal government – is allowed to interfere in matters relating to the prescriptive or enforcing powers of another public entity, except in certain specific situations. These are described in the Constitution.

2.2 The Brazilian legal system: an overview

The Constitution is the cornerstone of the Brazilian legal system and performs several functions, such as:

- providing for the fundamental rights and guarantees of Brazilian citizens;
- governing the political and administrative organisation of the republic as a whole;
- defining the roles and powers of the executive, legislative and judicial branches;
- providing for extensive regulation of the tax system; and
- providing the basis of the socio-economic and financial policies to be followed by the government.

As the supreme law of Brazil, the Constitution has precedence over all other statutes, laws, rules and regulations. In order to be valid and legally effective, these must not violate or conflict with the principles, guidelines and provisions of the Constitution.

Each state has its own constitution. The federal district and municipalities have their own fundamental laws, which are normally referred to as 'organic laws'. Again, each of these must be aligned with the Constitution.

The following list shows the legal hierarchy that exists in Brazil:

- the Constitution and its amendments;
- ordinary laws, supplementary laws, international treaties, delegated laws and provisional measures; and
- decrees and resolutions.

According to the majority doctrine and the prevailing understanding of the Supreme Court, international treaties, whenever incorporated into the Brazilian legal system by means of the appropriate legal procedure, have the same status as ordinary law. Supplementary laws and ordinary laws are the main category of laws; they are created by the National Congress and sanctioned by the chief of the executive branch.

Certain matters regarding the structure of the state and its services must be regulated by supplementary law in line with the Constitution. Consequently, these laws require a larger quorum for their approval or rejection in Congress.

Supplementary laws are not superior to ordinary laws. The difference between them is simply that the scope of the former is limited by the Constitution.

According to the Constitution, Congress will not always participate fully in the drafting of laws. Laws can also arise from an act of delegation from the legislative to the executive. Once issued, these delegated laws are scrutinised by Congress to ensure that they agree with the specified mandate.

The enactment of provisional measures is largely done by the president in matters of urgency. These measures have the same status as ordinary laws. A provisional measure becomes effective as ordinary law as soon as it is published in the official press. Nevertheless, it must be approved or rejected by Congress within 60 days, renewable for another 60-day term; otherwise, it will automatically lose its legal effectiveness.

Apart from provisional measures, the president may propose bills to be examined and then approved or rejected by Congress. The president may also veto bills of law approved by Congress; however, these may in turn be overruled by Congress through special majority vote.

The executive is also empowered to issue decrees and regulations to facilitate effective compliance with ordinary laws and similar statutes. However, these cannot restrict rights or create obligations beyond the original statutes.

The Constitution also provides for two other varieties of law: legislative decrees and resolutions. Legislative decrees are necessary for the approval of international treaties by Congress. Senate resolutions, on the other hand, are required for certain international financial transactions entered into by the government. Since these two types of law have their particular scope set out in the Constitution, they entail no conflicts of hierarchy.

The Constitution governs the interaction between the federal, state, municipal and district governments, and stipulates the distribution of legislative, administrative and tax collection powers between them. The distribution of legislative powers, for example, is based on the principle of the predominance of interests, according to which federal legislative powers relate to matters of general interest, state legislative powers relate to matters of predominantly regional interest and municipal legislative powers relate to matters of predominantly local interest.

The Constitution also establishes certain guidelines for the concurrent legislative powers held by federal, states and local governments. Despite these, the government has exclusive authority to legislate on matters of civil, commercial, criminal, procedural, electoral, agrarian, maritime, aeronautical, space and labour law. Moreover, only the government may regulate expropriation, bodies of water, energy, computer science, telecommunications, radio broadcasting, the monetary system, exchange, credit policy, insurance, foreign trade, mining deposits, nationality, citizenship and other matters.

2.3 Brazilian courts

(a) General overview

The judiciary comprises both the federal and state courts. There is no municipal judiciary system. The judiciary is primarily divided into ordinary and specialised courts. The highest court in Brazil is the Federal Supreme Court, which has the power to examine constitutional issues and certain other limited matters. The Superior Court of Justice is the highest court for reviewing matters of federal and state law.

(b) Ordinary courts

Each state is divided into judicial districts, which are composed of one or more municipalities. Each judicial district has at least one trial court, which functions as a court of first instance for most cases. Judgments of the trial courts can be judicially reviewed following an appeal to the courts of justice (courts of second instance).

Each Brazilian state has only one court of justice. This consists of a court of appeal, which is tasked with reviewing decisions taken by the trial courts. The court of justice has the final word on decisions taken at the level of state law.

In turn, the jurisdictions of the federal courts encompass, among others, disputes in which the federal government has an interest and disputes involving foreigners, nationality rights or crimes against labour organisations.

First instance federal trial courts are located in major cities; their jurisdictions are divided among judicial districts. The five regional federal courts, which are the second instance federal courts, have jurisdiction over groups of several states.

(c) Specialised courts

Some fields of law, such as labour, electoral and military law, are dealt with by specific courts. For labour matters, for example, there are lower labour courts and regional labour courts. These are responsible for deciding labour cases at first and second instance. There is also the Superior Labour Court, which has a final say on labour matters unless constitutional issues are involved (in these cases the matter may also be reviewed by the Federal Supreme Court).

(d) Superior Court of Justice and Federal Supreme Court

The Superior Court of Justice has jurisdiction over special appeals relating to lower court decisions that:

- contravene a treaty or federal law, or deny its effectiveness;
- assess the validity of a law or act of local government that has been challenged in the light of federal law; and
- interpret federal law differently from another court.

As previously mentioned, it is also possible, through extraordinary appeals, to submit certain cases to the Federal Supreme Court. This has exclusive jurisdiction to:

- declare federal or state laws unconstitutional;
- order extradition requests from foreign states; and
- overrule decisions of sole instance courts which may violate the Constitution.

3. Principles related to investments and business

3.1 Constitutional principles

Since all statutes, laws, rules and regulations in the Brazilian legal system must be aligned with the Constitution and its principles, it is important to understand the main aspects of these.

The Constitution sets out the following principles as the foundation of the federal republic and the legal democratic state:

- sovereignty;
- citizenship;
- dignity of the human person;
- the social values of labour and of free enterprise; and
- political pluralism.

Moreover, the Constitution establishes several fundamental rights and guarantees that derive from a main statement, according to which all persons are equal before the law. Thus, all Brazilians and foreigners living in the country are guaranteed the right to life, liberty, equality, safety and property. Among these fundamental rights, the following should be highlighted:

- No one may be obliged to do or stop doing something except when required by law.
- An individual's home is his or her inviolable refuge; no one may enter without consent, except in the event of an offence being committed, or a disaster, or to give help, or by court order.
- Correspondence and communications are secret, except in the latter case by court order for the purposes of criminal investigation.
- Work, trades and professions may be practised freely, in observance of any legally required professional qualifications.
- Property rights shall be guaranteed.
- The social function of property shall be maintained.
- Vested rights, the perfected juridical act and legal precedent shall be protected.
- No one may have his or her freedom or assets taken away without the due process of law.
- Any citizen may file a class action to nullify acts that are injurious to public or state property, to public order, to the environment or to Brazil's historic and cultural heritage.

In addition, the Constitution expressly states that all citizens have the right to an ecologically balanced environment, and that both government and society have a duty to defend and preserve it for present and future generations.

The Constitution also establishes the principles of an economic and financial order that is founded on an appreciation of the value of human work and free enterprise. The principles of the economic order encompass national sovereignty, private property, the social function of property, free competition and environmental protection.

The free exercise of any economic activity is also assured, regardless of government authorisation, with certain legal exceptions. The Constitution also states that, other than in certain cases, the state is allowed to exploit an economic activity directly only when required by national security or a relevant collective interest.

Based on this summary, we now present a more detailed analysis of certain principles and rights that are particularly important to doing business in Brazil, and in particular in the oil and gas industries.

(a) National sovereignty

National sovereignty entails a supreme and independent political power that cannot usually be limited by any national or international power. Sovereignty is equal to the supreme powers of other nations. As abstract as this definition may seem, it has significant concrete applicability.

For instance, a foreign law governing a given agreement may be considered valid and binding in the Brazilian courts if it does not contravene national sovereignty, public policy or good morals.[1] If the parties to an agreement do not expressly make such a choice, the Civil Code specifies that any obligations will be governed by the law of the country in which they are created.

Under Brazilian law, the law of the country where a person lives determines his or her legal identity, name, capacity and family rights. This avoids conflict with the laws of other countries. There are a few exceptions. For instance, issues relating to assets and properties are governed by the local law of where they are situated. This law determines whether property is movable or immovable, and whether an object may be subject to its own rights. Hence, real estate title and ownership, among other factors, are governed by local law. This also applies to movable property, except for those assets which are always carried with the owner.[2] Ships and aircraft are exceptions to this rule, because jurisdiction over their acquisition, mortgage and other aspects resides with the country in which they are registered.

As a general rule, a final judgment or arbitration award will be recognised and enforceable by the Brazilian courts once it has been ratified by the Superior Court of Justice. In order to be ratified, a foreign judgment or arbitration award must meet the following conditions:

- It must comply with all requirements for its enforcement under the laws of the place where it was rendered;
- It must have been issued by a competent court and after proper service of process. If this took place in Brazil, it must comply with Brazilian law or, after sufficient evidence of the parties' absence has been given, according to the applicable law;
- It is not subject to appeal;

---

1 According to Article 14 of the Introduction Law to the Civil Code (Decree-Law 4,657/42), if the judge does not have knowledge of the foreign law, he or she can require the party who invokes it to provide its text and validity. In addition, Article 337 of the Code of Civil Procedure (Law 5,869/73) provides that any party that invokes municipal, state, foreign or customary law must prove its content and validity if required by a judge.

2 In this sense, mortgage agreements over real property located in Brazil shall be governed by Brazilian law, as well as pledge agreements whenever the asset given in pledge is held by a person domiciled in Brazil.

- It must not contravene Brazilian national sovereignty, public policy or good morals; and
- It must be duly authenticated by the competent Brazilian consulate and accompanied by a translation into Portuguese, made by a certified translator.

Notwithstanding these conditions, the Brazilian courts will not recognise or enforce any foreign court decisions or arbitration awards if the underlying object of the dispute refers to a matter that is subject to exclusive Brazilian jurisdiction. This includes:

- issues relating to real estate located in Brazil; and
- probate proceedings of a deceased person's assets located in Brazil, even if the deceased was a foreigner and has lived outside Brazil.[3]

(b) Ecologically balanced environment

The Constitution devotes a whole chapter to the stewardship of the environment. This protects citizens' rights to an ecologically balanced environment as a common asset for society and a requirement for a healthy life. The duty to protect and conserve the environment is entrusted to government authorities and the civil community. In this way, the Constitution ascribes a dual status to the environment. It portrays it not only as the subjective right of every citizen, but also as a duty of the state. Room is thus provided for the public stewardship and individual protection of such an asset.

The Constitution confers a series of duties to the public authorities, including:

- the preservation and recovery of species and ecosystems;
- the preservation of the variety and integrity of genetic heritage, and the supervision of those bodies engaged in genetic research and manipulation;
- education about the environment at all levels, and the development of public awareness of the need to preserve the environment;
- the definition of territories that are eligible for special protection; and
- the compulsory assessment of the environmental impact of any activities that may cause significant ecologic degradation.

Furthermore, any person or entity that causes damage to the environment is subject to criminal and administrative penalties, and is also liable for redressing that damage.

The legislative authority of the federal government, states and municipalities over environmental matters also features in the Constitution. The government and states are concurrently competent to legislate on issues of environmental protection.

---

3 According to Article 55, Second Paragraph, of the Bidding Law (Law 8,666/93), as a general rule, the Brazilian courts shall have jurisdiction with respect to governmental contracts executed under the scope of such law. With respect to the choice of jurisdiction rules, the Code of Civil Procedure provides that Brazilian courts shall have non-exclusive jurisdiction whenever:
- the defendant, regardless of nationality, is domiciled in Brazil;
- the obligation is to be carried out in Brazil; or
- the controversy arises from a fact that occurred or an act that was performed in Brazil.

In such cases the Brazilian courts are likely to accept the decision of a foreign jurisdiction.

Thus, general rules for the environment are incumbent on the government, whereas the states must issue any supplementary rules. The right to legislate on matters involving water, energy, mines, biotechnology and nuclear activity is reserved to the federal authorities.

An activity or undertaking is subject to environmental licensing when its type, size or location may have a direct or indirect bearing on the physical, chemical and biological characteristics of the environment. These might include:

- the location, construction, set-up, expansion, change and operation of undertakings and activities that use environmental resources and may or actually pollute; and
- the undertakings that may cause an environmental impact in any way.

(c) Private property

The Constitution guarantees all individuals the right to private property. However, although this right is fundamental, it is not absolute. It is limited by the constitutional principles of the supremacy of public over private interests and the social role of property, which support the expropriation and creation of administrative easement over properties.

The basic distinction between expropriation and easement is that expropriation entails a loss of ownership of the expropriated property, whereas easement represents only a burden on part of the property.

Expropriation: There are two basic forms of expropriation in Brazil:

- that imposed due to economic or social interest as required by governmental authorities whenever there is no identical or similar asset available, against the payment of an indemnity (the so-called 'expropriation fee'); and
- deprivation determined in special cases, such as if the asset has been used in criminal circumstances relating to drug trafficking.

Prevailing law gives the federal, state and municipal authorities jurisdiction to expropriate by means of either of the following two procedures:

- administrative, where the parties agree on the amount of the indemnity; or
- judicial, where there is no agreement regarding the amount of the indemnity.

Expropriation without indemnification occurs whenever the property has been used in criminal circumstances. Otherwise, the expropriation act gives the property owner an indemnification right against the government. The value of this will be calculated according to how much is considered necessary to compensate the owner of the expropriated asset.

Easement: An easement is typically a restriction to a third party's property right for the benefit of another interest. In general, Brazilian law recognises two types of rights of way:

- private (or civil) easement; and
- administrative easement.

Civil easement is a right to use the property of another person, creating a burden on a property for the benefit of another belonging to a different owner.

Administrative easement is a right whereby a property is submitted to public use. It thus affects the right of the owner to use and enjoy the property. Administrative easement is usually defined by Brazilian legal scholars as a public right that authorises government authorities to use the property to execute works and services in the interest of all.

No specific rule governs administrative easements. The legal provision that deals with them is the same as that which regulates expropriations for public use. Administrative easements must always be preceded by an executive decree (a declaratory act of easement or decree of public use), by which the public interest to create them is declared.

Administrative easements become effective only through a public deed executed with the private individual and registered with the relevant real estate registry. If the parties fail to agree, the authorities should turn to the judiciary. The court's decision will then be registered accordingly.

The owner of the property may be entitled to an indemnity. This will be calculated on a case-by-case basis according to the actual losses in the use of the property. If there is no loss, no indemnity is payable.

In principle, an administrative easement is definitive because it is aimed at making the provision of a public service feasible, to be maintained as long as the need gving rise to it remains. However, subsequent facts may arise that lead to the end of the easement, such as the state's decision to stop using the property concerned.

Finally, the Brazilian Petroleum Law (Law 9,478/1997) establishes that the Brazilian Petroleum Agency (ANP) is responsible for proceedings with a view to declaring public utility for expropriation or administrative easement in any areas necessary for:

- the exploration, development and production of oil and natural gas; and
- the construction of refineries, pipelines and terminals.

(d) Free enterprise

The principle of free enterprise confers the right to exercise freely any economic activity, regardless of governmental authorisation. In other words, every citizen has the right to participate in deals and business, either solely or jointly with partners, at his or her own risk.

Exercising this principle must take place within the limits of the law and according to competitive and fair market practices. The entrepreneur must be free to control his or her business and choose the direction of the firm – including, for example, choosing what to produce, in what quantities and under what means and prices. However, such rights and liberties can be exercised only in accordance with other constitutional principles. These include the principle of social justice, which governs economic policy and protects citizens against the abuse of economic power.

With regard to the freedom of enterprise, the exploitation, production, import and refinement of oil and gas in Brazil were under strict government monopoly until the enactment of Constitutional Amendment 9/1995 and the Petroleum Law (9,478/1997).

Article 177 of the Constitution lists the following oil and gas activities as the exclusive preserve of the state:

- the exploration and production of deposits of oil, natural gas and other fluid hydrocarbons;
- the refining of domestic or foreign oil;
- the import and export of the above products and basic by-products; and
- the maritime transportation of domestic crude oil and basic petroleum by-products produced in Brazil, and the pipeline transportation of crude oil and its by-products, and natural gas.

Constitutional Amendment 9/1995 authorised the state to contract these activities to national or private companies. In doing so, it reduced the government's monopoly over the oil and gas industries. A new law was required to govern such contracts; this was enacted two years later as the Petroleum Law.

The purpose of the Petroleum Law was to regulate and implement Constitutional Amendment 9/1995 and bring greater flexibility to the Brazilian oil and gas industries. Private and state-owned companies in Brazil were subsequently authorised to perform activities that had previously been restricted to Petrobras.

The Petroleum Law restated the state's ownership of deposits of petroleum, natural gas and other fluid hydrocarbons found within the national territory. It also confirmed the state's monopoly over the activities referred to in Article 177. Accordingly, all exploration and production rights for oil and natural gas in Brazil belong to the government. In general, the ANP is responsible for managing these rights.

The principle of free enterprise now applies to the oil and gas industries under certain limitations. The activities listed above are regulated and inspected by the government, through ANP, and may be performed by companies incorporated under Brazilian law and headquartered in Brazil.

(e) Vested rights, perfected juridical act and res judicata

The Constitution's protection of vested rights, perfected juridical acts and *res judicata* places a limit on ordinary legislative power. Vested rights are those rights guaranteed to their owner and not generally subject to changes in the law.

A perfected juridical act is considered to exist whenever it has been completed with regard to the law at that time and has satisfied all requirements necessary to become fully effective.

Res judicata refers to those matters in a lawsuit or legal proceeding in which a final and non-appealable decision has been rendered, and is therefore not subject to reconsideration or modification in either the same or a different court. This not only prevents future judgments from contradicting earlier ones, but also prevents a multiplicity of judgments on the same matter involving the same parties.

These constitutional principles are connected to one of the pillars of the Brazilian legal system: the non-retroactivity of legal provisions. This principle is based on the *ex post facto* doctrine, or the non-applicability of a statute or regulation to events that pre-date its issue. It is intrinsically connected to the principle of the perfected juridical act.

To this end, the Law of Introduction to the Civil Code (Decree-Law 4,657/42) states that laws will come into effect with immediate and general observance of vested rights, perfected juridical acts and legal precedent.

Nevertheless, in some cases new laws are applicable to previously existing regulations. These exceptions include public policy provisions, such as rules related to government economic plans, and amendments to the Constitution, which by its supreme enforcement shall trump rights that already pertain to the equity of individuals or legal entities.

The rescissory action is an exception to the principle of *res judicata*. So long as the applicable legal requirements are met, it allows a party a two-years timeframe within which to contest the validity of a final and non-appealable court decision.

3.2 Civil law and corporate principles

(a) The principles of civil law

Any contract that is subject to Brazilian law must be drawn up according to the following principles:

- the freedom to contract;
- the social function of contracts;
- the obligation to perform;
- objective good faith; and
- the observation of subjective, objective and formal prerequisites for validity.

Except in some cases, freedom to contract applies to four fundamental points in the lifetime of an agreement:

- the ability to contract;
- freedom to select the counterparty;
- freedom to elaborate the contract's contents; and
- the ability to ask the state to ensure that the demands of the original arrangement are met.

There are exceptions and limitations to the freedom to contract. The Consumer Protection Code, for example, states that monopolistic suppliers of public services cannot choose whether to enter into a contract with a consumer. Other restrictions concern public policy and state intervention, which in some cases impose contracts and definitions of rights and obligations (eg, labour law), and empower judges to transform the contract and set out conditions for its enforcement.

According to Article 421 of the Civil Code, the freedom to contract must observe the contract's social function. Article 422 additionally states that the parties to a contract must do so in objective good faith and probity. Objective good faith relates to a party's adequate behaviour in a cooperative legal relationship, as opposed to subjective good faith, which is the party's awareness of acting according to the law.

The principle requires that the contract be executed according to any foreseeable events, and that both parties should gain the intended returns. Objective good faith thus goes beyond the obligation not to harm afforded by subjective good faith, to ensure that each party's obligation to cooperate in obtaining the expected results.

If the parties do not observe the necessary requirements, the contract is invalid. Subjective requirements are those that relate to the competence of the parties, while objective requirements relate to the legality, possibility and determination of the object of the contract. Validity does not generally depend on any particular formal requirements, except in certain circumstances.[4]

As a general rule, contracts executed abroad must be signed before a notary public and then sent for legalisation with the nearest Brazilian consulate. The contract must also be translated into Portuguese by a certified translator in order to be presented to public authorities and registries in Brazil.

Notwithstanding the above, the Public Registry Law[5] requires the following documents to be registered with the Registry of Deeds and Documents:

- documents resulting from deposits or pledges to assure the performance of contractual obligations;
- letters of guarantee;
- all documents originating from other countries; and
- assignments of claims and credits, and instruments of subrogation and payment in kind.

(b) Foreign capital and the principles of corporate law

Foreign capital in Brazil is governed by the Foreign Capital Law (4,131/1962) and Law 4,390/1964. Both laws are regulated by Decree 55,762/1965. According to Law 4,131/1962, 'foreign capital' means "any goods, machinery and equipment that enter Brazil, with no initial disbursement of foreign currency, for the production of goods or services, as well as any funds brought into the country for investment in economic activities, provided that in both cases they belong to individuals or legal entities resident, domiciled or headquartered abroad".

The Brazilian exchange rules changed significantly in early 2005, culminating in an unprecedented liberalisation of currency exchange. They are governed by National Monetary Council Resolution 3,265/2005. These rules:

- set out the principles to be observed by banks in each and every transaction – namely, the validity of the deal, its economic reasons and the parties' responsibilities and liabilities as defined in any supporting documents;
- restrict exchange transactions through non-resident bank accounts (which must be used exclusively in transactions on behalf of the account holder); and
- introduce new classifications for exchange transactions, which must be reported electronically to the Central Bank of Brazil.

---

4 In the case of a mortgage of an immovable asset created to secure an obligation, for instance, the law establishes that such an agreement must be made through a public deed drawn up by a public notary.

The 1995 constitutional reform made the following significant economic breakthroughs:

- It removed the concept of a Brazilian company as one holding domestic capital, and re-established the traditional concept of a Brazilian company as one organised under Brazilian law and headquartered and managed in Brazil;
- It allowed private companies to operate telecommunications, radio and/or television services either directly or through concession, authorisation or licence;
- It eased government monopolies, allowing private capital to be invested in prospecting for, researching, refining, trading or transporting petroleum, and exploring gas pipelines;
- It allowed the various Brazilian states to operate piped gas services, directly or via concession; and
- It lifted constitutional restrictions on offshore companies engaged in coastal shipping services.

Despite this, certain prohibitions and limitations are still imposed on foreign capital. For instance, foreign capital is prohibited from the following activities:

- nuclear energy;
- health services;
- post office and telecommunications services;
- domestic flight routes; and
- the aerospace industry.

Limits on foreign investments are also in relation to the ownership of rural land, business in border areas, media companies and financial institutions, among other things.

There are no such restrictions on foreign investment in the oil and natural gas industries. The Petroleum Law requires that foreign companies taking part in an invitation to bid, either individually or as part of a consortium, produce evidence of their technical capability, financial solvency, fulfilment of legal and fiscal obligations and other documentation. Additionally, there must be a commitment to establish a company under Brazilian law (in the event of being awarded a public contract), with its main offices and management located in Brazil. The execution of a concession contract is conditional on the foreign actor establishing the Brazilian company in question.

Foreign capital must be registered with the Central Bank of Brazil through its online registration system, such as the foreign direct investment (RDE-IED) function applicable to limited and closely held companies. Foreign capital must be registered when bringing funds into Brazil, remitting profits abroad, repatriating capital and registering reinvestments. Investments are registered either in the foreign currency in which they are actually made, or in Brazilian currency if the funds originate from a non-resident account properly kept in Brazil or from other assets located in the country.

Cash investments do not require preliminary official authorisation. Investments to subscribe for capital or to buy a stake in a Brazilian company must be remitted through a bank that is authorised to deal in foreign exchange. To complete the exchange transaction, the Brazilian investee–foreign investor identification number must be entered using the RDE-IED function. For tax purposes, foreign investment entities must be enrolled with the National Registry of Legal Entities. Individual foreign investors must be enrolled with the Individual Taxpayers Registry.

Currency investments must be registered within 30 days of the corresponding event, on the basis of the information provided by the representative of the Brazilian investee and/or foreign investor through the RDE-IED function.

There are usually no restrictions on the distribution and remittance of profits abroad. Since 1996, profits and dividends declared and distributed abroad are exempt from income tax. Under this legislation, reinvestments are those profits made by Brazilian companies and allocated to persons or companies domiciled abroad which have been reinvested in Brazil. Should the foreign investor decide to reinvest rather than remit profits, such profits must be registered as foreign capital, along with the original investment, through the RDE-IED function.

Foreign capital registered with the Central Bank may be repatriated at any time without preliminary authorisation. Remittances in excess of the registered amount are treated as capital gains for the foreign investor, and are thus subject to income tax.

A foreign company may also operate directly in Brazil, instead of incorporating a Brazilian company as a subsidiary. However, the authorisation process is subject to strict requirements, such as the submission of an application to the Brazilian government for approval. The constituent documents must be published in the official press and filed with the Public Register of Companies. Only after all formalities have been completed will the foreign company be allowed to begin activities in Brazil.

(c) General aspects of corporate law

Brazilian companies are subject to the principle of corporate social duty. This calls for the preservation and optimisation of the production of goods, assets and resources by a company whenever this is economically possible. According to Brazilian scholars, this principle requires a company to create job positions and respect and preserve the environment and the wider society. In this way, it can earn profits efficiently and obtain better and more transparent results that can sustain its activities.

Generally speaking, a shareholder's liability is limited by how much it has committed to contribute to the company's capital. In principle, shareholders should not be held liable for any amount in excess of such contributions. As a general rule, there are no minimum capital requirements for the incorporation of companies. The capital stock may be allocated between parties at their own discretion.

However, according to the doctrine of disregard of the legal entity, the courts may reach beyond the shareholders' personal assets in order to enforce the company's obligations whenever its assets are insufficient to meet its debts. Following case law, this doctrine is to be understood and applied as an exception to the general rule of the separation of a company's assets and liabilities from those of its partners. Nevertheless, statutes have endorsed the doctrine, making it a statutory and not simply academic consideration.

In general terms, the basic prerequisites for the court to disregard the legal entity of a company and therefore consider its shareholders personally liable for its debts are as follows:

- The company does not have sufficient assets to meet its obligations; and
- The situation results from a deliberate and malicious manoeuvre by the shareholders to frustrate enforcement of the company's debts.

The officers and administrators of Brazilian companies must comply with the basic duties of diligence, good faith and loyalty. Such senior managers must conduct the company's activities with the same care and probity as they would their own business. The duty of diligence is tied to the duty of good faith assumed by the manager in performing his or her functions. Finally, the duty of loyalty requires senior managers always to act in the best interests of the company.

Members of management bodies – including the fiscal board, board of directors and executive office – are liable for any damage resulting from dereliction of their duties and from acts performed negligently or in bad faith, or which violate the law or the company's bylaws. Criminal liability may also apply. Senior managers are prohibited from any of the following acts:

- discretional acts at the company's expense;
- any acts not authorised by the general meeting or board of directors, when such authorisation is required;
- lending of the company's funds or assets; or
- unauthorised receipt of any direct or indirect personal advantages from third parties, on account of their position.

Moreover, a senior manager cannot take part in any business decision when a conflict of interests is held to exist.

That said, an officer will not, in principle, be personally liable for damages caused by acts performed in the normal course of business, in the best interest of the company, under the provisions of the law and company bylaws. Otherwise, he or she could be personally liable for any damages caused to the company, its shareholders and third parties. An officer is liable not only for his or her own actions, but also for his or her omissions. This includes when acting in error, even if not maliciously, if that error falls below the standards expected of a diligent and careful officer in the same situation.

Furthermore, in principle, an officer shall not be held liable for unlawful acts carried out by his or her peers, unless he or she has acted in collusion or actually participated in such an act. If an officer is held liable for any damage to the company, a suit for damages may be filed by the company following a resolution of the general meeting. Such a lawsuit will be additional to any other court remedies available to the shareholders or third parties directly injured by the officer's acts.

3.3 Principles of public administration

(a) *Strict legality*

As expressly stated in the Constitution, all public administration entities, including public companies and mixed-capital companies, are subject to the principle of strict legality. Therefore, the public administration is allowed to act only within the limits that are established by law, while citizens and private parties are allowed to practise any lawful act without restrictions. In punitive proceedings, for example, this means that private parties will be penalised only for explicit infractions of the law, and the public agent is allowed to impose only those penalties that have been established in the law for the relevant infraction.

(b) *Supremacy of the public interest*

Unlike private agreements, contracts executed with the public administration involve a vertical relationship, by which the private party is subject to the public interest represented by the administrative authority. Therefore, administrative-public contracts are subject to potential amendments, so long as the financial and economic balance between the parties is maintained.

On this principle, the public administration may change the conditions of the contract, so long as it is judged to be necessary and does not substantially alter its qualitative terms. This principle supports several actions that may be taken by the public authorities, including the expropriation and establishment of administrative easements over properties.

(c) *Public bidding*

The Constitution establishes that the public administration[6] must comply with several specific principles, such as lawfulness and arm's-length relations, morality, impartiality, disclosure and efficiency. Consequently, works, services, purchases and disposals involving public administration entities must, as a rule, be contracted through a public bidding process[7] designed to provide equal conditions to all competitors.

The general rules for public bidding processes in Brazil are set out in the Public Bidding Law (Law 8,666/1993),[8] which reaffirms the principles to be observed in transactions with the public administration.[9] These include the following:

- Principle of equality – this establishes that all private parties are entitled to

---

5 Law 6,015/ 1973.

6 The federal government, states, municipalities and federal district, as well as public companies, mixed-capital companies and their foundations, are encompassed within this concept.

7 The public bidding procedure consists of a competitive administrative proceeding, comprising a chain of acts to choose the most advantageous bid.

8 The states and municipalities can have their own legislation, but the general precepts of Law 8,666/1993 should be observed. Mixed-capital companies can establish a simplified bidding system, but the constitutional principles of the administration should be observed and respected.

9 According to Article 3 of this law, "the bidding procedure shall guarantee observance of the constitutional principle of equality before the law and selection of the most advantageous bid for the Public Administration, and shall be processed and judged in strict observance with the basic principles of lawfulness, arms-length relations, morality, equality, disclosure, administrative good conduct, abidance by the announcement to bid, objective judgment and issues related thereto".

participate in bidding processes under equal conditions, and that the corresponding bid invitation cannot establish discriminatory clauses or conditions that grant or imply any favour to any of the bidders over their competitors.

- Principle of impartiality – this establishes that the rights and obligations of all bidders must be treated equally, and that the public administration must be guided by objective criteria in making its decisions. The administration cannot, therefore, take into account the personal conditions of the bidder or any advantages the bidder may offer that are not set forth in law or in the bid invitation.
- Principle of morality (honesty) – this requires that the public administrator abide by the standards of morality and proper behaviour, and that its conduct primarily keep in mind the public interest.

The Public Bidding Law sets forth the events and situations in which public biddings may be waived or be deemed inapplicable. Some of the situations in which public bidding may be waived are as follows:

- when there are no interested parties at a first bidding, and such a process cannot be properly repeated without harming the public administration; in this case all conditions established in the failed bidding process must be maintained;
- when the conditions offered for acquiring goods or services needed for a specific international agreement approved by the Congress are clearly advantageous to the public administration;
- whenever the exclusivity of the original supplier is required for purposes of the warranty of domestic or foreign components or parts; and
- when acquiring or contracting services to supply items to military vessels, boats, aircraft or troops and their means of transportation, during short-term stays in ports, airports or places other than their headquarters while deployed or taking part in training activities.

Bidding will not apply when competition is impossible, such as when there is an exclusive supplier for certain materials or equipment, or when contracting unique technical services from specialist professionals or companies.

Should an overpricing be detected in bids that have been waived or are non-applicable, the supplier or service renderer and the responsible public agent shall be jointly and severally liable for any damages caused to the Treasury, further to any other applicable sanctions.

(d) Abiding by the bid invitation

This principle determines that the bidders and the administration must abide by the rules, conditions and awarding criteria established in the bid invitation in all phases of the bid process.[10] If, in the course of the bid, the public administration deems it

10 Article 45, Law 8,666/1993

necessary to change any part of the invitation, then it must restart the entire bidding process, re-publish the invitation and allow all interested parties to submit new offers.

The principle of objective judgement is strictly related to abidance to the bid invitation, since the decision will always be made according to the objective criteria it establishes. Therefore, the public administration must choose the offer that best suits the public interest.

4. Conclusion

It is evident from the above that Brazil enjoys a stable and organised legal framework based on a system of civil law, supported by fundamental principles that arise mainly from the Constitution. Such principles in turn serve as guidelines to several corporate, civil and administrative concepts that must be considered when doing business in Brazil.

As the basis of the Brazilian system, such constitutional, administrative and corporate principles, along with their derivative concepts, should be observed whenever a Brazilian or foreign actor decides to participate in the Brazilian oil and gas upstream industry.

The Brazilian upstream sector operates under international standards in terms of contract structures, environmental and maritime rules, and elsewhere. Brazil is a signatory to the main international conventions that apply to the upstream industry and almost all the main actors in the sector are active in the country. Moreover, there is also a solid business environment in the industries that make up the upstream sector, particularly in the lease and charter of assets dedicated to such business. This is supported by sophisticated structures and various benefits that are felt across the industry.

Governmental authorities: the CNPE, the Ministry of Mines and Energy and the ANP

Andrea Falcão
Lawyer

1. Introduction

The political and administrative organisation of the Federative Republic of Brazil comprises the union, the states, the federal district and the municipalities.[1]

Under Brazilian law the union is a legal entity of internal public law,[2] vested with a sovereign legal personality. It operates within the legal system through direct and indirect federal administrations.

The direct federal administration includes the presidency and ministries, while the indirect federal administration includes autarchies, public companies, private and public joint-stock corporation, and public foundations. Each is responsible for managing the union's assets and the services under their jurisdiction.[3]

Mineral resources, including those underground,[4] and including all the oil, natural gas and fluid hydrocarbon reserves found in Brazil and in the country's territorial waters, are owned by the union. They are therefore managed by the direct

---

1 Constitution, Article 18: "The political/administrative organisation of the Federative Republic of Brazil includes the Union, the States, the Federal District, the Municipalities, all autonomous, pursuant to the terms of this Constitution."

2 Civil Code, Article 41.

3 Decree 200/1967, Article 4 specifies that the federal administration comprises:
- the direct administration, which is comprised of those services integrated in the administrative structure of the presidency and the ministries; and
- the indirect administration, which includes the following types of entity, each with its own independent legal personality:
  - autarchies;
  - public companies;
  - public and private joint-stock companies; and
  - public foundations.

Article 5 defines these entities as follows:
- an autarchy is an autonomous service with independent legal personality, assets and revenues to provide activities typical of the public administration, which require decentralised administrative and financial management to operate best;
- a public company is a private entity with its own assets and union capital that is created to pursue economic activities that the government is required to conduct;
- public and private joint-stock corporations are private entities for pursuing economic activities organised as a joint-stock corporation whose shares with voting rights are mostly owned by the union or by the indirect administration; and
- a public foundation is a private, not-for-profit legal entity, created by legislation to develop activities that are not required by public law, agencies or entities. It is administratively autonomous; its assets are managed by its directors and its operating costs are paid for by the union and other sources.

and indirect federal administrations.

Furthermore, although the Brazilian economic order is based on an appreciation for human labour and free enterprise,[5] Article 177 of the Constitution sets aside the following activities as state monopolies:

- the research and exploration of oil and gas deposits;
- the refining of domestic or foreign oil;
- the import and export of products and basic by-products resulting from oil activities;
- the maritime transportation of domestic crude oil or basic oil by-products produced in the country; and
- the shipment through pipelines of crude oil, its by-products and natural gas.

The Ministry of Mines and Energy (MME) manages these resources and activities on behalf of the direct federal administration and the National Agency of Petroleum, Natural Gas and Biofuels (ANP) on behalf of the indirect federal administration.

The president and the National Council of Energy Policy (CNPE) also direct the exploration and production of oil and natural gas in Brazil.

Petróleo Brasileiro S/A, or Petrobras, may also be considered a government agent, but because of its nature as a business it will not be covered by this chapter.

2. A short history of the present government agencies

In the 1960s and 1970s Brazilian development was characterised by the strong presence of the state in the economy. State-owned companies, which were organised as holdings/subsidiaries, were expanded to form large conglomerates. Among these was Petrobras, then the holder of the country's oil and gas monopoly.

The strong presence of state-owned companies diminished in the 1990s as the Brazilian economy opened up to foreign investment. The consequent growth in foreign trade and the privatisation of the economy led to the end of several state-owned companies.

The oil and gas industry trod a similar path. Petrobras's monopoly was reduced and it took up a new position, no longer as the executor of the monopoly on behalf of the union but as a concessionaire like any other player that had begun to operate in Brazil. It was during this time that the ANP was formed to regulate the industry.

However, the discovery in 2008 of vast oil reserves in the so-called pre-salt layer, led to intense discussions about whether to change the existing legal situation.

The president at that time, believing that it was necessary to change the law, sent four bills to the Brazilian Congress. He argued that the changes they called for were crucial to the government's strategic objectives, especially regarding how best to exploit the wealth that this new oil frontier would generate.

These bills were passed in the National Congress and subsequently ratified by the president. As a result the legal environment was significantly changed, and

4 Constitution, Article 20.

5 Constitution, Article 170: "The economic order, based upon the appreciation for human labour and free enterprise, is intended to ensure to all a dignified existence according to the precepts of social justice".

introduced the greater intervention of the state in the oil and gas industry. This called for a new distribution of responsibilities among government agencies, especially for the MME in relation to the ANP.

2.1 The creation of the CNPE

The easing of the state's monopoly on oil and gas introduced by Constitutional Amendment 9/1995[6] was followed by Law 9,478, the Petroleum Law, which was approved on August 6 1997. This created a new legal environment for the Brazilian oil industry and saw the creation of the CNPE[7] and the ANP.

The structure and operations of the CNPE are governed by Decree 3,520/2000, as amended.

The CNPE is an office assisting the president. It is comprised of nine state ministers, among whom the minister of mines and energy also acts as its chairman, as well as one representative for each state and federal district, one representative of society who must be an expert in energy, one energy expert from a Brazilian university, the president of Empresa de Pesquisa Energética (EPE) and the executive secretary of the MME.[8]

The representatives of the states, federal district, society and the university are appointed by the president for a two-year term, renewable for another two years.

2.2 The creation of the MME

The MME was created by Law 3,782/1960. Between 1990 and 1992, however, it was closed under Law 8,028/1990. During this time its responsibilities were transferred to the Ministry of Infrastructure, which was also responsible for the transportation and telecommunications industries.

The MME was reinstated on May 13 1992 when Law 8,422 came into force. The following matters were placed under its jurisdiction:

- geology;
- mineral and energy resources;
- the use of water-powered energy;

---

6 EC N.9, of November 9 1995, amending Article 177 of the Constitution. The first paragraph of this article is now worded as follows: "the Union may contract State owned or private companies to carry out the activities contemplated in subsections I to IV of this article, pursuant to the conditions set forth in the law".

7 Petroleum Law, Article 2: "The National Council of Energy Policy – CNPE is hereby created subordinate to the President of the Republic and presided by the State Minister of Mines and Energy with the attribution of proposing to the President of the Republic national policies and specific measures".

8 Decree 3,520/2000, Article 2 lists the following as members of the CNPE:
• the state minister of mines and energy, who will act as chairman;
• the state minister of science and technology;
• the state minister of planning, budget and management;
• the state minister for the treasury;
• the state minister for the environment;
• the state minister for development, industry and foreign trade;
• the chief of staff for the presidency;
• the state minister for national integration;
• the state minister for agriculture, cattle raising and supply;
• one representative from each state and the federal district;
• one representative of society who is an expert in energy;
• one representative of a Brazilian university who is an expert in energy;
• the president of EPE; and
• the executive secretary of the MME.

- mining; and
- metallurgy.

Only in 2003, with Law 10,683, were oil, fuel and electricity (including nuclear power) specifically added to this list.[9]

The MME is an office of the direct federal administration responsible for implementing national energy policy and setting the rules and guidelines for the energy industry. It has five secretariats:

- an executive secretariat;
- an electrical energy secretariat;
- an energy planning and development secretariat;
- a geology, mining and mineral transformation secretariat; and
- a petroleum, natural gas and renewable fuels secretariat.

In this context the Programme for Mobilisation of the National Oil and Natural Gas Industry (PROMINP) should also be mentioned. This was created in 2003 under the jurisdiction of the MME to help increase the participation of Brazilian companies in goods and services in the industry.[10]

2.3 The creation of the ANP

As mentioned above, the ANP was created by the Petroleum Law.[11]

At that time, the policy decision was made to move to a 'regulatory state' that would replace the 'manager state' that had prevailed until then. The aim was to increase the efficiency of economic activities through regulation.

In fact, the regulatory state model assumes that the state will focus on executing essential activities, transferring to private interests roles that they can play more efficiently. The regulatory role is reserved for the state.

It was in this spirit of decentralisation that lawmakers created the ANP, using legal parameters to shape its regulatory and administrative activity.

As a special autarchy linked to the MME, the ANP is a legal entity of public law and a member of the indirect federal administration, subject to the usual prerogatives and limits of state functions the legal personality of which requires autonomy. The ANP therefore has its own assets, revenues and personnel.

Because the ANP is a regulatory agency it is important that it is statutorily independent and able to separate itself as far as possible from economic and political interests.

---

9 Law 10,683/2003, Article 27 lists the following as coming under the jurisdiction of the Ministry of Mines and Energy:
- geology, mineral and energy resources;
- the use of water/powered energy;
- mining and metallurgy;
- oil, fuel and electrical energy, including nuclear.

10 A minimum percentage of local participation is required for goods and services purchased in concession contracts, and in 2004 PROMINP prepared a method for calculating this amount of local content. This method is known as the Local Content Book of Instructions.

11 Petroleum Law, Article 7: "The National Agency of Petroleum and Natural Gas and Biofuels – ANP is hereby created, being an entity of the Indirect Federal Administration subject to the special autarchy regime, as the Regulatory Authority of the industry of petroleum, natural gas, its by-products and biofuels, linked to the Ministry of Mines and Energy."

It was founded in 1998 by Decree 2,455, which also approved its organisational structure. This structure was revoked in 2011 by Administrative Ruling 69, which approved new internal rules for the ANP and re-shaped its organisational structure.[12]

The ANP is run by a collegiate board, comprised of a general board of directors and four directors, all of whom are appointed by the president and confirmed by the federal Senate. The term for each member is four years, with the possibility of renewal.

The new organisational structure defined in 2011[13] set the number of superintendencies at 15. These in turn are subordinated to the directors' offices in the following manner:

- Subordinate to the general director:
  - the Superintendency for Planning and Research;

---

12 ANP Regulation 69/2011, Article 1: "Pursuant to the terms of the Annexes hereof, the Internal Regulations of the National Agency of Petroleum, Natural Gas, and Biofuels are approved. Annex II hereof defines the type and the organisational structure of the Agency." Article 2: "Administrative Rulings no. 160, August 2 2004, no. 213, of November 26 2007, and no. 304, of December 20 2010, are hereby revoked."

13 Administrative Ruling 69/2011, Annex I, Article 2 states that the ANP should have the following organisational structure:
- a collegiate board;
- a general board of directors;
- Directorate I;
- Directorate II;
- Directorate III;
- Directorate IV;
- an executive secretariat;
- a General Attorney's Office;
- an Office of the General Director;
- the audit office;
- internal affairs;
- Superintendency for Defining Blocks;
- Superintendency for Technical Data;
- Superintendency for Bidding;
- Superintendency for Exploration;
- Superintendency for Development and Production;
- Superintendency for Government Participation;
- Superintendency for Refining and Processing Natural Gas;
- Superintendency for The Sales and Shipment of Petroleum, its By-Products and Natural Gas;
- Superintendency for Supply;
- Superintendency for Inspecting Supply;
- Superintendency for Biofuels and Product Quality;
- Superintendency for Planning and Research;
- Superintendency for Communication and Institutional Relations;
- Superintendency for Financial And Administrative Management;
- Superintendency for Human Resources Management;
- intelligence office;
- coordination of operational security;
- environmental coordination;
- coordination of technological development;
- coordination of fair competition;
- coordination of local content;
- coordination of the budget;
- parliamentary coordination;
- Department for The Inspection of Operational Safety in Exploration and Production;
- Centre of Inspection of Measurement of Production of Oil and Natural Gas;
- IT Department;
- Department for Technological Research and Analysis;
- Documentation and Information Department;
- Department of Consumer Relations;
- headquarters;
- a main office; and
- regional administrative units.

  - the Superintendency for Communications and Institutional Relations;
  - the Superintendency for Human Resources Management; and
  - the Superintendency for financial and Administrative Management.
- Subordinate to director I:
  - the Superintendency for Development and Production;
  - the Superintendency for Technical Data; and
  - the Superintendency for Government Participation.
- Subordinate to director II:
  - the Superintendency for Defining Blocks;
  - the Superintendency for Exploration; and
  - the Superintendency for Bidding.
- Subordinate to director III:
  - the Superintendency for Inspecting Supply;
  - the Superintendency for Supply; and
  - the Superintendency for Refining and Processing Natural Gas.
- Subordinate to director IV:
  - the Superintendency for Biofuels and Product Quality; and
  - the Superintendency for the Sales and Shipments of Petroleum, its By-Products and Natural Gas.

The Audit Office, internal affairs and Prosecutor's Office are further independent departments within the ANP. The Prosecutor's Office coordinates the agency's legal services, approves the legal opinions written by its attorneys and interacts with the Public Prosecution Office when initiating a case of public interest on behalf of the ANP.

Finally, the following departments are also part of the agency:

- Intelligence Office;
- coordination of operational security;
- environmental coordination;
- coordination of technological development;
- coordination of fair competition;
- coordination of local content;
- budget coordination;
- parliamentary coordination;
- Department for the Inspection of Operational Safety in Exploration and Production;
- Department for the Inspection of Measurements of Production of Oil and Natural Gas;
- IT Department;
- Department for Technological Research and Analysis;
- Documentation and Information Department;
- Department for Consumer Relations;
- headquarters;
- main office; and
- regional administrative units.

3. Current responsibilities of each government agent

The provisions of the Petroleum Law and of Law 12,351/2010 (the Law of Shared Production Regime) represent the current legal situation for exploring oil and gas in Brazil. These laws are complementary and distribute responsibility for these monopolised activities between the CNPE, the MME and the ANP.

The MME supports and prepares the main proposals that the CNPE submits to the president. It is also responsible for dictating national policy on the oil business.

To do this the MME has the responsibility of planning the use of oil and gas and, following comments from the ANP, proposing to the CNPE the definition of the blocks that will be the subject of concessions or shared production.[14]

The Law of Shared Production Regime also introduced changes to the Petroleum Law. These began with an expansion in the responsibilities of the president and the CNPE. This increase in power, without consultation with Congress, implies a increasing role for the state.[15]

The expanded responsibility of the CNPE[16] now includes proposing to the president those areas, besides the pre-salt area, that are to be considered strategic and

---

14 Law of Shared Production Regime, Article 10, lists the following among the responsibilities of the Ministry of Mines and Energy:
- planning the use of petroleum and natural gas;
- proposing to the CNPE, after comments from the ANP, the definition of those blocks that will be the subject of concession or shared production;
- proposing to the CNPE the following technical and economic parameters for shared production contracts:
  - the criteria for defining the union's excess oil;
  - the minimum percentage of the union's excess oil;
  - Petrobras's minimum participation in the consortium considered in Article 20; this must not be less than 30%;
  - the limits, deadlines, criteria and conditions for the contracted party to calculate and appropriate, the cost in oil and the volume of production with respect to the royalties due;
  - the minimum local content and other criteria related to the development of the national industry; and
  - the signing bonus, as well as the portion to be allocated to the public company, as described in Article 8;
- setting the guidelines to be followed by the ANP in promoting the bidding process referred to in Article 8, as well as preparing drafts of notices to bid and of shared production contracts; and
- approving these drafts prepared by the ANP.

Article 10 also states that at the end of each semester the Ministry of Mines and Energy must within 30 days issue a public report on activities related to shared production contracts.

15 Law of Shared Production Regime, Article 67: "The 1st paragraph of Article 23 and Article 27 of Law no. 9,478/1997 are hereby revoked." The 1st paragraph of Article 23 gave the ANP the power to define which blocks would be the object of concession contracts. Article 27 dealt with the individualisation of production, indicating that the ANP would be responsible for determining, based on an arbitrage report, how the rights and obligations related to the blocks would be equitably appropriated. Both cases are examples of the ANP's reduced power to intervene and the respective increase in power of the MME and the president in economic activity.

16 Law of Shared Production Regime, Article 9 defines among the CNPE's responsibilities the duty to propose the following to the president:
- the schedule for assigning blocks under the shared production system, and the development and capacity of the national industry to supply goods and services;
- those blocks that will be assigned to a direct contract with Petrobras under the shared production system;
- those blocks that will be auctioned off under the shared production system;
- the technical and economic parameters of the shared production contracts;
- the delimitation of other regions classified as pre-salt areas or as strategic, according to current geological knowledge;
- the sales policy for any oil allocated to the union in the shared production contracts; and
- the sales policy under consideration for any natural gas included in the shared production contracts, with consideration for the priority of the domestic market.

that fall under the regime of shared production. It is also responsible for suggesting which, under the regime of shared production will be directly contracted with,[17] and which will be auctioned off. However, even in areas that have been auctioned off the winning companies must form consortia with Petrobras and the national oil company (PPSA), created by Law 12,304/2010.[18]

The CNPE is also responsible for dictating the schedule for assigning blocks under the shared production regime, allowing it to monitor the development and capacity of the local companies to supply goods and services. In this way the policy of local content may become a reality across the country.

The president is therefore responsible for deciding on proposals from CNPE that relate to the following:

- delimiting strategic and non-strategic pre-salt areas;
- the blocks that will be subject to the shared production or concession regime;
- the blocks to be assigned directly under the shared regime with Petrobras and those that will be auctioned off;
- the schedule to assign blocks under the regime of shared production according to the policy of minimum domestic content;
- the technical and economic parameters of the shared production contracts; and
- the union's oil sales policy.

The notices to bid, the bids themselves and the block contracts fall under the jurisdiction of the ANP, following subsection IV of Article 8 of the Petroleum Law.[19]

---

17 The Law of Shared Production Regime, Article 12: "The CNPE shall propose to the President of the Republic the cases where, to preserve the national interest and pursue the other objectives of the energy policy, Petrobras will be contracted directly by the Union for the exploration and production of oil, natural gas and other fluid hydrocarbons under the shared production regime. The contracting parameters mentioned in the introduction shall be proposed by the CNPE, pursuant to subsection IV, Article 9, and subsection III of Article 10, when applicable."

18 Law 12,304/2010, Article 1: "The Executive Branch is hereby authorised to create a public joint stock company called *Empresa Brasileira de Administração de Petróleo e Gás Natural S.A. – Pré-Sal Petróleo S.A.* (PPSA), linked to the Ministry of Mines and Energy, for an undefined length of time. PPSA shall have its headquarters and venue in Brasília and main office in Rio de Janeiro."
Article 2 of the same law states: "PPSA's purpose shall be to manage the shared production contracts signed by the Ministry of Mines and Energy and the contracts to sell oil, natural gas and other fluid hydrocarbons owned by the Union. PPSA shall not be responsible for directly or indirectly executing the exploration, development, production and sales of oil, natural gas and other fluid hydrocarbons."

19 Petroleum Law, Article 8 states that the ANP is responsible for:
- implementing the national policy on oil, natural gas and biofuels, with an emphasis on guaranteeing the supply of petroleum by-products, natural gas and its by-products and biofuels throughout the country, and protecting consumer interests in relation to price, quality and supply;
- promoting studies for delimiting blocks for concession or the shared production of exploration, development and production;
- regulating geology and geophysics services in prospecting for oil, to identify technical data for non-exclusive sale;
- preparing notices to bid; promoting bid rounds for concessions for exploration, development and production; and signing and enforcing the resulting contracts;
- authorising the refining, liquefaction, regasification, loading, processing, treatment, transportation, storage and packaging of oil and gas products;
- determining the criteria by which to calculate pipeline transportation fees;
- inspecting the activities of the oil, natural gas and biofuels industry, as well as applying any applicable administrative and pecuniary sanctions;
- initiating applications for a declaration of public utility for the purpose of expropriation. and creating administrative easement where necessary for the exploration, development and production of oil and natural gas, and the construction of refineries, pipelines and terminals;

The MME will be responsible for setting the guidelines relating to the blocks set aside for the shared production regime. These will be followed by the ANP during the bidding processes and during the preparation of drafts of notices to bid and shared production contracts. Once the drafts have been approved by the CNPE, the bidding processes are conducted by the ANP[20] and the contracts are signed by the MME.[21]

- enforcing compliance with good practices of conservation and the rational use of oil, natural gas, their by-products and biofuels, and the preservation of the environment;
- stimulating research into and the adoption of new technologies for exploring, producing, transporting, refining and processing;
- organising and keeping a collection of information and technical data related to regulated activities in the oil, natural gas and biofuels industry;
- consolidating and disclosing, on an annual basis, information related to the national reserves of oil and natural gas as submitted by the companies;
- inspecting the correct operation of the National System of Inventory of Fuel and complying with the Annual Plan of Strategic Inventory of Fuels referred to in Article 4 of Law 8,176/1991;
- interacting with the other regulatory authorities in the energy sector in areas of common interest, including providing technical support to CNPE;
- regulating and authorising activities to do with the national supply of fuels, inspecting these activities directly or through agreements with other agencies of the union, states, federal district or municipalities;
- regulating and authorising activities to do with the production, import, export, storage, transportation, transfer, distribution and retail sale of biofuels, as well as assessing their compliance and certifying their quality, either directly or through agreements with other agencies of the union, states, federal district or municipalities;
- requiring regulated agents to send information about the production, import, export, refining, improvement, treatment, processing, transportation, transfer, storage, distribution, retail sale, allocation and sale of its products;
- specifying the quality of the by-products of oil, natural gas and biofuels;
- regulating and inspecting access to the pipeline capacity;
- promoting public hearings for contracting natural gas transportation, according to the guidelines of the MME;
- registering contracts of transportation and interconnection between transportation facilities, including those from abroad, and sales contracts signed by market agents;
- informing of the origin or description of the reserves of natural gas contracted and to be contracted by market agents;
- regulating and inspecting the storage of natural gas, including in relation to the third parties' right to access the facilities under concession;
- preparing notices to bid and promoting the bid rounds for contracting concessionaires to explore the transportation and storage of natural gas;
- signing, by on behalf of the MME, the concession contracts for exploring the transportation and storage of natural gas under the concession regime;
- authorising sales of natural gas under the responsibility of the union;
- setting criteria to check the capacity of transportation and transfer pipelines; and
- interacting with state and environmental regulatory authorities to set compatible and consistent standards for the natural gas industry and its markets.

The ANP may also require the following from the agents it regulates:

- to keep minimum inventories of fuels and biofuels at their own facilities or third-party facilities; and
- to provide guarantees and evidence of their capacity to supply the fuel and biofuels market, by presenting, among other things, supply contracts.

Article 8A states that the ANP must supervise the handling of natural gas on the transportation network and coordinate it where necessary. The contingency committee will define the guidelines for coordinating these operations. The article also states that the ANP should:

- supervise data and information on the transportation pipeline control centres;
- maintain a permanently updated database on the natural gas handling system, and notify the MME if this needs to be reinforced;
- monitor the introduction and shipment of natural gas to and from the transportation networks, comparing the volumes shipped with the transportation contracts that are in force;
- disclose any unused capacity and propose ways to contract it; and
- set the standards and parameters for efficiently operating and maintaining the system for transporting and storing natural gas.

The article also states that transportation companies are responsible for providing the ANP with the relevant parameters and information for the supervision, control and coordination of the operation of natural gas pipelines.

The technical and economical parameters of the shared production contracts that must be defined by the MME are:

- the criteria for defining the state's excess oil;
- the minimum percentage of the state's excess oil;
- Petrobras's minimum participation in bidding consortia;
- the limits, deadlines, criteria and terms to be used by the contracted party for calculating and appropriating the cost in oil and the production volume that corresponds to the royalties payable; and
- the rules on the minimum local content and the signing bonus; and
- how much is to be allocated to PPSA.[22]

The Law of Shared Production Regime changed the ANP's responsibilities. In addition to regulating and inspecting those activities carried out under the shared production regime, as is currently done for those blocks under concession, it was also newly required to assist the MME in designating which blocks were to be assigned to the concession regime or to the shared production regime, and to prepare drafts of the shared production contracts.[23]

As a result, the ANP now prepares the studies that will support the political definitions that the MME will propose to the CNPE and that will be decided upon by the president.

The ANP will also conduct the processes for auctioning the pre-salt and strategic

---

20 Law of Shared Production Regime, Article 11 assigns the following functions to the ANP:
- promoting technical studies to help the MME delimit those blocks that will be the object of a shared production contract;
- preparing and submitting to the MME drafts of the shared production contracts and the notices to bid, at the start of a bidding process;
- promoting these bidding processes;
- enforcing industry best practices;
- analysing and approving, according to the provisions of subsection IV of this article, the plans for exploration, evaluation and the development of production, as well as the annual work and production programmes related to the shared production contracts; and
- regulating and inspecting activities carried out under the shared production regime, following Article 8 of Law 9,478/1997.

21 For a full list of the MME's responsibilities see note 14.

22 Law of Shared Production Regime, Article 8: "The management of the contracts contemplated in the introduction to this article shall be done by the public company created for that purpose."

23 For a full list of the ANP's responsibilities see notes 19 and 20.

24 Law of Shared Production Regime, Article 20: "The winning bidder shall form a consortium with Petrobras and with the public company contemplated in the 1st paragraph of Article 8 of this Law, pursuant to the provisions of Article 279 of Law 6,404, of December 15 1976."

25 Law 6,404/1976, Article 279: states that the consortium will be formed by a contract that specifies the following:
- the designation of the consortium, if any;
- the project that is the object of the consortium;
- the duration, address and venue;
- a definition of the obligations and responsibility of each member of the consortium, and their specific duties;
- rules for receiving revenues and sharing profits;
- rules for the management of the consortium, accounting, representation of the members of the consortium and management fee, if any;
- the method of deliberating over matters of common interest, with the number of votes each member of the consortium is entitled to; and
- the share of each member of the consortium for covering any common expenses.

The consortium agreement and any amendments must be filed with the board of trade and the filing certificate must be published.

areas to bidding consortia. These must be formed according to Article 20 of the Shared Production Regime Law[24] and Article 279 of Law 6,404/1976.[25]

In fact the ANP is responsible for signing the concession contracts for the exploration, development and production of oil and gas in blocks that meet the provisions of article 23 of the Petroleum Law.[26] The ANP is also responsible for managing the state's assets according to the national interest:[27] Article 21 of the same law sets out that all rights for the exploration and production of oil and natural gas in Brazil belong to the state and are managed by the ANP.

Finally, the ANP regulates and inspects the oil industry through administrative rulings and resolutions, which are administrative acts that follow the resolutions of its board. Administrative rulings are used in cases when the rights of the economic agents or of consumers and users of goods and services are not affected. Resolutions, on the other hand, are used for decisions that affect the rights of these parties. For this reason they are always preceded by public hearings that give these parties a chance to have their views heard.

ANP Resolutions 36 to 39 of 2007 are especially important. They respectively approve the agency's Regulations 06 to 09, which were drawn up to create and implement the model of certification and measurement of the local content[28] in oil and gas exploration and production. This was so as to accord with the guidelines of CNPE and the terms of the concession contract used in the seventh bid round, which required that the commitment of concessionaries to acquire goods and services locally be proven through a national system of certification.

4. Conclusion

As may be seen, changes to the legal circumstances of oil activity in Brazil have resulted in significant changes in the responsibilities of the government agents.

In trying to assess the present situation, four points in particular must be considered:

- The main factor for these changes was the government's choice to increase the state's intervention in such economic activity;
- These new responsibilities have not yet been tested;
- No draft of the shared production contract has yet been elaborated; and
- No bidding round has been announced under the new shared production regime.

Because of these it is too soon to make an appropriate evaluation of the new scenario.

---

26 Petroleum Law, Article 23: "The activities of exploration, development and production of oil and natural gas shall be carried out under concession contracts after a bidding round, according to the terms of this Law, or the shared production regime in the pre-salt and strategic areas, according to specific laws."

27 Petroleum Law, Article 21: "All the rights of exploration and production of oil, natural gas and other fluid hydrocarbons in the national territory, including land, territorial sea, the continent and the exclusive economic zone are owned by the Union and managed by the ANP, except in the cases where other agencies and entities have that responsibility, pursuant to the law."

28 Annex III of Regulation 6 allows the most recent version of PROMINP's book of instructions to be used when measuring local content. The ANP's Coordination of Local Content document, prepared on December 1 2009 and revised on December 2 2010, means to clarify the process of certifying local content.

Brazilian players: Petrobras, NOCs, IOCs and independents

Felipe Feres
Luiz Antonio Lemos
Luis Antonio Menezes
Marcelo Romanelli
Campos Mello Advogados

1. Introduction

This chapter aims to provide a global overview of the main players in the upstream oil and gas industry in Brazil, as well as the history of their creation and participation in Brazil.

1.1 A history of Brazilian oil and the incorporation of Petrobras

The discovery of oil in Brazil dates back to the colonial period. The existence of petroleum had already been recorded during the imperial regime when a licence to extract bitumen at Marau riverbanks in the state of Bahia, northeastern Brazil, was granted. At this time, the regulatory framework was very poor and the industry was basically composed of small companies and entrepreneurs.

In 1927, a specific law was proposed to the oil sector, by which exploration was to be performed exclusively by Brazilian individuals. In 1930, an agronomist became aware that a "dark mud" was being used to light the lamps of the residents located in a small city called Lobato, in the state of Bahia. After several tests, he provided a technical report to President Getúlio Vargas about the existence of oil. These events triggered the beginning of Brazilian regulation over oil and gas activities.

As a consequence, the Brazilian Constitution of 1937 gave the right to explore mineral resources only to Brazilian individuals or companies controlled by Brazilian shareholders.

In 1938 discussions led to the enactment of Decree 3,236, which created the National Petroleum Council (CNP), and decided that the exploration of reservoirs was a monopoly of the state. In 1941 the Brazilian government announced the first Brazilian commercial oil field in the city of Candeias, in the state of Bahia. During the subsequent years, a natural gas field was found in Aratu and a petroleum field in Itaparica, both also in the state of Bahia.

In 1945, the Petroleum National Council decided to allow foreign investment in the Brazilian oil industry, as well as to open the downstream market by permitting the participation of national private companies in refining imported petroleum. This decision generated, in 1947, the campaign "The Oil is Ours", which called for

Brazilian autonomy in the oil sector. This campaign divided the country between those who wanted to have a Brazilian state company explore the oil, those who thought that the oil segment should be explored by all Brazilians and those who supported the presence of foreign private companies. The dispute lasted until 1953.

The first proposal prevailed, with the support of President Getúlio Vargas, and Petróleo Brasileiro SA (Petrobras) was incorporated by Law 2,004/1953. The state monopoly over the oil and gas industry was thus formalised.

In subsequent years, Petrobras improved its ability to operate and develop new technologies for exploring oil reservoirs. In 1968, it began to invest in a deep water exploration system. This led to the discovery of oil at the Campos Basin in 1974, which is still the largest oil producing basin in Brazil.

Despite these exploratory campaigns, oil production in Brazil was still incipient. At the same time the worldwide oil crises were beginning. In the 1970s, desperate to increase Petrobras's production and so fuel Brazil's growing economy, the government decided that the company should execute production 'risk contracts' in order to guarantee domestic oil supply. At this stage private companies were once more welcome to perform upstream activities. However, due to a lack of regulatory background, these contracts were frequently contested by Brazilian public opinion.

1.2 The 1988 Brazilian Constitution and the current oil framework

The 1988 democratic Brazilian Constitution maintained the federal union's monopoly, by expressly prohibiting the participation of private companies in the oil and gas market.

As a result, Petrobras was prevented from embarking on further risk contracts, although those already executed between 1976 and 1988 remained in force.

In 1995, Congress approved Constitutional Amendment 9, which modified the existing provisions on the oil industry to allow the union to contract both private and state-owned companies to explore and produce natural resources. This amendment was followed by the Petroleum Law,[1] and was one of a number of measures taken by the government to open the Brazilian oil industry to foreign investors. Those measures paved the way for the entrance of the international oil companies (IOCs) and independent companies into the upstream oil and gas business in Brazil.

During the period from 1997 to 2007, which encompasses the first 10 years of the regulatory concession system, proven Brazilian oil reserves jumped from 7.1 billion to 12.6 billion barrels, and proven natural gas reserves increased from 228 billion cubic metres (m^3) to 365 billion m^3.

In that same period, annual oil production increased from 316 million barrels to 669 million barrels, and annual natural gas production increased from 9.8 billion m^3 to 18.2 billion m^3. The result is that the production of hydrocarbons in Brazil more than doubled in 10 years.

The participation of many domestic and foreign oil companies was instrumental in achieving these results. In April 2008, 72 economic groups – 36 from Brazil,

1 Federal Law 9,478/1997.

including Petrobras; and 36 from 19 other countries, including Angola, Canada, Singapore, Colombia, South Korea, the United States, France, the Netherlands, India, Norway, Portugal and the United Kingdom – were active in Brazil in exploring and producing of oil and natural gas.

1.3 The discovery of the pre-salt fields and the new regulatory regime

On November 8 2007, the National Council of Energy Policy (CNPE) announced its first assessments of a promising new Petrobras prospect, named Tupi, located in the Santos Basin. The initial estimate was that the Tupi reservoir contained 4 billion barrels, but more accurate studies indicated that this discovery alone holds approximately 8 billion barrels of oil equivalent (BOE). This which would increase Brazilian hydrocarbon reserves by more than 50%.

The announcement initiated a series of statements on the possible existence of gigantic reserves in an exploratory frontier area named the 'pre-salt' layer. The name arises from the fact that these reserves are placed below a thick layer of salt, on average around 7,000 metres (m) deep. The pre-salt area is located approximately 170 kilometres (km) from the Brazilian coast, distributed throughout a range approximately 800 km wide, between the coast of the States of Espírito Santo and Santa Catarina.

As a result, a debate emerged in Brazil regarding what would be the most profitable and efficient regime for exploring and exploiting these new-found reserves.

In July 2008, an inter-ministerial commission was formed to study the regulatory framework and propose any necessary changes with respect to oil and gas exploration and production for the pre-salt areas. The commission was formed of five ministers: the minister for mines and energy, who was also the chairman of the commission; the chief of staff; the minister for development, industry and foreign trade; the minister for finance; and the minister for planning; as well as the presidents of the Brazilian Development Bank, the National Agency of Petroleum, and Natural Gas and Biofuels (ANP) and Petrobras.

Following studies carried out by the commission, in 2009 the president submitted bills of law to Congress that contained the new regulatory framework for the pre-salt area.

Among other laws that were enacted at this time, Law 12,351 (the PSA Law) introduced a new contracting system, the production sharing agreement (PSA) regime. This applies to exploration and production activities in the pre-salt areas and in areas that may be declared as "strategic" by the CNPE.[2] IOCs and independent companies are allowed to take part in bidding rounds for pre-salt blocks that will be granted under this regime. However, the new regime limits the participation of these players:

- Petrobras will be the sole operator of all blocks explored under this system;
- The federal government may directly hire Petrobras or hold bidding rounds

2 Note that the PSA Law does not describe exactly what should be considered strategic. It sets out that the government may use a federal decree to determine what should be considered a strategic area for the purposes of the PSA.

in which private companies can freely participate; and
- Petrobras will be granted a minimum 30% participating interest in areas that are auctioned, and it may also participate in the auction with the aim of increasing its interest in these areas.

The PSA Law creates a new player, the Brazilian Oil and Natural Gas Management Corporation – Pre-Salt Petroleum (PPSA), to represent the nation's interests in the PSA Regime.

2. Petrobras

Petrobras was created by Law 2,004/53, which established the following activities as a monopoly of the federal union:
- the exploration and production of oil reserves and other fluid hydrocarbons and rare gases;
- the refining of national or foreign oil; and
- the maritime transport of national crude oil or by-products produced in the country.

Created as a mixed capital corporation, in which the Brazilian government holds the majority of voting shares, Petrobras started to operate in January 1954.

With the flexibility of the oil monopoly, Petrobras began to figure as an exploration and production concessionaire. For this purpose, concession agreements were executed with the ANP that reflected those areas in which Petrobras had already entered a production phase. In order to protect the company's previous investments, such agreements were excused from the necessity of a bidding round. Most of those areas that were being explored by Petrobras were granted a three-year term for further exploration.

Petrobras acts in the Brazilian market as an economic agent and in competitive conditions with other players, without being subject to the Bid Procedures Law (Law 8,666/1993) for its own procurement activities. Yet Petrobras still has to follow certain procedures for contracting goods and services under a statutory, but simplified bid process, as per Decree 2,745/1998.

In terms of market value Petrobras is the largest company in Brazil and the eighth largest company in the world, with a presence in more than 28 countries across the five continents.

The company currently holds more than 100 oil production platforms, 16 refineries, 30,000 km of pipelines and 8,000 gas stations around the world. Its operations rely largely upon a fleet of 172 vessels, of which 52 are owned directly by the company.

Petrobras's daily production is in the order of 2.583 billion barrels per day (bpd) and 428,000 barrels of liquefied natural gas. Its proven oil reserves are estimated at around 16 billion barrels of oil. The goal is to double this number in the coming years. Petrobras's refineries generate 2,052,000 barrels of by-products per day.

The value of the trademark PETROBRAS is estimated at around R19 billion, with a net income of R213 billion and net profit of R35 billion. The investments made by the company total R76 billion, and its number of shareholders is around 580,000.

Petrobras's research centre (Cenpes) is the biggest in Latin America. It is in continuous growth due to the company's investments in research and development of new technologies to overcome the challenges that arise from its different businesses.

The board of directors of Petrobras approved its business plan for the period between 2010 and 2014 with a total of investment in the order of $224 billion, representing an average of $44.8 billion per year.

The plan is based on integrated growth, profitability and social/environmental liability, with 95% ($212.3 billion) to be invested in Brasil and 5% ($11.7 billion) to be invested abroad. Investments with local suppliers total 67%, which means an annual level of contracting in the country of around $28.4 billion.

Oil production is estimated at 3.9 million BOE in 2014 with a projection of 5.4 million BOE in 2020.

With the discovery of the pre-salt area and this daring business plan announced by Petrobras, the company had to raise funds to meet the investments necessary for exploring and producing of oil and gas at this new frontier, as well as for supporting necessary investments in its other projects.

A capitalisation and public offering of stocks process was therefore conducted in 2010. This includes the major participation of the government who paid their share through an onerous transfer of the equivalent to 5 billion barrels of oil in the pre-salt area that belong to the union but have not yet been exploited.

The capitalisation process was an option for funding the debt, once the company has come close to its 35% legal limit of indebtedness. If this limit is surpassed, the company runs the risk of losing its investment grade, which may have negative consequences for Petrobras's investment plans.

2.1 The monopoly period

With the end of World War II, the national economic and strategic importance of oil and its by-products was clear. It was in this context that Congress enacted Law 2,004/1953, which established oil activities as a monopoly of the government and set out the guidelines for national petroleum policy and the attributions of the CNP, as well as the creation of Petrobras.

National oil companies (NOCs) were being created around the world at this time. Most countries emerged from World War II with a better understanding of the importance of control over oil to assuring national security. Additionally, the social and political changes taking place in the new states – ex-colonies formally subjugated by the great powers – started a series of nationalisation measures in strategic sectors of their economies such as oil.

It was also necessary to raise funds to counter the lack of financial resources for exploring and producing national oil; this was one of the reasons for the creation of Petrobras, for example.

Petrobras was therefore created as a mixed-capital corporation. It started operations with the relatively meagre funds of $165 million. In its early stages there was also a distinct lack of qualified technical personnel, since geology courses did not yet exist in Brazil. Several US engineers were hired to manage Petrobras's exploration and production activities.

Between 1950 and 1967, Petrobras focused its operations on the onshore areas of the Reconcavo and Amazon Basins, although without much success at first. The discoveries in Jequiá and Tabuleiro Martins, in 1957, were the first to open the oil production horizons of the Reconcavo Basin, and the later discovery of Carmópolis was the crowning success of northeastern Brazil.

At the end of the 1960s, driven by a large demand for oil created by industrial expansion, Petrobras decided to enhance its investments in the sea. It once again had to overcome the same problems it first encountered – a lack of experience and qualified personnel. Between 1967 and 1972, a huge gravimetric appraisal was made between the states of Rio de Janeiro and Pernambuco. These studies did not present optimistic opportunities, which led Petrobras to look for foreign oil and direct its investments to the downstream sector.

The pessimism regarding the reserves, especially those onshore, and the technological complexities of expanding the exploratory frontier meant that the rate of production fell below the rate required to sustain increasing consumption. The result was the first external oil crisis.

The implications of this on Petrobras were both positive, because oil prices escalated, and negative, because the company's image deteriorated. However, in 1973 a few new discoveries were made, most notably in the Campos Basin, which would solve the country's oil supply problem.

Since oil production in Brazil was not yet sufficiently effective during the period it took to develop the Campos Basin, Petrobras, as mentioned above, was forced by the government to enter into risk contracts in an attempt to guarantee the domestic oil supply. In 12 years, however, these contracts presented Petrobras with few positive results other than knowledge about areas not yet explored by the company.

Nevertheless, by the end of the 1970s the discoveries started to increase. In 1979, the year of the second oil crisis, Brazil produced 14% of the oil it consumed; by 1985 this number had increased to 50%. This was mostly due to the technological advances that Petrobras made in developing the Campos Basin. Fields such as Namorado, Enchova, Carapeba, Marimbá and Abacorra allowed Brazilian production to increase dramatically and come closer to meeting the country's consumption demands.

Between the mid-1980s and the mid-1990s, Petrobras was able to overcome several financial adversities and severe political uncertainty to make immense technological strides and several commercial discoveries. 3D seismic technology became more commonplace, and important discoveries were made in the Solimões and Santos Basin. And then, in 1996, the giant field of Roncador was discovered in the Campos Basin.

2.2 The period of liberalisation

A new Brazilian Constitution was enacted in October 1988. This established freedom of initiative as one of its foundations, limiting the direct intervention of the state in the economy. In several sectors, the state's role was limited to that of a normative and regulatory agent, with responsiblities for supervision, motivation and planning.

Following the opening of the global market and the tendency towards privatisation of the late 1980s, the Constitution was amended in 1995. The result was the favourable participation of foreign capital in different areas of the national economy, as well as the development of private companies to perform activities that had previously been subject to state monopoly. This included the oil and gas industry.

By authorising public or private companies to perform exploration and production activities by means of authorisations or concessions, Amendment 9/95 brought flexibility to the state's monopoly of oil and gas activities.

Exploration and production remained a monopoly of the union, but the government was now able to contract public or private companies to perform these activities by means of bidding rounds and a concession agreement, or through an administrative authorisation.

In August 1997 the Petroleum Law was enacted to regulate this newly opened market for oil and gas.

Under the terms of this law and the Constitution, the concessionaire becomes the owner of the oil and gas after its production, but must compensate the government accordingly.

The Petroleum Law sets out several other rules with respect to the regulation of the oil and gas industry. It also created the CNPE, which proposes national energy policies to the president; and the ANP, the industry's regulator, which is linked to the Ministry of Mines and Energy.

The main changes brought by Amendment 9/95 and the Petroleum Law are:

- the creation of a regulatory agency for the oil and gas industry (the ANP);
- the introduction of governmental participations as a compensation to be paid by the concessionaire;
- a mechanism for evaluating oil and gas prices in Brazil;
- the opening of the market to other companies, besides Petrobras; and
- incentives to develop local industry through local content requirements.

Decree 2,705 was enacted in 1998 so as to regulate some of the provisions of the Petroleum Law, especially with respect to governmental participation and the methods of calculation.

This new regulatory environment fostered the country's industry. Today there are approximately 80 Brazilian companies operating and investing in more than 300 concessions bid by the ANP, and relating to more than 750 blocks.

Following Amendment 9/95 and the enactment of the Petroleum Law, the ANP performed the so-called "Round Zero". This was a round of negotiations whose aim was to define Petrobras's share under the new regime.

Petrobras's rights over 282 production or development fields – divided into 115 concession blocks, and equivalent to an area of 450,000 km^2 – were ratified by concession agreements. Over the following years, more than 60 of those fields which had production at some point were returned by Petrobras; these areas became known as "marginal fields".

Throughout the next 10 bid rounds that took place until 2008, Petrobras's participation was very large, and the company was granted 403 blocks, or approximately half of all the concessions granted. Petrobras is the operator in 327 of these blocks, which means that it is the operator in 40% of Brazilian concessions.

This competition-driven environment, together with Petrobras's opportunity to work as an operator in private consortia, has given it a state-of-the-art position over technology for deep-water drilling, the environment in which most Brazilian oil is located. As a result Petrobras has become one of the world's leading companies in this field.

In 2010, Petrobras drilled a total of 116 wells, of which 67 were onshore and 49 offshore. Of the offshore wells, 31 were in pre-salt areas and 18 in the post-salt region. The hit ratio achieved was 57%, which is 17% more than the year before. Discoveries of oil and associated gas of excellent quality (46º API) have also been made in the Solimões Basin, and in the Santos Basin 3 billion barrels of recoverable oil, with a quality around 30º API, have been verified.

2.3 The mixed regimes period

The PSA Law was enacted on December 2010. This introduced the production sharing regime to the exploration of oil and gas within the pre-salt and strategic areas.

As a result, Brazil now has two different regimes for the oil and gas industry:

- concession agreements; and
- PSA for the pre-salt and "strategic" areas.

PSAs may be executed by the union directly with Petrobras, without need for a prior bid procedure, or following a bid procedure involving other industry players.

According to the PSA Law, Petrobras will be the sole operator of all blocks under the production sharing regime, and it must have a minimum participation of 30% when it is in consortium with other players.

Petrobras's sole operatorship of all blocks under the production sharing regime will lead to much questioning with respect to the company's economic and political capacity to support all the costs and liabilities this entails.

According to specialists, the pre-salt area will require massive technological investment to overcome the technical difficulties in exploring and extracting hydrocarbons at such a depth. This is besides the increasing need for material, financial and human resources to continue all those pre-salt projects.

Petrobras therefore estimates that more than $110 billion will be necessary before 2020 in order to achieve the desired production of 5 million bpd from the blocks that have currently been granted.

Additionally, in the pre-salt areas in which Petrobras is the sole operator, the risk of occasional environmental damage may be increased due to the new knowledge of this frontier that needs to be acquired over time. If this occurs, its costs will be completely supported by the company and its partners.

In this worst-case scenario, it will be important to separate the union's political influence over the company from any penalties to which it may be subject.

2.4 The future

Some experts are distrustful of Petrobras's investment plan for the next years, including the economic uncertainties in relation to its capacity to support the necessary investments in the pre-salt area, as described above.

Although Petrobras recently conducted a capitalisation process to raise the necessary funds for exploiting the pre-salt area, this new frontier remains mysterious and uncertain, and may require higher investments than those foreseen.

The government's interference in the company's businesses has also increased as a result of the onerous transfer made by the union during its capitalisation process. This, together with the other factors described above, has contributed to an approximate fall of 50% in the company's market value during 2011.

Although Petrobras has a very successful history in the exploration and production of hydrocarbons in new frontier areas, only once it has succeeded in developing its pre-salt operations will it be able to deflect the present criticims and distrust.

3. Pre-salt NOCs

3.1 Creation

On August 2 2010, the Brazilian Congress enacted Law 12,304 (the PPSA Law). Although it has not yet been implemented, this law authorises the government to create the PPSA.

The PPSA will be a state-run corporation whose capital will be completely owned by the union.

The PPSA's revenues will come from a portion of the signature bonuses, to be defined by the Ministry of Mines and Energy, for each PSA,[3] and from remuneration for managing the PSAs and the hydrocarbon commercialisation agreements. The amounts of this remuneration will be defined according to the phases of the agreements, the dimension of the blocks and fields, and other criteria. It is not yet clear what compensation the PPSA will receive for this management or who will be responsible for making these payments.

The company's bylaws will be established by an act of the president. However, the law has already established that the PPSA will be managed by a board of five directors:

- one nominated by the Ministry of Mines and Energy;
- one appointed by the Ministry of Finance;
- one appointed by the Ministry of Planning;
- one appointed by the Civil House of the Presidency; and
- the chief executive of the PPSA.

It is also known that its headquarters will be in Brasília and its central offices will be in Rio de Janeiro.

3 A signature bonus is a government take to be paid by the winners of the bid for each block.

3.2 Roles

According to the PPSA Law, the PPSA must represent the union in consortia formed by the parties to each PSA, and will be the union's voice on the respective operating committees. In this way it will manage the PSAs.

Additionally, the company will perform a technical and economic evaluation of any exploration, appraisal, development and production plans, and must monitor and audit their execution.

The PPSA will also enforce any contractual provisions regarding local content obligations, as well as monitoring and auditing any costs and investments related to the PSA.

Under Brazil's PSA framework, the union is not authorised to receive its share of oil profits in cash, but must receive it in profit oil, which it must then commercialise. (Profit oil is the production of oil, natural gas and other fluid hydrocarbons to be shared between the union and other parties to the PSA.) In this way the PPSA will represent the union in executing and managing commercialisation agreements for hydrocarbons. The PPSA will also monitor and audit the operation, costs and prices for selling hydrocarbons. Petrobras will probably act as the PPSA's agent/broker in marketing the union's profit oil, and may even purchase it directly.

Other relevant roles of the new state owned company include:

- analysing the seismic data furnished by the ANP and any contractors under the PSA regime;
- supplying the ANP with the information necessary for its regulatory functions; and
- representing the union in unitisation procedures when reservoirs extend into areas that have not been granted or that have been granted under the concession regime.

Finally, it is important to emphasise that the PPSA may not directly carry out exploration, development, production or commercialisation. This means that, in reality, the PPSA is not Brazil's NOC for the pre-salt area, but the union's representative and manager, and the supervisor of other parties' activities. In many ways, Petrobras will continue to be the country's de facto NOC.

3.3 The relationship between Petrobras and other players

Under the PSA Law, winning bidders must form a consortium with the PPSA and Petrobras. As mentioned before, Petrobras will remain the mandatory operator of all pre-salt and strategic areas, in addition to holding a minimum 30% stake in each PSA consortium. Petrobras's forced stake in each consortium implies its acceptance of the respective tender protocol and the winning bidder's offer in the bid round. Its rights and obligations will be calculated in proportion to its participating interest.

Consortia shall be managed by an operating committee. As the union's representative, the PPSA will have the prerogative of nominating 50% of this committee's members, including its president. The president will hold the power veto and a tie-breaking vote. In this way the union, through the PPSA, will always be in a privileged position in comparison to other players within a consortium in such areas as defining work programmes, approving budgets and hiring the main field contractors.

As for the commercialisation of the union's share of profit oil, the new regulatory regime allows the PPSA to contract Petrobras as its trading agent directly, without a prior bidding process.

3.4 The future

The industry's players and stakeholders are anxiously waiting for the government to produce the PPSA's bylaws and the form of the production sharing agreement. Only then will various questions about the Brazilian PSA regime begin to be answered. Some of these questions are as follows:

- Since, in principle, the PPSA Law gives quasi-regulatory powers to the PPSA, in terms of evaluating plans for exploration, development and production, and the enforcement of the contract's rules, does that mean that the ANP's regulatory powers and roles will diminish for PSA areas?
- Will the PPSA's representation of the union on the operating committees entail unnecessary political influence in committee decisions, and will it lead to the most financially and operationally sound decisions being rejected in favour of those that are in line with the government's wishes and interests?
- How will the relationship between the PPSA and Petrobras play out in cases where they disagree during the operating committee's meetings or on the terms and conditions of the union's hydrocarbons commercialisation agreements?
- Considering its complexity, let alone the fact that it comprises two different regimes (concession and PSA), how will the rules for unitisation determine which should prevail over the other?
- Lastly and most importantly, will this new regulatory regime attract private national and foreign players, as the concession regime has done, or will it mark the beginning of Petrobras's *de facto* monopoly of the Brazilian exploration and production industry?

4. IOCs

During the concession years, IOCs have positively influenced the development of the Brazilian oil industry. Despite the fact that Petrobras has remained the major player in the upstream and downstream activities, IOCs have contributed to the development of technology and the palpable growth of the industry.

The ANP's annual reports on the number of players in exploration and production fields confirm that IOCs have played an important role since the monopoly for upstream and downstream activities in Brazil was loosened.

Some IOCs are currently producing in Brazil and several are exploring the Brazilian concession fields.

4.1 Participation during the monopoly period

Before the Petroleum Law, there were few players in the Brazilian oil industry, and from 1953 Petrobras was the sole company operating the fields. The IOCs played a greater role in the downstream market.

Nevertheless, from 1976 to 1988 Petrobras made risk contracts with both IOCs and Brazilian service providers. These required the contracted party to perform the services until the start of the production operations, at its sole cost and risk.

Once production had started, all costs would be repaid to the contracted party, who would be entitled to a share of the production revenues of each field throughout the production period. Petrobras would take over production once development operations for each unit were finished by the contracted party.

Despite this rule, the risk contracts usually allow Petrobras to ask the contracted party to continue providing technical and operational services in any commercial field that they had discovered and developed. The conditions and principles for these arrangements would be established separately.

In this period 243 risk contracts were signed, but only a few commercial fields were actually discovered. The IOCs therefore dealt more with the downstream business, and mainly the distribution of kerosene and gasoline during this time.

4.2 Participation during the period of liberalisation

After the loosening of the monopoly, the market was finally open for other national and international companies to explore Brazilian oil and gas. This took place through participation in the rounds of bidding promoted by the ANP.

The competition-based regime created by the Petroleum Law and the ANP's regulations was transparent. The chance to extend exploration and production operations into Latin America's biggest economy, under a familiar concession regime – the world's most widely used – and a stable political environment made Brazil an attractive environment for IOCs.

The concession regime has won the interest of various IOCs over the years, including US companies Exxon Mobil and Chevron-Texaco, the Dutch-UK company Shell, Spanish outfit Repsol, the UK companies BG and BP, the Portuguese Galp Energia, and even Chinese company Sinopec. This last has partnered with Repsol in a venture that, according to the company's website, plans to invest more than $7 billion in exploration and production activities in Brazil.

The presence of these IOCs in Brazil has contributed greatly to the incredible growth – of more than 300% – of the oil and gas industry in the 14 years of the concession regime.

The interest of the IOCs in the Brazilian reserves remains high and new players continue to enter the country. These include Russian company TNK-BP, which is one of the world's top 10 oil producing companies and the first Russian company to enter the Brazilian exploration and production industry.

4.3 Participation during the mixed regimes period

As previously explained, the discoveries made in the pre-salt layer greatly increased the potential of Brazil's oil and gas reserves, causing the government to rethink its strategy for oil and gas exploration and development. As a consequence, the ANP excluded any potential pre-salt blocks from the last two rounds of bidding, held in 2007 and 2008.

The new regulatory framework was created by three bills of law and introduced a new contractual and legal regime for the pre-salt and other "strategic" areas: the Brazilian PSA. Among the changes set out were the creation of a new state-run company – PPSA – which will participate in all pre-salt blocks, and the provision that Petrobras will be the sole operator of any and all such blocks, holding at least a 30% interest in any consortium formed with other parties.

While the PSA regime might appear less attractive for both independent producers and IOCs, it may still retain an interest for the IOCs. Although the Brazilian PSA has a lot of non-traditional features, PSA regimes are widely known and used throughout the global industry and are familiar to most IOCs. Even though there is no possibility of operation, the geological risk in the pre-salt area is smaller than in other offshore areas in Brazil, which may improve the security of investments.

4.4 The future

The political situation in Brazil has been stable since the early 1990s, and the country's ever-growing economy is strong and diversified. This allows strides to be made by the exploration and production supply chain. In fact, the scale of investments required by Brazil's infrastructure is enormous – estimates approach almost $500 billion over the next 10 years dedicated to oil and gas.

Most of these investments will be needed for exploring and developing the pre-salt area, which entails expansions to the refining and petrochemical sector, and the infrastructure for transporting and distributing gas and power. The multitude of large and intricate projects on the horizon is likely to present good opportunities for suppliers and partners, especially integrated companies that already have downstream activities in the country.

According to data from the Ministry of Mines and Energy, only 28% of the pre-salt's total area has so far been granted under concession. This means that 72% of the Brazilian pre-salt layer, or 107,228 km^2, remains unexplored.

Furthermore, Petrobras's success rate to date in drilling pre-salt areas is over 90%, and the discoveries it has already made may amount to 14 billion barrels. This is very encouraging for the future of the Brazilian oil and gas sector. In the following years Brazil will almost be able to double its oil production through such discoveries.

The Brazilian oil and gas industry is likely to remain dominated by Petrobras, with the continued presence of IOCs. Although there have not yet been any bidding rounds for new pre-salt blocks, there is a visible trend for new IOCs and NOCs entering Brazil, as shown by the recent arrival of Chinese companies Sinopec and Sinochem, the purchase by BP of Devon Energy's entire Brazilian operation and the entrance of Russia's TNK-BP.

5. Independents

The basic and most common definition of an independent oil and gas company is one whose revenues all or mostly come from upstream activities. These companies work exclusively in the exploration and production segment of the industry, with no downstream marketing or refining. However, for the purposes of tax the US Internal Revenue Service defines an IOC as one whose refining capacity is less than 75,000 bpd on any given day, or whose retail sales are less than $5 million for the year.

According to information from the Independent Petroleum Association of America, independents range in size from large publicly held companies to small proprietorships. Many independents are privately held small companies with few employees. The number of independents has gradually decreased over the last decade.

When referring to the Brazilian industry, the first thing to point out is that the definition 'independent producer' is not used. For this reason there is less information about the number of independents in the country. Nevertheless, taking the definition given above into consideration, it is safe to say that independents have broad activities across the upstream oil and gas sector in Brazil: there are several Brazilian independents and a multitude of international independents.

The Brazilian independents range from small companies, such as Lábrea Petróleo, to large, publicly held corporations, such as OGX, whose stock market flotation was incredibly successful. OGX currently holds more than 20 blocks under exploration, and so has a good potential of reserves.

HRT is another successful Brazilian independent. It began as a service provider and quickly evolved into an independent producer, holding concessions in the Solimões Basin in the state of Amazon, which also has good oil and gas potential. Petra Energia is another Brazilian independent with several blocks under exploration.

It is common for Brazilian independents to have international funding, including from pension and investment funds based outside Brazil. Two cases exemplify this situation well. Barra Energia, a recently incorporated company with highly qualified and experienced technical personnel. Its initial activities were supported by large investments from the First Reserve Corporation, a private investment fund and the world's leading investor in energy. OGX, before going public, also made large private placements, including some from Ontario Teachers' Pension Plan.

There are many international independents operating in Brazil. One of the largest independent oil companies in the world, Houston-based Anadarko Petroleum Corporation, has been performing exploration and production activities in the country for almost a decade. The same was true of the longtime US leading independent Devon Energy, before it sold its Brazilian operations to BP. Other important international independent players present in the country include Perenco, a group holding a worldwide portfolio of assets with operations in 16 countries across the globe; Vanco Exploration, which also holds oil and gas interests in offshore West Africa and the Black Sea; Karoon Gas, a major Australian gas company with assets in the Brazilian Santos Basin, and Woodside, Australia's largest independent oil and gas producer.

According to a study performed by the Independent Petroleum Association of America, a total of 10.8% of independent companies reported participating in international operations, with another 11.1% planning to do so within the next five years. Latin America was a popular venue, with relatively amenable political risk, although the political risk in Brazil is considerably smaller than that of other countries on the continent. The large-sized independents are active internationally, with 50% of the study's respondents indicating that they operated overseas and 37.5% planning to pursue international opportunities in the next five years.

5.1 Opportunities within the period of liberalisation

The Petroleum Law and the ANP's regulations after 1997 helped to create and implement a transparent and effective legal framework that was based on competition and sought to aggressively increase Brazil's oil and gas exploration and production. Competitive operating costs and the potential for large reserves also helped to create an attractive environment for independent companies.

Between 1999 and 2008, 10 bid rounds were performed by the ANP and 765 blocks were granted under concession agreements. Several Brazilian independents were formed and several international companies entered the country. Annual oil and gas production more than doubled in this period, allowing Brazil to become self-sufficient in oil and gas. According to the ANP, there are currently 79 economic groups performing exploration and production activities in the country; 40 of them are foreign and 39 domestic. A good number of these are independents.

5.2 Challenges during the mixed regimes period

After the discoveries made in the pre-salt layer and the strategic rethinking they demanded, extensive studies were performed into the legal-regulatory exploration and production regimes used across the global oil industry. These included a study sponsored by the Brazilian Development Bank that analysed the regimes of 11 different countries. Following this research the government drew up three bills of law with the aim of introducing a PSA regime.

This new regulatory framework appears less attractive to independents because Petrobras will be the only operator in all pre-salt blocks. Furthermore, each consortium's operating committee will be controlled by the government, since the PPSA will appoint half of its members, including its president. Petrobras will also be able to appoint its own representative(s) in proportion to its participating interest. There is therefore some legal uncertainty for current, and potential, independent companies.

Because the concession regime implemented in 1997 is transparent and has been such a success, it is understandable that both IOCs and independents are concerned about whether the new mixed regime will work efficiently.

On the other hand, despite this uncertainty, investing in the pre-salt may still be feasible and interesting. The operating costs are likely to be higher, but recent prospects suggest that the hit ratio for commercial reserves is considerably higher in the pre-salt area than in other offshore areas.

The main challenge with respect to independents in this mixed regimes period is maintaining their interest. In order to overcome the legal insecurity created by the PSA, the Brazilian government must implement a regime that is still attractive to independents. It must ensure that the mixed regime works efficiently and intelligently, and also that the respective concession and production sharing regimes can work together without conflict or confusion.

5.3 The future

The future for independents in Brazil is uncertain. Because there have been no bid rounds since 2009, and because Petrobras will be the sole operator of the pre-salt blocks, there has been a recent trend for foreign independents to leave the country.

Investments are also being made, especially by Brazilian independents such as OGX and HRT, in new exploration frontiers, such as the onshore blocks in the Parnaíba and Solimões Basins. These areas have not yet been labelled as "strategic" by the ANP, and therefore do not yet come under the PSA regime. These areas show good potential, especially for discoveries of natural gas.

The participation of independents in the huge reserves of the pre-salt area depends mostly on the strategy adopted by the Brazilian government. In order to attract independents to the pre-salt blocks, the government will need to elaborate and implement measures in the PSA template to increase its attractiveness to these companies. The overall potential for the exploration and production of oil and gas in Brazil is immense. However, the new mixed regime has reduced the opportunities and desire for independents to invest.

6. Conclusion

Three main issues, of paramount relevance for the future of the oil and gas industry in Brazil, remain unresolved:

- unitisation;
- local content; and
- the rules of governance under the PSA regime.

6.1 Unitisation

Vast extensions of offshore areas, already granted or yet to be granted by either concession or PSA, may be joined as a common reservoir. This issue will particularly be very relevant for the pre-salt area, considering the potential size of the reserves and the current format of the concession blocks, which follow a cell-like structure, much like that in the Gulf of Mexico.

The Brazilian concession regime already presents several obstacles to unitisation, and the PSA will certainly generate complex new ones, with the possibilty arising of unitisation between one area under concession and another under a PSA. The current legislation has no answer for which regime would apply, what type of remuneration the government would receive – whether tax and royalties, or profit oil – or how the operational aspects of two such blocks would be resolved and who would be the operator of the unitised area.

6.2 Local content

It will be a challenge to meet local content requirements with the technological demands of the production chain. The PSA will therefore create a monopsonistic market, with Petrobras the market's sole buyer. Although local industries will be contracted to supply the needs of exploration and production activities, their capacity to export might be compromised under the PSA regime as they would only meet Petrobras's operational requirements.

This might cause the local supply chain to become one-dimensional, and therefore unable to develop suitable products for IOCs and independents or even receive the input of those companies. The lack of a contractual relationship in Brazil thus reduces its competitiveness in the international market.

6.3 Governance under the PSA regime

The main questions here include:

- the actual regulatory role of PPSA with respect to the existing regulatory power of the ANP;
- the level of political influence on the PPSA's representatives on consortium operating committees;
- the relationship between PPSA and Petrobras in case of divergences in decision making; and
- the attractiveness of the PSA regime to private national and foreign players, considering that its template has not yet been elaborated.

The expectation is that 2012 will see definitions for the actual implementation of the PSA regime, followed by a resumption of bid tenders for the pre-salt and concession areas by the ANP.

Only once the bid tenders have resumed under the PSA regime will we have a better picture of the practical challenges of the mixed regulatory regime, including those addressed in this chapter.

The authors would like to thank Saulo Padua and Bruno Vignal for their kind assistance in the preparation of this chapter.

Concessions and the licence regime

Daniela Ribeiro Davila
Vieira, Rezende, Barbosa e Guerreiro Advogados

1. Introduction

In the last decade, the Brazilian government identified its main goals as monetary stabilisation and fighting inflation. As a result, it was compelled to reduce the amount of investment it made in infrastructure.

It was therefore necessary to provide the country with appropriate mechanisms for obtaining domestic and international capital that could help to quickly increase the domestic production of oil and natural gas, and the capacity of refining, transportation and the supply sector as a whole.

To reach these goals, the executive branch submitted a constitutional amendment (Amendment 9/95) that would ease the state monopoly on oil and natural gas. This led to Law 9,478/1997 (the Petroleum Law), which established a new legal framework for the Brazilian oil industry, that is, the concession regime.

2. The union's ownership of gas and oil deposits

The Brazilian Constitution of October 5 1988 established the union's ownership of "mineral resources, including those underground."[1]

Note that the broad term of "mineral resources" includes oil and natural gas. However, as pointed out by Alfredo Ruy Barbosa:[2]

the current biochemical discussions on whether or not to classify petroleum as a mineral are irrelevant from a legal standpoint, considering the standardized treatment always given by the Brazilian Lawmaker and Constitutional Lawmaker.

Despite controversy in the specialised doctrine,[3] deposits of oil, natural gas and other fluid hydrocarbons are neither public goods for common use, nor special use property for a particular public purpose. They are public goods to be used in economic activities, that is, used for economic and not public purposes. They are therefore assets of the union.

Hely Lopes Meirelles defines public property in the following terms:[4]

Available dominion assets or patrimony are those that, although they are a part of public domain like other assets, are different due to the ever-present possibility of being

1 See Article 20: "The following are Union assets: [...] IX – mineral resources, including those underground".
2 Barbosa, Alfredo Ruy, *A natureza jurídica da concessão para exploração e produção de petróleo e gás.*
3 In the opinion of Alexandre de Moraes they are public assets, not domain assets. In Moraes, Alexandre de, *Constituição do Brasil Interpretada e Legislação Constitucional*, 7ª ed., São Paulo, Atlas, 2007, p. 2021.
4 Meireles, Hely Lopes, *Direito Administrativo Brasileiro*, 18ª ed, São Paulo, Malheiros, 1993, p. 433.

used for any purpose, or even disposed of by the government as they see fit. That is also why they are referred to as available patrimonial assets, or as patrimonial items for tax purposes. These assets comprise the assets of the State as an object of real or personal right, meaning that the government exercises ownership powers, *as per the precepts of constitutional and administrative law, in the authoritative opinion of Clovis Bevilaqua.* (Emphasis added.)

Although the union's ownership of assets covers their use, enjoyment and disposal,[5] in the specific case of hydrocarbons deposits the union may exercise only use and enjoyment, exploring them for the purpose of economic advantage. The right to dispose of these deposits remains theoretical.

This is because even if the union could theoretically sell its deposits, the Constitution restricts their exploitation to state monopoly. Any potential buyer of these assets may therefore not use or enjoy them.

Having defined hydrocarbon deposits as the union's dominion assets, we must analyse the union's constitutional monopoly over activities related to them.

3. The monopoly of exploration and production activities

The state monopoly over activities in the oil and natural gas industry was established by Law 2,004/1953. This created Petrobras and assigned it exclusive rights to these monopolised activities.

In constitutional terms, the exploration and production of oil and natural gas was dealt with in the Constitutions of 1967 and 1988.

The liberalism of the Brazilian Constitution should be noted. This can be ascertained by reading the principles of Article 170. Among these, the principle of free competition stands out. The introduction to this constitutional provision should also be mentioned, which expressly states that "the economic order, grounded on the appreciation of human labour and free enterprise, is intended to ensure to all a dignified existence, according to the principles of social justice, following these principles".

The state's action as an entrepreneur in oil and gas is therefore exceptional, as may be seen in Article 173 of the Constitution.[6] Here, except for certain cases, the direct exploration of economic activity by the state is limited to the imperatives of national security or the relevant collective interest.

The state's interference in the economic order is therefore legitimate only in restricted cases, as in cases of public monopolies expressly provided for in the Constitution. Among these is the monopoly over oil and natural gas activities, which is provided for in Article 177.[7] This provides for state intervention, and reserves the exploration of these activities for the state. The union's monopoly therefore refers only to the exercise of exploration and production.[8]

This reservation of economic activity by the state, through public interest,

---

5 See Article 1,228 of the Civil Code: The owner has the right to use, enjoy and dispose of the object, and the right to take it back from anyone who unjustly owns it or holds it.

6 See Article 173: "Except in the cases contemplated in this Constitution, the direct exploration of an economic activity by the State will only be allowed when necessary for the imperatives of national security or relevant collective interest, as defined in the law".

prevented private enterprises from economically exploring these deposits. The first paragraph of Article 177 states that "the monopoly contemplated in this article includes the risks and the results in the activities mentioned in that article. The Union is prohibited from assigning or granting any type of interest, in kind or for payment, in the exploration of deposits of oil or natural gas."

That, thus, constituted the state monopoly of exploration and production of oil and natural gas, established by Law 2,004/1953, and elevated to the status of a constitutional provision in the Constitution of 1967, fully incorporated into the Constitution of 1988, where the state intervention in such economic domain was upheld, under exceptional monopoly. Petrobras featured as its sole and exclusive executor until the loosening introduced by Amendment 9/95.

4. The loosening of the monopoly

As described above, the 1988 Constitution established strict rules for activities related to the oil industry, raising them to the status of constitutional provision. Any contracting of such activities or participation in their results was strictly banned.

To government authorities in the early 1990s this provision was an obstacle to the development of petroleum activities. It was considered necessary to provide legal mechanisms to attract both domestic and international private capital to Brazil, and to increase and accelerate the implementation and growth of oil and natural gas activities.

To achieve these objectives, the Chamber of Deputies and the Senate enacted Amendment 9/95, which changed the first paragraph of Article 177 to the following: "The Union may contract with state-owned or private companies the activities forth in subsections I to IV of this article, pursuant to the terms provided by law."

This so called "loosening of the monopoly", expressed in the expression "may contract" became a right of the union to hire these activities from state-owned or private companies. This condition was approved with the Petroleum Law, which repealed Law 2,004/1953 and created a new legal framework that allowed private participation in the oil industry. The Brazilian Petroleum Agency (ANP) was instituted as the regulatory authority and enforcer of these activities.

In fact, the easing of the oil monopoly came in the wake of the privatisation process, which included removing the barriers to free enterprise and free competition that the Constitution safeguarded for those monopolies.

Amendment 9/95, however, achieved only an intermediary stage of privatisation. The monopoly was loosened, in essence representing a new constitutional principle

---

7 See Article177: "The Union has the monopoly over the following:
I – the research and exploration of the deposits of oil and natural gas and other fluid hydrocarbons;
[...]
§1º The Union may hire State-owned or private companies to provide the activities contemplated in subsections I to IV of this article, pursuant to the conditions of the law.
§2º The law mentioned in the 1st paragraph shall govern:
I – the warranty of provision of oil by-products throughout the national territory;
II – the contracting conditions;
III – the structure and attributions of the authority regulating the Union's monopoly.
[...]".

8 The other activities related to oil and natural gas were not mentioned here since they are beyond the scope of this essay.

in which private companies were able to compete to provide an activity under monopoly. In fact, the Petroleum Law was published two years after Amendment 9/95, and until then Law 2,004/1953 remained in force. During that time Petrobras continued to run the union's monopoly on an exclusive basis.

The loosening therefore granted the union new authorisation to dispose of the exploration of its hydrocarbon deposits differently from the practice under the monopoly regime. With the enactment of the Petroleum Law and the introduction of the concessions regime, the monopolised activities were no longer directly explored by the state, but became the object of bidding between state-owned and private Brazilian companies.

It may thus be said that Amendment 9/95 admits the co-existence of two constitutional principles: the monopoly of the union and the flexible monopoly. The amendment therefore confirms the state's monopoly on the exploration and production of hydrocarbons, but allows state-owned and private companies to be hired to carry out these activities. There is therefore a possible choice for the lawmaker between maintaining the monopoly system or adopting a system that would allow competition.

This opinion is shared by Alexandre de Moraes,[9] who goes further:

It is, therefore, a new concept of monopoly, no longer related to the state intervention in the economic domain exclusively controlling the means of production (intervention by absorption), but related to the monopoly of choice by the government, which may, in accordance with the constitutional rules, choose between confirming the exploration and production of the deposits of oil, natural gas and other fluid hydrocarbons by a single company or contracting with state-owned or private companies.

Constitutional Amendment No. 9/95 ended the state monopoly over the economic activity related to oil and natural gas while retaining the monopoly of the activity itself, i.e., the exploration and production of the deposits of oil and natural gas and other hydrocarbon fluids still constituting a monopoly of the Union, in the sense that only the government may decide who can carry out this economic activity. This is what we refer to as the monopoly of choice by the government. *(Emphasis added.)*

The fundamental conclusion, therefore, is that the current constitutional rule is a "monopoly of the choice by the government", that is, the union's choice to hire out monopolised activities or carry them out itself.

Another important question is whether Amendment 9/95 chose concession as the method by which to contract the activities related to oil and natural gas, or if it simply opened up the possibility of third-party contracts according to methods that were later defined in ordinary law.

It is essential, before any debate on this issue, to read the following passages by Luis Roberto Barroso. These deal with collisions of constitutional rights[10] and discuss methods for interpreting constitutional texts that greatly help in understanding the issue at hand:

The constitutional principles are the set of rules that reflect the ideology of the

9 De Moraes, Alexandre, op.cit, p. 2024.
10 Barroso, Luis Roberto, *Temas de Direito Constitucional*, 2nd ed., Rio de Janeiro, Renovar, 2002, p. 65.

Constitution, its basic principles and its purposes. In short, they are the rules elected by the original Constitutional lawmakers as the foundations or essential qualifications of the legal order. The interpretation of the Constitution should start by identifying the leading principle governing the issue examined, starting from the most generic to most specific, until the concrete rule governing the topic is formulated. It is important to note that the distinction of the past between rule and principle no longer applies. The modern dogmas endorse the view that the statutory rules in general and the constitutional rules, specifically, can be classified in two different categories: the principles and the rules. The latter is restricted to specific situations to which they apply. The principles are normally more abstract and for a more prominent purpose within the system. There is no hierarchy between the two categories. That, however, does not prevent the principles and rules from playing different roles inside the legal order. Thus, according to the principle of hierarchic-normative unity, rules of the original Constitution should never be considered without effect, nor may the reader deliberately choose one to prevail over the others. The Constitution is widely known to be a dialectic document, the product of political compromise and, for that very reason, it covers potentially conflicting principles and rights. When actual conflict situations arise – such as, for example, situations where free enterprise and the state's intervention in the economic scene face off, or between the ownership right and the principle of the social role of property – the interpreter is responsible for seeking the possible conciliation between apparently opposing propositions by weighing values.

The weighing of values is the technique through which the interpreter seeks to deal with constitutional values in a line of collision. Since there is no abstract criterion that makes one value prevail over the other, reciprocal concessions should be made to lead to a socially desirable result, sacrificing the least of each one of the opposing fundamental principles or rights. The lawmaker cannot arbitrarily choose one of the interests at stake and ignore the other, risking violating the constitutional text. Remember: the rules apply to all or nothing, while the principles must be weighed.

With the reflux of positivisms – normative, historicist and sociological – the legal principles gave a new configuration to the theoretical framework of the post-positivism, introducing or deepening concepts such as balance, reasonableness, equality and secondary liability, among others. The interpretation of the Constitution, while using the limits and possibilities offered by the principles to seek a fair solution for a concrete case, increases the creation power and the subjectivity of the interpreter. Consequently, the predictability and certainty of the decisions lose, although the written rule will always remain as an objective parameter, demarcating the boundaries of action. However, what is sacrificed in terms of safety is returned with a gain in the best implementation of the constitutional justice.

The conclusion reached is that the constitutional rules require methods of interpretation that go beyond the traditional. This initial explanation is necessary because, upon first reading Amendment 9/95, the contracting of monopolised activities authorised by Article 177 would be limited to the method of concessions. This may be inferred from subsection II of the second paragraph of this amendment, which states that the law allowing flexibility of the monopoly "shall govern the structure and the attributions of the authority regulating the Union's monopoly".

This first impression derives from the exegesis of said article, through the traditional and widely known methods of interpretation.

In fact, from the writings of the renowned jurist Vicente Raó on the analysis of texts as the initial interpretation of legal rules,[11] we learn that, in the grammatical process (also known as the literal process), "words represent the first expression of things as conceived by the intellect and ... should never be examined separately, but as a whole and contrasted against each other, as part of the text".

Ráo, resorting to the provisions of the Chilean Civil Code, then states that: "The words of law shall be complied with according to their natural and obvious sense, according to their general use. However, when expressly defined by the lawmaker in certain matters, the words of law become those matters, according to their legal sense."[12] He closes with the following remarks: "The technical words of any science or art shall be interpreted according to the meaning given by those teaching the same science or art, except when clearly revealed that they were employed in a different meaning."[13]

According to this interpretation, the expression "the regulatory authority of the Union's monopoly" contained in Amendment 9/95 indicates that the Constitution's author chose for activities to be contracted exclusively by concession.

The expert in interpretation will also apply a logical approach. According to De Plácido e Silva[14] this "will probe the lawmaker's thinking to adapt the law to the facts, taking into consideration the fact governed by the law, the analogy and the similarity between the facts". This would justify the creation, under the privatisation process taking place in the mid-1990s, of regulatory agencies.

Finally, the same can be said about the method of systematic interpretation. This "seeks the true intent of the law based on the relationship of the words and the thought with a natural reasoning, justice, order and common good, to reach, through legitimate and justified conclusions the true or most normal meaning of the text and applies it according to the lawmaker's intent".[15]

However, all this interpretation effort yields to the fact that what is being interpreted is a constitutional text. As previously seen, this should be examined according to specific rules of interpretation. For that it is necessary to distinguish between principle and constitutional rule; not because there is a hierarchy between them but because the principle is general and the rule is specific.

In fact, one can assert that Amendment 9/95 introduced a new constitutional principle: that is, the principle of a flexible monopoly that would allow the union to contract public and private companies to undertake activities under state's monopoly. The amendment also describes what the law should contain, but this represents a response to the circumstances of the time. Its details are more appropriate to subsequent law than the constitutional text.

---

11 Ráo, Vicente, *O Direito e a Vida dos Direitos*, v. 1, Tomo III, 2nd ed. São Paulo, Resenha Universitária, 1977, p. 467.

12 Ráo, Vicente, *op. cit.* p. 467

13 Ráo Vicente, *op cit.* 467

14 Silva, De Plácido, *op. cit.*, p. 764

15 Silva, De Plácido, *op. cit.*, p. 764

The authors of the 1988 Constitution therefore focused on the principle of the monopoly of exploration and production of oil and natural gas. The lawmaker in 1995 went in the opposite direction and changed that rigid principle, allowing monopolised activities to be outsourced.

The principles should govern not only the relations anticipated and considered by the legislature, but also new or different relations that may fall under them. In addition, the constitutional text should be broad and flexible enough to withstand any future changes in society and admit all infra-constitutional laws that may subsequently be approved. We may therefore conclude that the Constitution's authors wanted to give the union broad authorisation to contract monopolised activities to third parties.

As we know, the Petroleum Law permits a concession regime for contracting exploration and production activities in Brazil. This law does not preclude the authorisation of other methods of contracting. Indeed this happened in 2010 with the passing of Law 12,351, which allowed the co-existence of a production sharing regime. To make this co-existence possible a new nomenclature was created for areas of exploration of oil and natural gas on the Brazilian continental shelf. These were pre-salt areas, strategic areas and areas of concession.

The pre-salt area is the underground region formed by a vertical prism of unknown depth. The geographical coordinates of this are defined in the addendum to Law 12,351, but further regions may be defined by the executive branch as geological knowledge increases.[16]

The strategic area is the region of interest for national development defined by the executive branch. It is characterised by a low exploratory risk and a high potential for the production of oil, natural gas and fluid hydrocarbons.[17]

The concession areas are those auctioned off under the concession regime described in the Petroleum Law.

5. The concession contract

The Petroleum Law chose the concession regime[18] for the exploration and production of oil and natural gas in the areas considered non-strategic and outside the pre-salt area. Law 12,351/2010 (the Law of Production Sharing) introduced for the same reason the production sharing regime to the pre-salt and strategic areas.

Unlike under the shared production regime, where the union keeps the exploration results, under the concession regime a third party will explore the deposit for its own benefit. Hence the need for a legal instrument related to these assets of the union. The Petroleum Law, supported by the Constitution, stipulates that the concession regime will always be preceded by a mandatory bidding process.

However, the fact that the exploration of these assets is not governed by public (administrative) law does not make the concession a private law. This is because the

16 Compare subsection IV of Article 2 with subsection V of Article 9 of Law 12,351/2010.

17 Compare subsection V of Article 2 with subsection V of Article 9 of Law 12,351/2010.

18 Law 9,478/1997, Article 23: "The exploration development and production of oil and natural gas shall be carried out under concession contracts preceded by a bidding process according to the terms of the Law."

contracting party of the concession is an entity of the public administration, the ANP, a special autarchy that operates as the regulatory authority in the oil, natural gas and biofuels industry. This circumstance affects the balance between the public and private interests of the parties and admits the prerogatives of the state.

A concession for the exploration and production of oil and natural gas is a concession to the economic exploration of a public asset. This is different from a concession for the exploration of minerals, which is a concession to the use of a public asset.

We should also stress that the concession being examined is not a unilateral act by the government. On the contrary, it is an economic bilateral contract which cannot accommodate exorbitant conditions and unilateral changes, which are typical of administrative contracts, although it has all the characteristics of an adherence contract.

Article 21 of the Petroleum Law[19] assigned the management of all of the union's rights of exploration and production of oil and natural gas to the ANP. That is why the ANP regulates the industry and signs the concession contracts.

The parties to the concession contracts are, therefore, the ANP, representing the Federal union, and the state-owned or private company, formed according to Brazilian law to carrying out the exploration, development and production of oil and natural gas in the concession blocks.

The ANP promotes bidding rounds of these blocks on the suggestion of the Ministry of Mines and Energy and approved by the Brazilian National Energy Policy Council. The ANP publishes the draft of the contract to be used for that round, along with the notice to bid.

The following phases take place in organising a bidding round:[20]

- definition of the blocks;
- announcement of the round;
- publication of the pre-tender protocol and the draft concession contract;
- a public hearing;
- payment of participation fees and offer guarantees;
- making available of the data package;
- an environmental-technical seminar;
- a legal-fiscal seminar;
- publication of the notice to bid and the concession contract;
- opening of the qualification phase for bidding companies;
- the auction for the submission of offers; and
- signing of the contracts.

After bidding, the concession contracts are signed by the ANP, on behalf of the

19 Article 21: "All the rights of exploration and production of oil, natural gas and other fluid hydrocarbons in the national territory, including the continent, the territorial sea, the offshore platform, and the exclusive economic zone are owned by the Union and managed by the ANP except in the cases of jurisdiction of other authorities and entities expressly defined in the Law."

20 MME-EPE Work Group, *Conceptual Aspects of the Regulatory Systems of Exploration and Production of Oil and Natural Gas and the International Experience', Report of Phase A.*

union, and the winning companies. The ANP follows the implementation of these contracts. They cover the following:

- payments for the occupation (or retention) of the areas;
- payment of royalties;
- payment of special participations for fields of high production volume or high profitability;
- conditions for returning the areas;
- the term and duration of the contract, and deadlines and work programmes for exploration and production;
- the commitment to acquire goods and services from domestic suppliers (ie, local content);
- the commitment to abide to the minimum exploratory programme proposed in the winning bid;
- the mandatory adoption of measures for preserving reservoirs and other natural resources, the safety of personnel, equipment and the protection of the environment;
- the mandatory adoption of best industry practices and adherence to the relevant technical and scientific standards and procedures, including those related to recovery techniques, so as to rationalise the production and control the decline of the reserves;
- the responsibility of concessionaires to rationalise production and control the decline of the reserves;
- the responsibilities of concessionaires to the environment; and
- the investment of 1% of gross revenue in exploration and production (all fields paying special participation are subject to this fee).

The concession contracts begin by invoking the legal definitions of the oil industry found in Article 6 of the Petroleum Law and Article 3 of Decree 2,705/1998.

The object of the contract is always the implementation of a minimum exploratory programme by the concessionaire, for which consistent financial guarantees must be presented, and for the concessionaire to identify a petroleum reservoir within that area. Terms and duration are agreed in compliance with the phases of exploration, discovery and evaluation until a declaration of commerciality for the discovery is made.

The exploration phase is divided into two periods. The first is compliance with the minimum exploratory programme. Once the work obligations of that programme are fully complied with the concessionaire may inform the ANP that it intends to proceed to the second exploration phase. It hereby retains only those areas of the block required by the evaluation plan and immediately returns the remainder. It also presents financial guarantees for this new exploratory period. Once the concessionaire considers the exploration phase completed it will retain only those areas to be developed, immediately returning the remainder to the ANP. The entire concession area may also be returned, in which case the exploratory programme must be completed.

When a discovery is made the concessionaire will evaluate it during the exploration phase. If it wishes, the concessionaire may issue a declaration of commerciality and notify the ANP.

The production phase comes next, with the approval of the development plan, the date of initial production, and annual production programmes, including measurements, deliveries and the availability of production.

From the initial date of production of each field, the volume and the quality of the oil and natural gas produced are estimated regularly, at the concessionaire's expense. This cost includes the methods of measurement and any equipment and instruments considered in the development plan and inspected by the ANP.

The concessionaire takes ownership of the oil and natural gas measured according to the terms of the concession contract.

The ANP monitors and inspects the execution of all these operations. If the minimum exploratory programme is not met, the agency may enforce the financial guarantees. In the event of a commercial discovery and subsequent production the ANP will participate in its measurement, delivery and availability.

Once a concession area is delivered, the concessionaire will keep the union exempt from all damages or losses, and undertakes full and objective responsibility for all damages and losses to the environment or third parties that result from its operations. It is also liable for all expenses and costs incurred in the abandonment, removal and return of assets.

6. Government take in the concession contract

The government take is how the government receives revenues generated by oil. It is defined in various statues, including the Petroleum Law, Decree 2,705/1998,[21] ANP Administrative Ruling 10/1999 and Law 7,990/1989, and in the notices to bid and concession contracts.

The technical definition of the government take, given in Decree 2,705/1998, describes it as the payment to be made by the concessionaires who are exploring and producing oil and natural gas. Article 45 of the Petroleum Law established the following under the government take: signing bonus, royalties, special participations and payments for the occupation or retention of an area. This article also defines royalties and special participations as mandatory.[22]

6.1 Signature bonus

The signature bonus, the minimum amount of which is defined in the notice to bid, is defined in Article 46 of the Petroleum Law[23] as a payment equal to the amount offered by the winning bid to obtain a certain concession. It is payable by the winning bidder upon the signing of the concession contract.

Consequently, it is one of the criteria used for judging the proposals presented by

21 Articles 47, 50 and 51 of Law 9,478/1997 led to the publication of Decree 2,705/1998.

22 Article 45: "The concession contract shall cover the following government participations contemplated in the notice to bid: I – signing bonus; II – royalties; III – special participation; and IV – payment for the occupation or retention of area."

23 Article 46: "The minimum amount of the signing bonus shall be defined in the notice to bid and will be equal to the payment offered in the proposal for the concession, payable upon the signing of the contract."

each bidder. It is also a requirement for signing the concession contract and is included and regulated in the notice to bid.[24]

Since the signature bonus is a payment made before the exploration phase begins and is unrelated to the success of the exploration, it is included under the exploratory risk.[25]

The minimum signature bonus is set by the ANP in the notice to bid as appropriate for each block. Known geophysical, geological, geochemical data and other applicable information for the area, indicating the likelihood of a recoverable oil and/or natural gas reservoir, are all taken into account in its calculation.

For this reason the ANP classifies the blocks to be bid upon as "new frontier", "mature basin" and "high potential".

In other words, taking into account the data already known in relation to the area to be bid upon, the minimum bonus is set from a combination of the following probabilities included within the exploratory risk:

- the probable existence of a reservoir; and
- the greater or lesser capacity of recoverable oil.

In Brazil, current knowledge suggests that the areas of high potential are in very deep waters. They therefore require high investment and are difficult to prospect. The ANP therefore also determines the technical and financial qualification of each operating company, classifying them as A, B and C; A being the best qualified and C being the least qualified. The blocks themselves are similarly classified as A, B and C.

Therefore, when determining the signature bonus, the ANP links its figure to the characteristics of the block, taking into account the block's attractiveness and its need for investment. Those blocks with a higher signature bonus in the notice to bid are those with the least exploratory risk, in spite of their high cost and complexity of development and production.

On the other hand, for the purposes of the bidder's offer, there is no maximum limit for the signature bonus. However, it cannot be lower than the amount described in the notice to bid; otherwise the bidder will be disqualified.

Should the winning bidder pay the bonus but withdraw from the deal before signing the concession contract, they will waive its payment. The ANP may then call the second highest bidder to make a new payment and sign the contract, or remove that block from the bidding round.

Decree 2,705/1998 defines the criteria for calculating and collecting the government participation. In relation to the signing bonus, it covers only the following:

- that the winning bidder makes a single payment; and
- that the funds from the bonus be allocated to the ANP to pay for its operational needs.[26]

---

24 The two other criteria relate to the commitment to acquire goods and services locally in the exploration and development phases.

25 MME-EPE Work Group, *Conceptual Aspects of the Regulatory Systems of Exploration and Production of Oil and Natural Gas and the International Experience, Report of Phase A*. Sub item 3.1.2.

6.2 Royalties

Royalties represent financial compensation payable by concessionaires. They are paid on a monthly basis in relation to each field, beginning in the month when initial production takes place. No deductions are allowed according to Decree 2,705/1998.[27]

Royalties were introduced by Law 2,004/1953, which deals with their payment and application.[28]

The legislation governing this government participation has been amended several times, especially in the following laws: Law 7,525/1986, Law 7,990/1989, the Petroleum Law and Law 10,195/2000. All of these, with the exception of the Petroleum Law, deal solely with the application of the funds obtained through royalties.

Law 7,525/1986 amended Law 2,004/1953 to state that the oil royalties could only be applied in energy, the paving of highways, the supply and treatment of water, irrigation, environmental protection and basic sanitation.

Three years later, Law 7,990/1989 introduced the strict prohibition on using royalties to pay debt and permanent payroll. That law, however, was amended by Law 10,195/2000, which stated that this prohibition does not apply to the payment of debt to the union and its entities.

It is furthermore important to highlight the changes to the application of oil royalty funds caused by the Petroleum Law.

In addition to expressly revoking Law 2,004/1953, the Petroleum Law increased the new maximum limit for royalties from 5% to 10% of total production volume.

Article 47 of this law states, however, that the ANP may include in a block's notice to bid a reduction of this percentage to the minimum of 5% of the production

---

26 Decree 2,705/1998, Article 9: "The signing bonus described in subsection I of Article 45 of Law nº 9.478, of 1997, shall be the amount offered by the winning bidder in the proposal to obtain the concession of oil or natural gas, and shall never be lower than the minimum set by the ANP in the notice to bid.
Sole paragraph. The winning bidder shall pay, upon the signing of the respective concession contract, the full amount of the signing bonus in a single payment."
Article 10: "Part of the signing bonus shall be paid to the ANP, according to the provisions of subsection II of Article 15 of Law nº 9.478, of 1997."

27 Decree 2,705/1998, Article 11: "The royalties contemplated in subsection II of Article 45 of Law nº 9.478, of 1997, represent the financial compensation payable by the concessionaires of exploration and production of oil or natural gas and shall be paid on a monthly basis for each field, beginning in the month the respective production begins. All deductions are hereby prohibited."

28 Law 2.004/53 – "Article 27. The company and its subsidiaries are required to pay compensation equal to 4% (four percent) to the States or Territories and 1% (one percent) to the Municipalities of the price of the oil, the shale bitumen and the gas extracted in their respective areas where oil is explored.
1st para. – The amounts mentioned in this article are set by the National Petroleum Council.
2nd para. – The payment of compensation shall be made on a quarterly basis.
3rd para. – Except for the funds allocated to the Ministry of the Navy, the other funds mentioned in this article shall be applied by the States, Territories and Municipalities exclusively in energy, paving of roads, the supply and treatment of water, irrigation, environmental protection and basic sanitation.
4th para. – Compensation is also payable to the bordering States, Territories and Municipalities, when the oil, bitumen shale and gas are extracted from the continent, at the same rate of 5% (five percent) set in the introduction to this article, of which 1.5% (one point five percent) is paid to the Municipalities and their respective geo-economic areas; 1% (one percent) paid to the Ministries of the Navy, to cover the costs of inspection and protection of the economic activities in said areas; and 1% (one percent) to form a Special Fund, to be distributed among all States, Territories and Municipalities.
5th para. – (vetoed).
6th para. – The central States, Territories and Municipalities with lakes, rivers, river and lake islands where oil, bitumen shale or gas are explored, shall be entitled to the compensation described in the introduction to this article."

after taking into consideration the geological risks, the expected production and other relevant factors.[29]

Consequently, the portion of the royalties equal to the minimum of 5% of the production shall be applied according to Law 7,990/1989; when those royalties exceed 5%, Article 49 of the Petroleum Law will apply.[30]

Article 49 distributes the excess according to percentages and purpose, summarised as follows: whenever exploration takes place on land, lakes, rivers, or river and lake islands, the funds shall be divided between the state, the municipalities, and the Ministry of Science and Technology. When the exploration takes place on the continental shelf, however, the funds will be divided between the states, the municipalities, the Ministry of the Navy, Special Fund and the Ministry of Science and Technology.

The criteria for calculating and collecting government participations, including royalties, are defined in Decree 2,705/1998. This arose as a consequence of the Petroleum Law, which demanded:

- criteria by which to calculate royalties;
- the regulations for special participation;
- the regulations for payments for the occupation or retention of an area.

Article 13 of this decree[31] states that when a field encompasses two or more

---

29 Law 9,478/1997, Article 47: "Given the geological risks, the expectation of production and other applicable factors, the ANP main include in the corresponding notice to bid the reduction of the royalties set forth in the introduction to this article to an amount equal to at least five percent of the production."

30 Law 9,478/1997, Article 49: "The portion of the royalty exceeding five percent of the production shall be distributed as follows:
I – when the exploration takes place on land or lakes, rivers, river and lake islands:
a) fifty two and five tenths percent to the States where production occurs;
b) fifteen percent to the Municipalities where production occurs;
c) seven and five tenths percent to the Municipalities affected by the operations of loading and unloading of oil and natural gas, according to and at the discretion of the ANP;
d) twenty five percent to the Ministry of Science and Technology to fund programs of scientific research and technological development applied to the oil industry;
II – when the exploration takes place on the continental shelf:
a) twenty two and five tenths percent to the bordering producing States;
b) twenty two and five tenths percent to the producing Municipalities;
c) fifteen percent to the Ministry of the Navy, to cover the costs with inspection and protection of the production areas;
d) seven and five tenths percent to the Municipalities affected by the loading and unloading of oil and natural gas, according to and at the discretion of the ANP;
e) seven and five tenths percent to form a Special Fund, to be distributed among all States, Territories and Municipalities;
f) twenty five percent to the Ministry of Science and Technology to fund programmes of scientific research and technological development applied to the oil industry.
1st para. From all the funds payable to the Ministry of Science and Technology at least forty percent will be applied in training and scientific and technological development programmes in the Northern and Northeastern regions.
2nd para. The Ministry of Science and Technology shall manage the programmes supporting the scientific research and technological development described in the introduction to this article, with the technical support of the ANP, complying with the terms of subsection X of Article 8, and under agreements with the universities listed in a decree by the President of the Republic."

31 Law 9,478/1997, Article 13: "In the cases of fields encompassing two or more concession areas where differ concessionaires operate, the agreement signed by the concessionaires for the individualisation of the production, contemplated by Article 27 of Law nº 9.478, of 1997, shall define the participation of each one in regards to the payment of royalties."

concession areas, and two or more concessionaires, the amount of government take from each will be defined according to the production agreements between them.

Article 11 of the same Decree 2,705/1998[32] states emphatically that royalties are financial compensation to be paid by oil and gas concessionaires.

To corroborate this assertion one need only note that when the union grants a certain block for exploration it is also granting the results of that exploration. As a consequence, since the oil is a domain asset of the union the results of its production extend beyond the union's assets and become part of the concessionaire's entitlement. The royalty is therefore financial compensation paid for the use of state-owned property for economic purposes.

6.3 Special participations

The special participations were introduced by Article 45 of the Petroleum Law. Article 50 of the same law required both the notice to bid and the concession contract to make the government participation mandatory, and for it to be regulated by presidential decree; this is Decree 2,705/1998.

Article 21 of this decree[33] defines the special participation as a special financial compensation payable by oil and gas concessionaires in cases of large production volume or high profitability.

Although the Petroleum Law[34] assumes that the special participation will be applied to gross production revenue – minus royalties, the exploration investment, the operating costs, depreciation and taxes – it is clear that Decree 2,705/1998 in fact defines the criteria for estimating this government take, together with ANP Administrative Ruling 10/1999, which defines the calculation procedures to be used by the concessionaires.

Decree 2,705 states that each field of a certain concession area must pay the special participation quarterly, beginning in the quarter when initial production begins. It also states that progressive rates will apply to the quarterly net production revenue of each field, according to the location of the site, the number of years of production and the inspected quarterly production volume.

To best understand this calculation method it is useful to define net production revenue and inspected production volume.

The net production revenue is the gross production revenue after deductions for royalties, investment in exploration, operating costs, depreciations and taxes that are directly related to field operations dispersed under the concession contract. It is

32 Decree 2,705/1998, Article 11: "The royalties described in subsection II of Article 45 of Law nº 9.478, of 1997, represent financial compensation payable by the concessionaires of exploration and production of oil or natural gas and paid on a monthly basis, for each field, beginning in the month the production begins. All deductions are prohibited."

33 Decree 2,705/1998, Article 21: "The special participation contemplated in subsection III of Article 45 of Law nº 9.478, of 1997, represents a special financial compensation payable by the concessionaires of exploration and production of oil or natural gas, in the cases of large production volume or high profitability, according to the criteria of this Decree, and shall be paid in relation to each field of a certain concession area, beginning in the quarter when the respective production begins."

34 Law 9,478/1997, Article 50: "1st para. The special participation shall apply to the gross production revenue, minus the royalties, the investments in the exploration, the operating costs, the depreciation and the taxes contemplated in the laws currently in force."

calculated according to the rules of ANP Administrative Ruling 10/1999.[35]

The inspected production volume is the total volume of oil or natural gas in each field in cubic metres, as measured at the relevant production measurement point.[36]

Payments for the Special Participation are therefore conditional upon both revenue and production volume, regardless of the fact that the Petroleum Law and Decree 2,705/1998 both state that they will be due in cases of large production volume or high profitability. In this case profitability means net revenue.

In fields that encompass two or more concession areas but with one concessionaire, the special participation is based on the total net production revenue and inspected production volume of those fields.

If there are different concessionaires, then the individualisation agreement between them will define their respective contribution to the net production revenue, therefore the amount of special participation.

ANP Administrative Ruling 10/1999 sets out how to calculate the special participation. It lists the following deductions from gross production revenue that must be made when calculating net production revenue:

- the costs incurred in paying the signing bonus;
- the costs incurred in exploring the deposits of oil and natural gas, and the drilling of wells;
- the costs incurred in the development and production of oil fields;
- the amount set aside to cover future expenses in the decommissioning and environmental restoration of the field area; and
- the actual costs incurred from the decommissioning of wells during their production phase, above those included in the amount already set aside.

It should be stressed that the signing bonus itself is expressly excluded from the list of qualifying expenses for the exploration of oil and natural gas deposits.

Furthermore, the signing bonus may already be deducted from gross revenue, that is, from the calculation base of the net production revenue, under Article 13 of this ruling.[37]

However, it should be said that the special financial compensation resulting from large production volumes and high profitability was created so that the concessionaire could pay it without suffering losses, since the net production revenue, which is the basis for calculating the special participation, is arrived at from gross revenue which allows for full but well-defined deductions.

Income from the special participation must be distributed according to the terms of Articles 24 and 27 of Decree 2,705/1998 and of Article 50 of the Petroleum Law. These allocate 40% to the Ministry of Mines and Energy, 10% to the Ministry of the

35 Decree 2,705/1998: "VIII – Net Production Revenue: for each field of a certain concession area, the gross production revenue minus the payment of royalties, investments in exploration, operating costs, depreciations and taxes directly related to the field operations, actually disbursed, during the term of the concession contract until the time of estimation, calculated based on the ANP rules."

36 Subsection X of Article 3 of Decree 2705/98.

37 ANP Administrative Ruling No. 10/1999, Article 13: "The following may be subtracted from the gross production revenue in each base period, to calculate the respective net production revenue: I – the costs incurred by the concessionaire to pay the signing bonus of the concession contract, if any."

Environment, 40% to the state where production occurs or that borders the continental shelf where the production occurs, and 10% to the municipality where production occurs or that borders the continental shelf where production occurs.

It is worth mentioning that payment of the government take differs between the pre-salt and strategic areas. Special participation is not charged, for example.

7. Conclusion

In the approximately 10 years between the enactment of the Petroleum Law and the discovery of the pre-salt deposits, the global oil industry was dramatically affected by the changes in wealth resulting from a high number of mergers and acquisitions, by changes in the market's supply and demand structure, and new regulatory arrangements in the leading producing countries. Add to that the continuing rise in the international price of crude oil after a long period (from 1986 to 1998) of relatively low prices.

It was in this international scenario that in July 2007 Petrobras revealed the potential of the pre-salt area covering the sedimentary basins of Santos, Campos and Espírito Santo. It concluded that the estimated recovery volumes for these deposits could in the medium term place Brazil among the world's main producers of oil and natural gas.

In that new reality, which initiated a growing interest of the international oil market in Brazil, the country's executive branch once more focused its attention on oil industry legislation. It took advantage of the monopoly held by the union to explore economically the oil and natural gas deposits in the pre-salt region through production sharing contracts. The executive decided that this was the best way to safeguard the interests of future Brazilian generations.

That change in the exploratory model took into consideration the large estimates of recoverable hydrocarbons and the low exploratory risk. In all exporting countries of the world these are factors that influence how much oil revenue is received by governments and much is received by companies that contract with those governments. However, in Brazil the necessity and wisdom of changing the regime for the pre-salt and strategic areas remains to be seen.

The concession regime allowed international players to carry out the exploration and production of hydrocarbons in Brazil under clear rules and a strong regulatory agency. Petrobras was inserted into a competitive environment. Here, freed from the burden of monopoly, the company grew and developed to the point of discovering, in unimaginable conditions and at tremendous depths, the immense pre-salt reserves.

The discovery of the pre-salt therefore proves the success of the concession regime. It is yet to be seen whether the shared production regime will prove attractive to international players, whose participation in the industry is both healthy and necessary.

The new petroleum regime

Felipe Feres
Luiz Antonio Lemos
Luis Antonio Menezes
Marcelo Romanelli
Campos Mello Advogados

---

1. Introduction

On November 8 2007, the National Energy Policy Council (CNPE) announced the assessment of reservoirs of Petrobras's largest oil province, called "Tupi", located in the offshore Santos Basin. Accurate studies indicated that this area holds approximately 8 billion barrels of oil equivalent (BOE), which would increase Brazilian hydrocarbon reserves by more than 50%. This was just days before the start of the National Petroleum, Natural Gas and Biofuels Agency's (ANP) Ninth Bidding Round for petroleum and natural gas upstream concessions.

This announcement initiated a series of statements on the possible existence of gigantic reserves in an exploratory frontier that came to be known as the "pre-salt" layer. This name arises from the fact that these reserves are situated below a thick layer of salt, on average around 7,000 metres deep. The pre-salt layer area is located approximately 170 kilometres (km) from the Brazilian coast, with a width of approximately 800 km, between the coasts of the states of Espírito Santo and Santa Catarina, in the south and southeastern regions of Brazil. This new exploratory frontier might place Brazil's oil reserves among the largest in the world.

As a result of these significant discoveries, the CNPE decided to withdraw 41 of the 311 blocks offered in the ANP's Ninth Bidding Round. All of these blocks were located in the pre-salt area. The justification for this action was that in consideration of Brazil's strategic interests, extensive studies were necessary to evaluate the suitability of the existing concession regime in relation to the new prospects.

In July 2008, an inter-ministerial committee was created to analyse the various alternatives and suggest modifications to Brazil's exploration and production concession regime, which has been in effect since 1997. The committee's goal was to present the president with options for the reform of the then-current legislation, principally Law 9,478/97 (the Petroleum Law).

After a year-long discussion, in August 2009 the Brazilian government presented to Congress bills of law that introduced:

- a Brazilian production sharing agreement (PSA) regime that would apply to the pre-salt layer and other strategic areas;
- the creation of a social sovereign fund to receive oil revenues due to the union;
- the creation of a state-owned company to manage the PSAs (the PPSA); and
- the assignment by the union to Petrobras of rights to explore and produce 5 billion BOE within certain pre-salt areas (the Petrobras Assignment Agreement).

2. The new regulatory regime

2.1 The Brazilian production sharing regime

At the end of December 2010, Federal Law 12,351 (the PSA Law) was finally enacted. This amended the Petroleum Law and introduced the PSA as an additional legal-regulatory regime for exploration and production in Brazil. The PSA regime applies to upstream activities performed in the pre-salt layer and in strategic areas to be defined as such by the federal government.

Under the PSA Law, although the union does not bear any of the risks of exploration and production activities, any exploited hydrocarbons are the original property of the union. However, once a commercially feasible hydrocarbon discovery is made, the union gives over part of its production as reimbursement for the exploration, development and production costs incurred by those oil companies that are party to the agreement. This is known as 'cost oil'. The union then shares in the rest of the production with these companies at a rate established in the agreement. This is known as 'profit oil'.

The PSA Law prohibits the union from receiving its share of profit oil in cash. Therefore, when selling the union's share of the profit oil, the PPSA may enter into commercialisation agreements with Petrobras. These do not require a prior public bidding process.

Furthermore, those oil companies that exploit hydrocarbons under PSAs, including Petrobras but excluding the union's share of the profit oil, will pay certain government participations as compensation for the granting of the PSA and the exploitation of the hydrocarbons. These government participations comprise royalties and signature bonuses, but not special participations; these are paid under the concession regime.

Royalties and signature bonuses receive the same overall legal treatment under the PSA regime as they do under the concession regime. Thus, royalties are a constitutionally granted financial compensation for the exploitation of hydrocarbons, payable and distributed to certain municipalities, states and the union. The signature bonus is the amount to be paid by the winning bidders to the union as consideration for granting and executing the relevant PSA. However, it should be noted that the applicable rates and distribution rules for royalties payable under PSAs are still being debated by Congress. It is likely that they will differ from the distribution rules that apply to the concession regime.

The ANP is still drawing up the PSA template. Many practical, operational and financial questions concerning the regime are therefore still to be analysed and answered. These include:

- the types of costs and restrictions to them that may be included in cost oil, and how these will be audited;
- the rules and regulations regarding how profit oil will be shared between the different parties to the agreement;
- provisions for unitisation;
- the operating committee's governance rules and quorums for approving matters that are submitted to it; and
- the rules for settling disputes.

Five basic state entities are involved with the PSA regime (including Petrobras, as a mixed-capital, state-controlled corporation):

- the CNPE, which decides:
  - when the ANP bidding rounds will take place;
  - the pre-salt blocks and strategic areas that will be offered under the PSA (including the definition of what a strategic area would be); and
  - the technical and economic parameters of the PSAs;
- the Ministry of Mines and Energy (MME), which approves the drafts and executes the PSAs on behalf of the union, and proposes to the CNPE several technical and economic parameters of the PSA, such as:
  - Petrobras's minimum interest in the consortia (explained further below);
  - any specifications concerning the cost oil; and
  - the amount of the signature bonuses for each PSA to be auctioned;
- the ANP, which, among other things:
  - performs technical studies to help the MME decide which blocks will be granted under the PSA Regime;
  - prepares the PSA template;
  - promotes the bidding rounds; and
  - regulates and supervises activities under the PSAs, in similar fashion to its role under the concession regime;
- the PPSA, which, among other things:
  - manages the PSAs;
  - represents the government on the respective operating committees; and
  - sells the union's share of profit oil (as explained further below); and
- Petrobras, which will be the sole operator of all PSAs awarded and will have a minimum 30% interest in each agreement.

As occurs under the concession regime, the ANP will, subject to the CNPE's authorisation, promote public bidding rounds for each PSA. Any oil company that meets the necessary technical, legal and financial qualification criteria set out in the tender documents may participate in these rounds. The winning bidders will enter into a consortium agreement with the PPSA and Petrobras, mindful that Petrobras will be legally entitled to a minimum 30% interest in each consortium under the PSA. On top of this mandatory interest, Petrobras may itself participate in bidding rounds and so increase its participating interest in the relevant PSA. Should it choose not to participate directly, Petrobras must accept in advance the terms and conditions of the tender document (including the relevant signature bonus) and is legally bound to the offer made by the winning bidder(s). In the ANP bidding rounds, the winners are determined solely according to the percentage of profit oil to be allocated to the union.

It is important to note that certain provisions in the PSA Law differ in many respects from the international PSA experience. It is known that, historically, the main purpose of PSAs has been to tempt international oil companies into developing a host country's exploration and production sector, while guaranteeing the state more control and exclusive ownership over hydrocarbon reserves and production.

One issue that may affect the plurality of oil companies in Brazil is Petrobras's mandatory operatorship in the agreements, and the fact that Petrobras will not be allowed to assign its operatorship or part of its interests below the 30% floor to any other oil company. It is well known that partnering between oil companies is crucial in the exploration and production industry, as they are able to share and mitigate the risks of the activity and exchange know-how. It is common for operators to exchange positions in different blocks and also to share rigs that they have hired. This ultimately helps them comply with contractual-regulatory commitments, especially in exploration and development programmes, which is when the highest expenditures are made.

However, as a state-controlled corporation, Petrobras is subject to strict debt limits and other restrictions. As a mandatory operator, with a considerable minimum participating interest in each PSA but certain budgetary restrictions, it may have difficulty fulfilling all its financial, operational and regulatory obligations in a timely fashion. This might especially concern those commitments related to minimum exploratory programmes and development plans. Hence, Petrobras may find that the privileges conferred to it under the PSA Law may become a great burden and could slow the exploration and development of new fields under the PSA regime.

Moreover, the PSA Law provides for strict governmental control over operational and financial decisions within the PSA's operational committees. Although it does not contribute to the consortium (financially or otherwise) or share in its liabilities and risks, the PPSA will represent the union's interests in each consortium. It will be entitled to appoint half of the members of the consortium's operational committee, including its president, regardless of the overall number of members. The committee's president will have veto powers and a casting vote in matters to be addressed by the PSA template. These remain to be defined and will affect the attractiveness of the Brazilian PSA regime.

It should be noted that the committee makes the most important decisions in an exploration and production project. These concern exploration plans, reservoir evaluations, annual work programmes, overall project budgets and the statement of marketability of hydrocarbon discoveries. In most major oil producing countries that are open to foreign investments, such matters are generally decided in common agreement between the parties involved, with little or no government interference.

Finally, Brazil already has a regulator for the exploration and production industry in the ANP. According to the Petroleum Law, this agency is charged with reviewing and approving plans for exploration and development, annual work programmes and production programmes, as drafted and approved by the operational committee. By law, the ANP's revisions and controls have to be based on technical and legal requirements. The agency thereby ensures that the projects are being carried out in accordance with best industry practices and with the oil companies' contractual obligations, such as assumed local content commitments. It also ensures that the production will not cause reservoir depletion. Under the PSA Law, the PPSA will act as manager of the PSAs. According to Federal Law 12,304/10 (which created the PPSA), in order to manage PSAs the agency will, among other things, evaluate, monitor and audit exploration, development and production programmes and plans, as well as an oil company's compliance with local content commitments.

Therefore, it is foreseeable that there may be dual governmental control over the operations under the PSAs – that is, from the ANP and the PPSA. This has the potential to increase bureaucracy in exploration and production projects. It is also likely that the PPSA's decisions, unlike the ANP's, will contain and be directed by political elements and thinking.

2.2 The reserve fund

As mentioned above, the PSA Law also created Brazil's sovereign oil fund, in which the union's oil revenues will be deposited. In terms of its objectives, the Social Fund, as it is called, bears characteristics of the three main types of sovereign wealth funds found internationally:

- It is a savings fund, insofar as the PSA Law provides that the Social Fund will be used to constitute long-term public savings;
- It is a strategic fund, as its resources may be used for social and regional development programmes, comprising investments in:
  - education;
  - culture;
  - sports;
  - public health;
  - science and technology;
  - the environment; and
  - mitigation of and adaptation to climate change; and
- It is a stabilisation fund, because the PSA Law provides that its resources may be used to mitigate the potential negative effects (eg, the Dutch disease) on the national economy caused by the inflow of large volumes of oil revenues.

The PSA Law also established that the following financial resources will be mandatorily deposited into the Social Fund:

- a portion of the signature bonuses as provided for in the PSA;
- the royalties due to the union, in accordance with the terms of the PSA;
- the revenues deriving from the sale of the union's share of profit oil;
- the royalties and special participation revenues due to the union regarding pre-salt areas that have already been granted under the concession regime;
- the fund's financial earnings; and
- other resources allocated to the fund in accordance with the law.

The Social Fund will have an investment policy that aims to achieve financial stability and sustainability, as well as to advance the fund's objectives as described above. Overall, the fund's financial investments will be made in assets located outside Brazil, in order to avoid any negative impact on the national economy due to the inflow of large volumes of oil revenue. As a general rule, only the fund's financial earnings (return on capital) may be spent on social and regional development programmes.

The investment policy will be established by the Social Fund's Financial

Management Committee. This will be made up of the minister of finance, the minister of planning and the president of the Central Bank. The committee will have the legal obligation to set:

- the annual amount that may be withdrawn from the fund, so as to ensure its financial stability;
- the minimum return expected from its investments;
- the types and levels of risk of the investments that may be made by the fund;
- the minimum and maximum investment percentages that may be made abroad; and
- the minimum capitalisation required before any of the fund's resources may be used for the objectives set out in the PSA Law.

The Social Fund's Advisory Board will recommend to the president the priority and allocation of the fund's resources to the social and regional development programmes listed above. In evaluating the proposed investment programmes, the board must take into account the effective impact on the populations and regions that will receive these resources, with the main purpose of reducing the country's regional inequalities. The president has yet to publish the advisory board's organisational rules and statutes.

Finally, the PSA Law sets certain controls on the fund. The fund's financial statements must be prepared and assessed twice a year in accordance with the applicable legislation and the presidency must present to Congress, on a quarterly basis, the fund's performance report. The parameters for this are yet to be set out in the fund's by-laws.

2.3 The new national oil company

The PSA Law also authorised the government to create the PPSA, a state-run corporation whose capital is completely owned by the union, and whose main purpose is to act as the manager of each PSA awarded.

The PPSA's revenues will come from a portion of the signature bonuses, to be defined by the Ministry of Mines and Energy for each PSA, and from remuneration for managing the PSAs and the hydrocarbon commercialisation agreements. The amount of this remuneration will be defined according to the phases of each agreement, the size of the blocks and fields, and other criteria. It is not yet clear what compensation the PPSA will receive for this management or who will be responsible for making these payments.

The company's by-laws are yet to be established by an act of the presidency. However, the PSA Law has already established that the PPSA will be governed by a board of five directors:

- one nominated by the Ministry of Mines and Energy;
- one appointed by the Ministry of Finance;
- one appointed by the Ministry of Planning;
- one appointed by the Civil House of the Presidency; and
- the chief executive of the PPSA.

It is also known that its headquarters will be in Brasília and its central offices will be in Rio de Janeiro.

According to the PSA Law, the PPSA will manage the PSAs. In support of this, its main roles will be:

- to represent the union in consortia formed by the parties to each PSA, and to be be the union's voice on the respective operating committees;
- to perform the technical and economic evaluation of and monitor the execution of any plans for exploration, appraisal, development and production;
- to enforce any contractual provisions regarding local content obligations, and to monitor and audit any costs and investments related to the PSA;
- to represent the union in executing and managing hydrocarbon commercialisation agreements – these will most likely will be entered into with Petrobras without a prior bidding procedure; and
- to represent the union in unitisation procedures when reservoirs extend into areas that have not been granted or that have been granted under the concession regime.

Finally, it is important to emphasise that the PPSA may not directly carry out the exploration, development, production or commercialisation of hydrocarbons. This means that, in comparison to the international experience, the PPSA will in reality not act as Brazil's national oil company for the pre-salt area. (If one considers that national oil companies are, by definition, *de iuris* and *de facto*, a country's oil company, and are directly involved in upstream and/or downstream activities.) In many ways, Petrobras will therefore continue to be the country's *de facto* NOC, especially in view of the increased role and importance it has under the PSA regime.

3. The licence regime

3.1 What happened to the licences awarded in the pre-salt area?

Petrobras claims that in 2006, two years after the first major deep water exploratory campaigns in the offshore Santos Basin, it successfully drilled 7,600 metres below sea level. Here it discovered significant natural gas and condensate formations in the pre-salt. Already aware of the pre-salt's potential, that same year Petrobras and its partners discovered gigantic light oil formations in the Tupi area.

All such drilling campaigns that led to the discovery of pre-salt formations in the Santos and Campos Basins have been made under concession agreements awarded after 1999. Approximately 30% of the 149,000 km^2 pre-salt area is currently granted under the concession regime. Such contracts are held by several national and international oil and gas companies. These include Petrobras, of course, as well as Shell, Exxon, BP, Anadarko, Eni, Chevron, Statoil, Galp and Repsol-Sinopec. Many of these companies have recently announced pre-salt discoveries.

Despite rumours of possible expropriation and contract termination circulating in the months following the announcements of the pre-salt's potential, the government has officially stated that all currently awarded concession agreements with pre-salt potential will be duly respected. Any operations carried out in these areas may do so in accordance with the legal framework of the concession regime.

3.2 What will happen in future rounds?

As mentioned above, following the enactment of the PSA Law in December 2010, all remaining pre-salt and strategic areas will be granted under the PSA regime, for which the government may hold public bidding rounds or hire Petrobras directly. Concession agreements will still apply to those areas with no pre-salt potential or areas that are not deemed strategic by the government.

No PSA bidding rounds have yet been held and no PSAs awarded. This is mainly due to the fact that Congress has yet to pass the PSA royalty distribution rules. These will most likely will differ materially from those of the concession regime. One bill of law that establishes such distribution rules has so far been passed in the House of Representatives and is being examined in the Senate. However, it is not possible to know exactly when, or whether, this bill will be passed into law.

Due to the risk of lawsuits from the states and municipalities that currently receive royalties and special participations, the federal government has repeatedly stated that it will not award any new PSAs until this law is enacted.

4. The Petrobras Assigment Agreement

On June 30 2010, Federal Law 12,276 was enacted to authorise the union to assign to Petrobras the exploration and production rights to oil, natural gas and other fluid hydrocarbons in certain pre-salt areas not already granted under Concession Agreements. It limited the production volume to 5 billion BOE. This law also permitted the union to capitalise Petrobras with federal treasury bonds, during the company's 2010 major public stock offering.

As occurs under the concession regime, Law 12,276/10 states that Petrobras will have original property rights over any hydrocarbons produced from the assigned pre-salt areas. It must also pay royalties as financial compensation for its production. Royalties under the Petrobras Assignment Agreement are paid in accordance with the provisions of the Petroleum Law, which also apply to the concession regime. However, this law does not expressly mention the payment of special participations. For this reason, the federal government understands that these are not due under the Petrobras Assignment Agreement.

On September 3 2010, Petrobras, the union and the ANP entered into the Petrobras Assignment Agreement, which advanced the purposes of Law 12,276/10. Among other things, this agreement provides for:

- the area covered by the assignment, consisting of seven pre-salt exploratory blocks, all of which are located close to the Tupi mega-discovery, within the offshore area that borders the states of Rio de Janeiro and Sao Paulo;
- the volume that Petrobras may extract from the area, which is limited to 5 billion BOE;
- the price to be paid for the assignment of the rights, as explained below;
- the terms and conditions of the subsequent revision of the contract price;

- the term of the agreement, which is limited to 40 years, extendable for an additional five years;
- the minimum local content percentage; and
- the supervision of Petrobras's exploration and production activities by the ANP, similarly to that agency's role under the concession regime.

According to the Petrobras Assignment Agreement, Petrobras paid around R74.8 billion for the assignment from the union. Most of this was made using federal treasury bonds issued by the union to pay for additional Petrobras shares acquired during the company's public stock offering at the end of September 2010.

The Petrobras Assignment Agreement should not be considered an additional legal-regulatory regime in Brazil. It applies only to Petrobras, to certain offshore areas, and is limited in time and to the production volume described above. In short, this agreement is a legal device created by the government so as to give highly promising pre-salt reservoirs to Petrobras, without performing a prior public bidding procedure and in advance of the arrival of the PSA regime. At the same time it also considerably increased the union's equity interest in Petrobras's capital.

5. Conclusion

It has been four years since the last ANP bid round (Round 10) and six years since the last one that granted access to pre-salt and other promising offshore exploratory areas (Round 8). The government has stated that it will not auction any exploratory area under the PSA regime until Congress has passed legislation that sets out the rules for distributing PSA royalties. Since Brazil is a lively democracy, with dozens of pro-government and opposition parties, this task may take several months to complete, to say the least. The ANP has stated that it intends to have a new concession regime bid round in the near future, and that this will include new onshore exploratory frontiers and offshore areas excluding the pre-salt layer.

In spite of heated discussions within the academy and within Congress, there is an overall sense that these are exciting times in Brazil. The exploration and production industry has great growth potential and there is the possibility of unprecedented benefits for the general population. We are hopeful that the two legal regulatory regimes may coexist in harmony for the benefit of future generations, and that they will be able to attract the investment required to carry out so many costly upstream projects. Needless to say, in a world in which renewable energy sources and biofuels are playing an ever-greater role, now is the time for Brazil to exploit and benefit from its huge hydrocarbon reserves.

The authors would like to thank Saulo Padua and Bruno Vignal for their kind assistance in the preparation of this chapter.

Joint ventures

José Virgilio Lopes Enei
Leonardo Miranda
Machado, Meyer, Sendacz e Opice Advogados

1. Industry background in Brazil

The exploration and production (or upstream) sector of the oil and gas industry is, traditionally, capital and risk intensive. The need to share risk and capital requirements means that there are many joint ventures among industry players worldwide.

This profile of capital and risk is particularly applicable to today's Brazilian oil and gas industry.

The recent sub-salt discoveries[1] are expected to add 50 billion to 100 billion barrels of oil to the Brazilian oil reserves,[2] but will probably require investments in production activities in excess of $500 billion.

In addition to the sub-salt blocks, other offshore and onshore upstream opportunities are already anticipated that will require further investment. The 11th bidding round for non-sub-salt concessions has been scheduled for 2012. This will include blocks in the so-called equatorial region (extending from Rio Grande do Norte to Amapa states, in the north and northeast regions of Brazil) that possess a geological configuration similar to very profitable blocks on the West African coast.

The 12th bidding round, which is for sub-salt concessions, should follow soon after in 2012 or 2013. This is subject to pending regulation that will complete the new sub-salt legal framework. Political debates as to how sub-salt royalties should be divided among producing and non-producing states have delayed this new bidding round.

Apart from upstream opportunities, there are also investments to be made in new refineries, oilducts, pipelines, liquefaction and re-gasification plants, and other midstream and downstream projects.

---

1 The sub-salt, as defined by the so-called Production Sharing Law (Law 12,351/2010), is the "subsoil area in the shape of a vertical prism with indeterminate depth, and its polygonal base defined by the geographical coordinates of its vertices, as set forth in the Annex [t]hereto, as well as other areas that come to be delimited by the Executive Branch in accordance with progress made to geological knowledge". In broader terms, the sub-salt is located in ultra-deep waters in the exclusive economic zone of Brazil, between 5,000 and 7,000 metres (m) below the sea surface, in an area of approximately 150,000 square kilometres (km) and about 200 km away from the coast within the Espírito Santo, Campos and Santos Basins. It thus adjoins the states of Espírito Santo, Rio de Janeiro and São Paulo. By the end of 2011, approximately 28% of the sub-salt areas had already been granted under concession to Petrobras and private companies such as BG, Galp and Repsol. Therefore, 72% of these areas are yet to be granted to investors under the new production sharing agreement regime.

2 Apart from sub-salt discoveries, proven reserves in Brazil were estimated at 14 billion barrels of oil equivalent (boe) by 2011. The sub-salt reserves may increase that quantity many times over. Oil production in Brazil reached approximately 2 million barrels a day in 2011. It is expected that only the first sub-salt blocks to be developed will meet this production level before 2020.

Petrobras alone, as indicated in its business plan of July 22 2011, has anticipated investments of $224.7 billion for the period from 2011 to 2015. Other players on the Brazilian market operate at a smaller, but still very large scale, and will also face challenging capital demands.

With this in mind, this chapter discusses some of the main alternatives for raising long-term capital for the oil and gas industry in Brazil. These alternatives are:

- bringing strategic or financial equity partners into a joint venture scheme;
- partnerships in the sub-salt regime;
- corporate finance and project finance;
- project bonds; and
- other structured and hybrid alternatives.

Particular focus is given to the M&A and farm-in types of joint ventures – that is, the first and second alternatives above – as well as to the exploration and production sector of the oil and gas chain.

2. Capital-raising alternatives for oil and gas projects in Brazil

2.1 Bringing strategic or financial equity partners into a joint venture scheme

The topic of joint ventures in the oil and gas industry is already widely studied in almost every oil and gas jurisdiction. Yet in Brazil, a civil law jurisdiction, it is of utmost relevance given the relatively recent history of the local oil and gas industry – under the so-called concession regime – but also because of the recently enacted additional legal framework, known as the sub-salt regime.

Both the concession and the sub-salt regimes are regulated by the ANP, as well as authorities that are not sector specific, but play a pivotal role in the oil and gas industry, such as the environmental and maritime authorities.

These laws and regulations create numerous obligations with corresponding liabilities, penalties and further burdens. These require close attention to the operations, and a knowledge of the Brazilian legal system. That overall legal framework is in line with international benchmark regulations and has a degree of sophistication that comes close to that in force in countries such as the United States and United Kingdom.

The industry's risks, obligations and liabilities allow room for partnerships between players. In the Brazilian case these are still predominantly with the national oil company Petrobras. In fact, although Petrobras no longer holds a monopoly in the concession regime (and its dominance is simply a fact), its presence is mandatory in the sub-salt regime.

The future challenges for upstream companies include substantial costs that must be met in the relatively short term (in the exploration and development phases). There has therefore been an increasing demand for sources of capital. Joint ventures with strategic or financial equity partners have served that purpose well.

Recent successful transactions include the Sinopec acquisition of minority stakes at Repsol and at Petrogal. Private equity funds are also investigating upstream opportunities in Brazil and might prove a good alternative. Other companies have been able to raise equity via capital market structures. The most notable examples here have been the OGX and HRT initial public offerings.

This chapter is intended to be a practical guide, presenting types of capital sourcing structures and within those highlighting the risks or main points of attention to create a successful joint venture in the Brazilian upstream oil and gas industry.

(a) Joint venture scheme in the equity level (M&A type)[3]

Foreign companies operating in Brazil have preferred to move through the acquisition of shares.

This typical M&A approach allows more flexibility than a pure asset transaction (farm-in/out), to the extent that:

- it allows transactions at a level above the ultimate target (ie, the Brazilian exploration and production company), which in most cases is incorporated in a jurisdiction outside Brazil. This may give more leeway to structure the transaction and accommodate tax costs, governance issues and more flexibility to certain cash flow issues related to the transaction. In an asset deal or M&A local target this theoretically means that the purchase or subscription price has to enter the asset/target jurisdiction and comply with foreign exchange controls;
- other than possible antitrust issues, a pure M&A transaction on shares, particularly in a layer above the Brazilian upstream company, is less likely to trigger regulatory concerns; and
- it is also less likely to require the involvement of third parties (such as counterparties to the joint operation agreement).

There are two main types of such a share-based M&A: the acquisition of existing shares of the selling shareholder (producing a 'cash-out' effect, where the purchase price is paid to selling shareholders rather than the company itself), or the issue of new shares by the joint venture entity ('cash-in'). In most cases the preferred structure will be determined by a combination of whether the upstream company needs further capital, with opportunities for financial and tax planning.

The most remarkable recent M&A transactions have been Repsol's sale of 40% of its Brazilian subsidiary to Sinopec for $7.1 billion in 2010,[4] and the purchase of new shares at Galp Energia by Sinopec for $4.8 billion. The latter has seen the acquisition by Sinopec of a 30% stake in Galp Energia, as announced on November 11 2011.[5]

Given the industry's early stage of development, transactions have so far had a common purpose and strategy: to bring in a new strategic partner (into the operations or the upstream company) to share the operational risks and costs and

3 This chapter assumes that the exploration and production company is the actual operator (or its joint operational partner) of the block (ie, a concessionaire or the holder of a production sharing contract). Nevertheless, the comments below apply to equity deals involving layers above the exploration and production company itself. In other words, the sale of stock other than shares of the company directly (as would be the case of shares in a holding entity) is also covered by the following notes, since the ultimate target of any such acquisition is Brazilian assets – that is, the blocks themselves.

4 Official website of Repsol: www.repsol.com/es_en/corporacion/prensa/notas-de-prensa/ultimas-notas/01102010repsol-brasil-sinopec.aspx

5 Official website of Galp: www.galpenergia.com/PT/investidor/Noticias/Paginas/GalpEnergia anunciaparceriacomSinopec.aspx.

strengthen the company's financial capabilities. Transactions with this in mind are generally performed within the exploration and development phases, when the costs are substantially more than in the later production phases.

On the other hand, few companies have divested their operations. Some small companies have done so, and the market perception was that the challenge was greater than the company itself. The only notable case involving a large company was the BP-Devon transaction, but this was part of a wider transaction. As reported by BP, Devon Energy was paid "$7.0 billion in cash for assets in Brazil, Azerbaijan and the US deepwater Gulf of Mexico".[6]

It is worth highlighting the main features of this type of transaction in Brazil that should be noted when structuring a transaction.

Due diligence: First of all, buying a regulated company is often more cumbersome than a more generic M&A. In Brazil, regulated sectors are in most cases formed through contracts with the government. The counterparty is therefore more robust and tends to have more leverage. The first task for a successful joint venture is knowing the regulations.

The oil and gas industry is no different. In fact it is one of the most regulated sectors in Brazil. Upstream companies (which, in the case of consortia, means every member of the consortium liable before the ANP) are subject to various regulations issued by a range of authorities. Particular among these is the sector's regulator, the ANP. Many of these regulations impose severe responsibilities upon the company.

Due diligence exercise is therefore key. Beyond the usual exercise recommended for any M&A transaction in a country that bears a complex legal system, there are certain areas in the oil and gas industry that require more attention. These are the environment, local content, obligations towards the ANP and relationships with joint operating agreement partners.

First of all, exploration and production companies are responsible for obtaining the applicable environmental licences before beginning their operations. The primary observation therefore concerns the state of the operations. If a licensing process is underway the buyer should carefully review its progress and confirm that there have been no unexpected delays or requirements from the authorities.

On the other hand, if the licences are already in place, it is important to follow up any conditions attached to their issue, as well as their validity with respect to the operations timeline.

Companies are also responsible for reporting environmental incidents to the ANP and the environmental authorities, and are directly liable to both. Members of a consortium are jointly liable, but the first burden will mostly likely be the operator's.

Another critical area is compliance with the requirements of local content.

Companies are bound to the commitment they made thorough the bid phase. Bidders must present a commitment to local content within a range set by the ANP for each bid. This sets the company's obligation to acquiring equipment and services locally in the phases of exploration and development.

---

6 Official website of BP: www.bp.com/genericarticle.do?categoryId=2012968&contentId=7060559.

Exploration and production companies are therefore contractually committed to purchasing local goods and services on a competitive basis. The goal is the development of local suppliers and technology, the mass creation of jobs and economic growth. The company has to complete a table that presents a scale against which it has to make its offer. This specifies not only the contract phase (exploration or production), but also the different equipment and services to be acquired during the life of the contract.

Penalties for non-compliance with those commitments may be substantial, and the ANP has already levied fines against some operators. Although there are some exceptions to these local content obligations (in cases of high prices, technology gaps, etc), new ownership or other changes particular to the company itself are not among these.

As mentioned above, exploration and production companies are subject to various requirements, which mainly come from the ANP. These include frequent reporting obligations, government takes and the general conditions imposed by industry best practices.

Exploration and production companies are further bound to plans and programmes they have submitted to the ANP. Any unauthorised deviations from these may result in penalties and even the closure of operations.

Finally, due diligence must also cover any guarantees required by the ANP. Two of the most relevant financial obligations are the guarantees covering the minimum exploratory programme and the performance guarantee from the controlling affiliate. The former is mandatory in every operation, while the latter is required only in certain cases. These are mainly when the bidder is relying on the capabilities of its affiliates rather than its own.

The buyer should investigate the status of those guarantees. If they do not conform to the ANP's rules the contract may be terminated.

In Brazil, the exploration and production company may be a consortium of companies. Although one of them already functions formally as an operator, each is considered a separate company by the ANP, with joint liability for the operations. On top of the mandatory consortium agreement, members to a consortium will also execute a joint operating agreement. This will regulate the details of the relationship between the partners over the joint operations of the concession block or production sharing agreement, including exploration, development and production activities.

Besides the usual checks for any existing or past controversies between partners, it is important to investigate whether there have been sole operations, deviations from the ANP-approved plans, any issues with contractors, indebtedness and so on.

Joint operating agreements, preemption rights, disclosure obligations, etc: Most Brazilian joint operating agreements follow the model of the Association of International Petroleum Negotiators. This is the industry's agreed standard for joint operations, although the terms may be subject to interpretation by the will of the parties, local laws, changes to circumstances and other principles of law.

Every joint operating agreement has requirements for transactions that involve either the assets or shares of the company. These include in certain cases (especially asset sales) the obligation to gain the other partners' consent before completing a transaction.

Many contracts contain industry-standard restrictions on the transfer of participation interests in the concession. These include, in particular, comprehensive pre-emptive rights. These are often drafted to cover direct and indirect transfers, through "assignment, merger, consolidation, sale of stock or other conveyance, other than with or to an affiliate".

While some joint operating agreements may attempt to impose pre-emption rights for nearly all direct or indirect transfers, others provide safe harbours. These include exceptions for initial public offerings, for indirect transfers that do not cause a change in control, or for package deals. (These last are the simultaneous sale of interests in different blocks or concessions, where no individual block or concession represents more than a certain percentage, such as 20% or 30%, of the overall deal price.)

This is clearly a sensitive issue which has to be checked early on. If a consent or preemption right does apply, an appropriate strategy can then be designed in good time.

ANP approval: According to the Petroleum Law, the ANP's rules and typical concession agreements, transferring a direct or indirect equity participation in the concession requires the ANP's approval only in particular circumstances. These are when the share transfer requires the ANP to release its role as parent guarantor, or means it will no longer be a controlling affiliate of the concessionaire, so introducing a new guarantor which has previously been approved by the ANP.

On the other hand, the ANP must give prior approval in the case of a straightforward transfer of participation interests in the concession, or any merger, amalgamation or spin-off of the concessionaire.

It is important to investigate whether the proposed transaction will involve circumstances that require prior approval from the ANP. This is time-consuming, and usually requires between two and 12 months to secure.

(b) Joint venture scheme in the asset level (farm-in approach)

In terms of local issues, there are few differences between an equity and an asset transaction (the so-called farm-ins and farm-outs). Essentially, the ultimate target is the same, and so most of the above summary also applies to equity transactions.

Nevertheless, the farm-in approach has been the choice of many companies. They either want to bring fresh money to particular operations (rather than the entire portfolio of an exploration and production company), or want to monetise part of their investments to meet obligations in other operations. Through a farm-in transaction, the 'farmer' does not bring the 'farmee' on as a shareholder, but as a partner in the consortium's joint operating agreement.

One of the most remarkable examples of this in the oil and gas industry was Statoil's sale of 40% of the offshore Peregrino field to Sinochem Group. According to Statoil's press release at the time, "Sinochem Group paid a total of US$3.07 billion in cash for the 40% share of the Peregrino field plus financial settlement from effective date to closing date".[7]

An asset deal allows the buyer to get closer to the asset that may be the actual target. From a seller's perspective, it concentrates the partnership in the asset, shielding the seller's other businesses. Indeed, many equity transactions may be preceded by corporate restructuring so as to split the target assets from others that the seller wants to retain sole control of.

Nevertheless, some regulatory specifics are worth noting with regard to farm-in/out deals.

Firstly, an asset deal is subject to the ANP's prior approval. The assignee must pass the same qualification test to which the assignor was subject when winning the bid (or acquiring the assets from a previous assignor, if that was the case).

The assignee is therefore required to comply with the qualification requirements set out in the tender protocol of the bidding round[8] in which the concession block was auctioned. The table on the next page summarises the documents that are usually required.

Secondly, if an asset deal does not benefit from certain exceptions, it will trigger prior consent and pre-emption rights under the relevant joint operating agreement. In other words, it indicates a direct transfer of the participating interest, and unless the joint operating agreements provides a clear safe harbour, pre-emption rights and consents are likely to apply.

(c) Capital raising via initial public offering

A third route, the initial public offering, is a valuable source of capital. There have been three successful cases in the Brazilian oil and gas industry: OGX's of R6.7 billion,[9] HRT's of $1.3 billion[10] and Queiroz Galvão's of $900 million.[11]

In September 2010, Petrobras completed the largest capitalisation in world history. It raised $70 billion in equity, most of which was for exploration and production of the sub-salt area. Petrobras is a mixed capital entity – that is, it is controlled by the Brazilian government, but a significant number of its shares are held by private investors. In April 2011 *Forbes* ranked it one of the 10 largest companies in the world.[12]

Petrobras's capitalisation was technically not an initial public offering, but a follow-on transaction. The company was already listed and its shares were already traded in both Bovespa and New York when the new shares were issued.

---

7 Official website of Statoil: www.statoil.com/en/NewsAndMedia/News/2011/Pages/14Apr_Peregrino_Sinochem.aspx.

8 By the end of 2011, the ANP had carried out 10 bidding rounds for exploration and production concessions in Brazil, representing hundreds of blocks onshore and offshore.

9 Official website of *Business Wire*: www.businesswire.com/news/home/20111110006922/en/ OGX—-Quarter-2011-Results

10 Official website of *International Financing Review*: www.ifre.com/equities-hrt-r$22bn-ipo-seen-comfortably-oversubscribed/610671.article.

11 Official website of *Best Growth Stock*: www.bestgrowthstock.com/stock-market-news/2011/05/ 25/brazil-oil-start-ups-shine-as-petrobras-worries-mount/.

12 Official website of *Bloomberg*: www.bloomberg.com/news/2010-09-24/petrobras-raises-70-billion-in-world-s-largest-share-sale-to-fund-fields.html.

Class	Document	Mandatory?
Participation fees	Payment of participation fees and evidence of this	√
Technical	Technical summary	For non-operators
	Technical summary*	For operators
	Summary of the professional curriculum**	For operators
Financial	Consolidated financial statement	√
	Independent accountant's opinion	In certain cases
	Bank reference	√
	Relevant obligations statement	√
	Details of medium-term planning	√
	Summary of financial statements	√
Legal	Legal opinion or organisation chart detailing the existing chain of control	√
	Declaration of all relevant legal or judicial claims	√

* The technical summary must show previous experience in:
- onshore, shallow-water and deep-water exploration and production operations;
- level of production in equivalent oil;
- exploration and production operations in adverse environments; and
- environmental aspects.

It must also show the amount of experience in exploration and production operations.

** For companies that can not prove their previous operational experience.

The particular feature of the oil and gas industry with regard to initial public offerings (or similar capital market deals) is that with the exception of Petrobras, companies do not have robust production. However, they can rely on the certification of their reserves by independent surveyors. This has proved sufficient, and the capital market has been a significant source of capital for companies like this.

In fact, the Brazilian capital markets were traditionally reluctant to accept project risk. This was overcome through OGX's remarkable initial public offering in 2008. OGX is one of the Eike Batista venture companies that make up the X Group, dedicated to the upstream oil and gas sector. By the time it launched in June 2008, it managed to achieve the highest amount of equity ever raised in a primary initial public offering in Brazil. Most remarkably, it was based only on greenfield projects and projections.

Despite such successes, an initial public offering is a time-consuming and costly transaction. It requires the involvement of various third parties and favourable opinions. The company must not only be prepared to face a new array of regulations (besides those of the oil and gas industry itself), but also be able to convince its potential investors that its assets are worth the capital asked for. Needless to say, some companies have failed to meet these challenges. They either are now preparing for a new attempt or have opted for more traditional and less complex means of capital sourcing.

At the time that Sinopec was completing its investment in Repsol, press articles indicated that Repsol had been pursuing a local initial public offering for its assets in Brazil, before it decided instead to effect an M&A with a strategic investor.[13]

In order to become public (the first regulatory step towards an initial public offering), a company must be listed as such with the Brazilian Securities Commission. Moreover, there are different levels of corporate governance. Compliance with these will be closely examined before the company makes a decision. They include:

- minorities protection and board membership;
- related-party transactions; and
- constraints on new ventures in Brazil.

On the one hand, an initial public offering is a powerful mechanism for raising substantial amounts of cash. But on the other hand, it requires a lot of work. Perhaps most importantly, the day after the initial public offering the company will suddenly be subject to numerous regulations and exposed to the market.

2.2 Partnerships in the sub-salt regime

It is worth noting some of the particulars of potential joint ventures under the new production sharing agreement regime.

Under the concession regime, subject to the usual legal, technical and financial requirements, companies are free to join one another under a consortium to bid for and execute the concession. They are free to agree on its governance and other provisions of the consortium and joint operating agreements. Under the production sharing agreement regime, however, companies will be required to partner with Petrobras, which will be entitled to a minimum 30% stake in the consortium. They

13 Official website of *Exame.com*: exame.abril.com.br/mercados/noticias/repsol-registra-pedido-ipo-cvm-586210>; official website of Uol.com: http://economia.uol.com.br/ultimas-noticias/valor/2010/10/01/apos-acordo-com-sinopec-repsol-desiste-de-ipo-no-brasil.jhtm.

must also accept political interference from the government which, represented by the Brazilian Oil and Natural Gas Management Corporation for Pre-Salt Petroleum (PPSA), will have veto rights over certain decisions of the consortium's operating committee.

Despite these restrictions, M&A transactions of equity and assets will be possible in sub-salt operations. Although the former do not present any further issues beyond what have already been discussed, the latter may be subject to more stringent regulation than under the current system of concessions.

In any case, depending on the initial structures of the production sharing contracts, the market expects that Petrobras will remain the main engine behind M&As in the industry, considering that it may sell any participating interests so long as it does not fall its mandatory 30% participation.

(a) The PSC regime

It is important first to recall that Petrobras will be the sole and mandatory operator, and is assured a minimum 30% participation in the consortium that is awarded the production sharing contract. The PPSA will also have a mandatory role, so as to represent the government's interests and appropriate its share in the production of the field.

Private parties or Petrobras itself is entitled to bid for the remainder of the production sharing agreement. The winner will be the entity willing to surrender the largest participation stake to the PPSA. Nevertheless, the PPSA's share is calculated from the net production (profit oil) – that is, the production remaining after a certain share has been set aside to cover all eligible costs (cost oil).

The law has left various subjects to be regulated by the production sharing agreement itself, including matters that will be subject to veto or special vote by the PPSA. A good deal of effort will therefore have to be applied by the private partners in negotiating the joint operating agreement so as to ensure reasonable governance rights.

(b) Governance of the sub-salt joint ventures

Petrobras will play a strong role in sub-salt exploration and production. Nevertheless, and irrespective of the legal prerogatives granted to it by the new legislation, there will be many opportunities for local and international private parties to make alliances with Petrobras or compete with it.

Having that said, the governance of joint ventures in the sub-salt areas tends to be the issue on which companies in partnership with Petrobras and the PPSA have least subsidies in the existing concession rules. In fact, even in those concessions where Petrobras is the operator (and controller of the main decisions), governance has come from the result of previous negotiations with Petrobras. However, under the new model, what was a factual situation has become mandatory.

Therefore, the homework for those companies entering into a partnership with Petrobras and the PPSA begins with identifying those aspects of corporate and operational governance either drafted under the new model (laws and model contract, and later on the regulation)[14] or left for the partners' negotiation. In the next phase these will consist of negotiating the agreements that will enable the private parties to ensure their decision-making powers under the new regime.

When preparing their investment plans and analysing the production sharing bid rounds, companies must account for a new agent that is strong and exempt from project costs (ie, the PPSA), plus the same old partner, Petrobras, which is now granted exclusive operatorship and a minimum stake of 30% of the project.

The production sharing regime intends to ensure that companies in partnership with the PPSA and Petrobras will never have exclusive control of the projects' governance (ie, control over the main decisions). For this reason only the PPSA has veto rights and a casting vote.

Now that the new model has been launched, the most important legal due diligence for companies that will contract with Petrobras and the PPSA should be reviewing the governance of the consortia. This will encompass those matters that require decisions from the operational committee, and within those, those matters that are subject to the control of the PPSA as chairman of the operational committee. The next step should be negotiating the contractual arrangements that allow balanced governance, by means of working on points that are not directly referred to by the law, or the application of those that are, or even the softening of all those points. In summary, this is no different from the usual legal work on joint ventures, where the parties practise their freedom to contract, taking care not to breach any mandatory principles of law.

On the other hand, the financial models must give consideration to a joint venture whose economical and political rights might not be entirely aligned, as the PPSA will retain important veto rights despite not sharing any project costs.

(c) Corporate finance and project finance

Apart from equity sources, oil and gas entrepreneurs will usually look for debt financing, like any other capital-intensive investor.

Although debt leverage brings financial risks to the borrowing company or its parent guarantor, it allows for improved returns on equity and, therefore, better dividends to shareholders.

An early stage exploration and production project will usually carry too many uncertainties and risks for a project finance lender. For this reason most will be developed under a traditional approach to corporate finance. This means that it will be one of many projects developed by a consolidated oil and gas company, funded by other cash generating activities, by equity sources and/or by traditional corporate finance.

Petrobras, for instance, holds directly most of the participation interests it acquired in the Brazilian exploration and production concessions.

Even upstream projects structured and developed as special purpose entities in the best fashion of project finance/risk isolation, are generally financed by equity contributions from its shareholders, or debt financing guaranteed by a strong sponsoring affiliate – usually a parent guarantor.

---

14 By the end of 2011, when this article was drafted, production sharing agreement laws had been enacted but required regulation; the standard form was still pending.

This has been the usual approach of BNDES and other Brazilian banks in lending to oil and gas companies in Brazil.

However, the oil and gas industry has always been innovative. If cost-effective project financing is not available to finance the full range of activities of an exploration and production project, it is frequently available for securing the use or ownership of certain assets, such as rigvessels, platforms, floating production storage and offloading vessels, and related equipment.

To that effect, a new affiliate or non-affiliate special purpose entity will be incorporated to raise finances under the highest debt-to-equity ratio (eg, 80: 20) allowed by the finance lenders, and to purchase or contract this equipment from a reliable third party contractor, under an EPC/turnkey arrangement.

In that case, so long as the usual project finance concerns are properly addressed, the upstream company will treat the charter fees as ongoing non-financial expenses. These will be recognised in the company's financial statements on an accrual basis – that is, alongside the use of the assets and not as a long-term debt. In other words, this structure accomplishes the off-balance effect. It is also off-budget for mixed capital entities in Brazil that are limited in the permitted amount of capital investments.

Project finance lenders will demand first priority security interests over virtually all assets and rights of the special purpose entity, including its charter/leasing revenues and the assets themselves.

These lenders are comfortable with lending on a project finance basis because if the special purpose entity defaults, they can rely on the revenues payable by the charteree/lessee or its parent guarantor. This is usually a consolidated and financially sound company. In addition, the equipment itself usually presents a reasonable market value and may be foreclosed and relocated if required.

Oil and gas midstream projects are even better suited for project financing. Project finance has been successfully deployed in Brazil for gas pipelines, gas processing units and gas-fired or fuel-based thermal powerplants. Project finance is also expected to be achieved for refining plants, gasification and liquefaction LNG plants and other major projects currently under development.

2.3 Project bonds

In summary, a project bond is a method of financing implemented through the local or cross-border issuance of debt securities such as debentures or international notes or bonds (eg, 144A or Reg-S).

Traditionally, project financing has been limited to a very specialised and selective group of financial institutions, export credit agencies or multilateral entities, such as the Inter-American Development Bank, the International Finance Corporation, US Exim Bank, Japan Bank for International Cooperation, KfW and a few commercial banks.

However, the appetite of commercial banks for project financing has increased and a larger pool of banks has recently been reached.

Institutional investors have generally become familiar with and interested in project financing investments. In the oil and gas sector, they can do so by purchasing debt securities of oil and gas project companies.

As for traditional project financing, projects more suited for this type of financing are those that involve the acquisition and construction of hard assets such as vessels and platforms, to be long-term leased or chartered to creditworthy exploration and production companies.

Except for Rota das Bandeiras,[15] the first true project bond experiences in Brazil have been to finance oil and gas equipment like this.

In October 2010 the Lancer Finance Company, a special purpose entity controlled by Schahin, issued senior notes in the United States, governed by 144-A and Reg S regulations, for $270 million. These were due in 2016 and paid interest of 5.85%. The proceeds were used to refinance the drilling vessel SC Lancer, and to construct the twin Black Diamond drilling vessels, all of which were chartered or to be chartered to Petrobras. The security package included the vessels, the charter revenues and shares in Lancer Finance.[16]

In November 2010, Odebrecht Drilling Norbe VIII/IX Ltd, an offshore special purpose entity controlled by Odebrecht Óleo e Gás, raised $1.5 billion by issuing 144-A and Reg S bonds abroad. These reach final maturity in 2021 and pay interest at 6.375% per annum. The proceeds were used to refinance the construction, in Korea, of two drilling vessels, Norbe VIII and IX. These were then chartered to Petrobras, under a project finance structure. The security package was comprehensive and included mortgage over the vessels, security over revenues, a pledge of shares and relevant contractual rights in the special purpose entity, and a parent guarantor for the risks of construction.[17]

In July 2011, a special purpose entity of Queiroz Galvão Óleo e Gas issued non-recourse project bonds in the form of seven-year $700 million senior notes, yielding 5.45% per annum. These were for the refinancing of the rig vessels Atlantic Star and Alaskan Star, which have been chartered to Petrobras for some years. Security included all revenues payable by Petrobras, among other assets and rights held by the issuer.[18]

Compared to traditional loan-agreement project finance, project bonds present certain challenges.

First of all, traditional project finance usually requires constant monitoring, authorisations and waivers by the lender. However, a project bond transaction often involves dozens of investors. How can these authorisations and waivers be timely and repeatedly obtained from such a large group of entities? If the bond indenture is silent on a particular matter, unanimity may apply and would be almost impossible to achieve. The usual solution is to set low voting quorums, so that authorisations and waivers can be granted if approved by a simple majority, or if not expressly denied by a certain percentage of investors.

15 This was a landmark toll-road concession financing, made in August 2010. It was made through the local issue of R1.1 billion-worth of 14-years debentures by an Odebrecht special purpose entity. These paid interest of 9.57% per year plus IPCA inflation.

16 Source: www.projectfinancemagazine.com/Article/2675490/Schahin-launches-Lancer-rig-bond-recapitalisation.html; and McLaughlin, Cathleen e Yessios, Dorina. "Why project bonds? Why now?" *Latin Lawyer Magazine*. April 2011, vol. 10, pp. 35–37.

17 Elected as the 2010 Bond Deal of the Year by Project Finance Magazine and Latin Lawyer. Source: www.odebrechtonline.com.br/relatorioanual/2011/pt/23_oleo_gas.php

18 Source: www.power.inf.br/site/petroleo-e-gas/7536-queiroz-galvao-oleo-e-gas-levanta-us-700-milhoes.

Another usual challenge is to mirror the traditional approach of releasing loan amounts in several disbursements hand-in-hand with the project milestones. This approach serves two purposes: lenders mitigate the risk of the funds being misused and borrowers do not have to pay interest on finance that is not yet needed.

However, it would be extremely burdensome for project bond investors to make piecemeal disbursements, paying for the bonds in installments. There is also the inherent risk of default. A reasonable alternative is to require bondholders to disburse in full, but place the proceeds into an escrow account so that they may be released on a gradual basis, as the project progresses. Although this solution may mitigate the risk of misuse it should not relieve the issuer from interest accrued from the original investors' date of disbursement.

2.4 Other structured and hybrid alternatives

There are cases where, differently from the more typical finance experiences reported above, the full array of upstream activities may be eligible for project finance at a non-prohibitive cost. This has been the case, for instance, for upstream projects that are able to present certified reserves or are already producing on a pilot scale, and that therefore offer a high chance of commercial discoveries and meaningful production.

This is so-called 'reserve-based lending', and it may be interesting for medium-sized or independent oil and gas companies who do not yet have access to more attractive sources of financing.

In these circumstances, the concession itself will often present an attractive market value. Lenders may be happy to lend money, on a project finance non-recourse or limited recourse basis, by taking the concession itself and its future production or revenues as security.

Strong and well-structured projects are sometimes also able to raise additional project financing to fund part of the equity required from shareholders, through subordinated debt taken at an intermediary holding level. This is the 'mezzanine' structure.

These specialised lenders are usually private equity funds. They will need to charge interest consistent with the higher risk of the projects. Indeed, repayment is dependent on the project generating sufficient cash to pay not only the original project finance lenders but also to distribute dividends generous enough to serve the mezzanine financing and leave a residual benefit for the final shareholders.

From the shareholders' perspective, the mezzanine structure allows higher debt-to-equity leverage, and thus increases even further their potential returns.[19]

The creativity of the oil and gas industry has already been mentioned, and it has traditionally encouraged the development of sophisticated legal and financial structures. Indeed, project financing itself is said to have been developed in the 1970s in the context of oil and gas projects that were being developed in the North Sea.

---

19 InfraBrasil and Darby-Stratus are known examples of such specialised lenders who have closed or offered mezzanine financing in Brazil.

For this reason, many other sophisticated structures (including securitisations, export prepayment and consortia) have been successfully implemented in Brazil. But given the limitations of this chapter it seems sufficient to mention so far successful experience which has gained recent notice in the Brazilian press.

'Projeto Sondas' is a project under which Petrobras has sponsored the creation of a new company, Sete Brasil. Petrobras is a minority 10% shareholder. Sete Brasil has been designed for raising local or offshore finances, on a project finance basis, to acquire initially 28 rigvessels to be used in upstream projects owned or operated by Petrobras. Seven of these rigvessels were contracted in 2011 and the remaining 21 will be in 2012. Sete Brasil, or its local or offshore subsidiaries, will own the rigvessels, but they will be constructed on an EPC/turnkey basis by shipyards in Brazil, such as Estaleiro Atlântico Sul.[20]

The rigvessels will then be long-term chartered or leased to Petrobras or its affiliates. The revenues gained may secure the repayment of project finance and offer acceptable equity returns to investors. The shareholding control of Sete Brasil was held by a Brazilian private equity fund independently managed by Caixa Econômica Federal (a robust financial institution, controlled by the government). This raised capital from institutional equity investors such as pension funds and financial institutions.[21]

The innovation here is clear: from the perspective of Petrobras or another off-taker, the structure offers simultaneous equity and project financing that may be raised in different stages so as to accommodate an increasing number of projects.

3. Conclusion

Taking into account the sub-salt areas and the other opportunities presented by the industry the financial challenges to be faced in the near future by oil and gas companies in Brazil are enormous. More than ever, lawyers and financial experts will be required to put together projects and their financing.

Nevertheless, the options presented above show a variety of means suited to raising capital for oil and gas projects, including in the exploration and production sector. All of them have already been successfully tested in Brazil, on a larger or smaller scale.

---

20 Source: exame.abril.com.br/negocios/empresas/noticias/petrobras-cria-empresa-de-sondas-do-pre-sal; br.noticias.yahoo.com/sete-brasil-encomenda-navio-sonda-r-1-35-161231174.html;

21 *Ibid.*

Transport and third-party access

Felipe Feres
Luiz Antonio Lemos
Luis Antonio Menezes
Marcelo Romanelli
Campos Mello Advogados

1. Pipelines

In general, the construction, operation and maintenance of pipelines for petroleum, natural gas and petroleum by-products are subject to Law 9,478/1997, as amended. Although the transportation, storage, liquefaction, regasification and commercialisation of natural gas are subject to the general rules of this law and to Ordinance 170/1998 of the National Petroleum Agency (ANP), they are specifically governed by Law 11,909/2009 (the Gas Law).

The Petroleum Law determines that any Brazilian company or consortium may be authorised by the ANP to build transportation facilities for petroleum, its by-products and natural gas, and carry out any related activities, whether for the internal market or for import and export.

The Petroleum Law classifies two types of movement of petroleum and natural gas: transportation and transfer. Transportation is the use of pipelines or routes of general interest. Transfer is the use of pipelines or routes that are of the specific and exclusive interest of the facility's owner or of the exploring entity. There are therefore generally two types of pipeline: transportation pipelines and transfer pipelines.

The ANP enacted Ordinance 170 in order to regulate the Petroleum Law's provisions and to establish rules for the construction and operation of transportation and transfer facilities. According to this ordinance, these activities can be performed only with the ANP's express authorisation, unless the pipes are contained within the boundaries of an industrial plant. Nevertheless, after the enactment of the Gas Law, the construction and operation of any natural gas transfer pipelines that are not part of exploration and production facilities require authorisation from the ANP.

This authorisation is granted in two stages: construction authorisation (CA) and operation authorisation (OA).

The CA request must be accompanied by:

- the latest version of the company's bylaws, registered by the Board of Trade;
- proof of enrolment with the federal and state revenues;
- the project's technical documents, such as its installation summary, in which the service to be performed is presented, the movement and storage capacity for each stage of the project's implementation, and other various technical data;

- the preliminary blueprints and the physical and financial schedule; and
- the installation licence from the relevant environmental agency.

The ANP must review the documentation within 90 days and may request additional information from the entrepreneur. Additionally, the agency shall publish in the *Official Gazette* a summary of the project, which shall remain open for comments and suggestions for 30 days.

In its turn, the OA request must be accompanied by

- an operation licence, issued by the relevant environmental agency;
- a certificate of commissioning of the work issued by a specialised and independent technical entity; and
- a summary of the facility's maintenance plan and its system of quality assurance for the period of its operation.

The ANP will have 30 days to review the documentation and request any further information.

If a pipeline is classified for transportation, authorisation can be granted only to companies whose sole business is the construction and operation of such pipelines.

After receiving the ANP's authorisation, the company is subject to several obligations. These include updating the maintenance plan and the quality warranty system, informing the ANP of any event that may pose a risk to third parties or the environment, and any interruption, reduction or modification to the quality of the services offered.

The ANP may revoke these authorisations should the authorised company enter liquidation or bankruptcy or fail to comply with its legal obligations, or at the company's request.

The ANP's Technical Regulation 2, approved through Regulation 6/2011, establishes rules for managing the safety of onshore oil and gas pipelines. It sets out the minimum requirements and safety standards for onshore pipelines, with the aim of protecting the facility, the operator's workforce, the environment and the general population. It applies to the operation, maintenance and deactivation of all pipelines, as well as to the planning and construction of new pipelines and extensions.

The transportation, storage, liquefaction, regasification and commercialisation of natural gas are governed by the Gas Law, Decree 7,382/2010 and the ANP's regulations enacted after Ordinance 170.

The Gas Law grants the pipeline transportation of natural gas to any company incorporated in Brazil, regardless of whether its controller is a domestic or foreign entity, by means of concession or authorisation. The Petroleum Law provides only for an authorisation system for constructing and extending transfer and transportation pipelines. Following the enactment of the specific rules of the Gas Law, the authorisation regime established by the Petroleum Law no longer applies to natural gas pipelines. (While several provisions of Petroleum Law still apply to gas pipelines, the Gas Law has now established more specific rules governing gas pipes and a new granting system.)

Transportation pipelines that are entirely within the Brazilian territory are subject to the concession system, which is preceded by a bidding process. Transportation pipelines that involve international agreements, such as the Brazil–Bolivia Gas Pipeline (GASBOL), which transports natural gas from Bolivia to major Brazilian consumer markets, are subject to the authorisation system, which is not preceded by a bidding process.

The authorisation system also applies to the construction, extension and operation of natural gas transfer pipelines.

The Gas Law also created a new classification for gas pipelines: the natural gas production flow pipeline. Natural gas production flow pipelines that are not part of an oil and gas exploration and production concession (ie, a facility that is not part of the assets of an upstream project, and thus is not included in the applicable plan of development for the field), are subject to the authorisation system without a bidding process. Neither transfer nor production flow pipelines are obliged to provide open access to third parties (see below). (Natural gas production flow pipelines may in fact be part of the assets of an upstream project. In this case, no specific authorisation from the ANP would be required, as the pipeline would already be described in the relevant plan of development approved by the agency.)

The ANP is responsible for organising and promoting the bidding rounds for transportation gas pipelines, and the tender protocols and concession agreements for their construction, extension and operation. These have a 30-year term, which is extendable for another 30 years. The ANP also executes these agreements, under the direction of the Ministry of Mines and Energy.

The Gas Law stipulates that it is incumbent upon the Ministry of Mines and Energy to:

- establish what gas pipelines are to be built or extended;
- establish the guidelines for contracting the transportation capacity; and
- determine whether the concession or authorisation system applies to a given pipeline.

1.1 Bid rounds and authorisations

Only companies or consortia whose head offices are in Brazil and that are incorporated in accordance with Brazilian law can construct, extend and operate pipelines and other facilities for natural gas (including LNG), petroleum and its by-products.

The rules for oil pipeline construction and operation are established by the Petroleum Law and Ordinance 170, and are simpler than those for natural gas pipelines. The authorisation system applies to all oil pipelines and there is no need for a bidding process.

Under the Gas Law, the bidding process for concessions to construct or extend natural gas transportation pipelines must be preceded by a public invitation for contracts. This must be promoted by the ANP, following the guidelines from the Ministry of Mines and Energy. The goal of such an invitation is to identify potential shippers and gain a measure of the demand for the new pipeline.

During the public invitation process, the ANP must calculate the maximum tariff that shippers will be charged. At the end of this process, shippers that are interested in using the pipeline must indicate their commitment to buy the requested capacity in a letter to the ANP. This letter of commitment is irrevocable and will become part of the tender protocol (see below).

The ANP will organise and promote the bidding process for concessions to natural gas transportation pipelines that are located within Brazil. This includes elaborating the tender protocol and the concession agreement. The agency will also execute the concession agreement with the winner of the bidding process, on behalf of the Ministry of Mines and Energy. The agreement will have a 30-year term, renewable once for a further 30 years.

The winner of the bidding process may be one of the following:

- the bidder that offers the lowest annual revenue, according to the tender protocol and the regulations;
- the bidder that offers the highest payment for using the public asset; or
- a combination of both criteria, in accordance with the tender protocol.

Among other things, the tender protocol must indicate:

- the route of the pipeline, the delivery and reception points, and the projected transportation capacity and the criteria used for its calculation;
- the maximum expected annual revenue and the criteria used for its calculation;
- the criterion for selecting of the best proposal, as described above;
- the bidders' requirements and any pre-qualification criteria;
- a list of the documents required and the criteria to be followed in evaluating the technical and financial capability, and the legal and tax good-standing, of the bidders, and the technical, economic and financial feasibility of the proposal;
- an express indication that the concessionaire will be responsible for compensating any expropriations and easements necessary to perform the agreement, as well as for any costs connected with acquiring the necessary permits, including environmental licenses;
- the exclusivity period that the initial shippers will have in which to exploit the new pipeline;
- the concession period and the possibility of its extension, if applicable;
- any mandatory items to be included in the technical proposal that will be presented with the financial proposal;
- the minimum percentage of local content in the gas pipeline;
- a list of those shippers who have written letters of commitment requesting transportation capacity, with the requested volumes and warranties of each; and
- the letters of commitment themselves.

When a concession is terminated, the concessionaire is obliged to continue with the transportation services until a new concessionaire is appointed, or until the gas pipeline is deactivated. It also possible to assign the concession agreement, provided that its terms and conditions stay the same.

Authorisations granted after the enactment of the Gas Law will have a 30-year term, extendable for an equal period; authorisations granted before the law was passed also have a 30-year term, but this is not extendable.

At the end of the concession or authorisation period, the assets associated with the transportation of oil and gas will revert to the union, following a public interest resolution and appropriate financial compensation. The assets will be administered by the granting power, according to specific regulations that are yet to be enacted. These assets may themselves eventually be offered as facilities within a new natural gas transportation concession.

1.2 Licensee third-party rights

The Petroleum Law states that any interested party may use transportation pipelines and offshore terminals, following appropriate remuneration to their owners.

The ANP's Ordinance 115 regulates this third-party access. Those pipelines that originate in petroleum and natural gas production areas, as well as those of less than 15 kilometres (km) length, are not subject to this ordinance. Third-party access to natural gas pipelines is also not covered, but is instead regulated by the Gas Law and other ANP rules.

The following are some of the main rules set out in Ordinance 115:

- The transporter shall provide access to any interested third parties to its available capacity, operational capacity and idle capacity.
- Any applicant that claims to be harmed by the access allocation proposed by the transporter may ask the ANP to intervene while the access allocation proposal is available.
- The owner of the transportation facility has right of preference for moving its own products.
- In the first 10 years of operation, the owner's preference will comprise the entire operational capacity, which corresponds to the maximum monthly volume of products which the transporter may transport between the reception and delivery points of a transportation facility.
- If a third party requests firm transportation over and above the pipeline's current operational capacity, and the owner chooses not to invest in expanding the capacity (which must always be limited to the maximum capacity of the pipeline – that is, is the maximum monthly volume of products that the transporter can move in a pipeline between receipt and delivery points, considering all pumping stations and tanks, as well as possible expansions and upgrades), the owner must accept that such expansion will be carried out by the third party. Despite such an investment, the expanded facilities will still belong to the owner.
- If a request for firm transportation requires the pipeline to operate at more than 90% of its maximum capacity, the transporter is obliged to report this fact in the *Official Gazette* and on the Internet. After publication in the *Official Gazette*, the interested party has 30 days to request firm transportation to the same pipeline. When this is done, the transporter must draft an allocation proposal to optimise the facility's operation within 15 days, and publish it in the *Official Gazette* with the appropriate justifications.

- Requests for firm transportation that requires the pipeline to operate at more than 90% of its operational capacity must also be reported by the transporter in the *Official Gazette* and on the Internet. In these cases, other interested parties will have 21 days to request firm transportation.
- The service agreements for firm transportation will last between five and 15 years, and each party must submit an extract of that agreement to the ANP.

Access to transportation pipelines of less than 15 km in length is regulated by Ordinance 255/2000. In this case, the transporter must provide access to any interested third parties according to the available operational capacity and the rules established in this regard.

The following are some of the main rules set out in Ordinance 255:

- The owner of the pipeline shall allow connection of third-party transportation facilities to its own, provided that the operational safety regulations are observed.
- The owner retains right of preference for moving its own products.
- The transporter must compile a transportation programme for the next month of all orders made before the 15th of the current month. This is so as to optimise the operation of the facility. The transporter must confirm this programme within three days. Orders made after the 15th may be included if operational capacity is available.
- Shippers with a confirmed order must make payment in full for transportations that are programmed but not executed due to their own fault. However, the shipper may assign this programmed capacity to a third party, as long as it agrees to the same conditions.
- The owner may not reserve capacity and not use it, except in case of proven acts of God or *force majeure*.
- The shipper and the transporter are responsible for product quality, and the transporter may use the principle of fungibility unless expressly otherwise provided.

Third-party open access to natural gas pipelines is governed by the Gas Law and Decree 7,382. Third parties may have open access to gas transportation pipelines only subject to the concession system. This ensures the publicity, transparency and participation of all interested parties. Third parties do not have open access to transfer or production flow pipelines.

First shippers are entitled to a period of exclusivity to new natural gas transportation pipelines. The Ministry of Mines and Energy, upon consulting with the ANP, will determine these periods of exclusivity on a case-by-case basis.

The period will be defined according to the following parameters:

- It will not exceed 10 years.
- It will consider the level of development of the market that is to be served.
- It may change according to the result of the public invitation, under the terms of the tender protocol.
- It will be terminated when the pipeline transportation reaches its maximum

contracted capacity, even if the deadline set out in the public invitation has not been reached, in accordance with ANP's future regulations.

Third-party open access to transportation pipelines is guaranteed in the following three different capacity allocations:

- using available capacity to contract a firm transportation service, on occasions when the transporter must programme and transport the daily volume of natural gas ordered by the shipper, up to the maximum capacity specified in the contract;
- using idle capacity to contract an interruptible or non-firm transportation service, on occasions when service may be interrupted by the transporter due to priority being given to firm transportation that has already been contracted; and
- using available capacity to contract an extraordinary transportation service, during the lack of a firm transportation arrangement, whose service is subject to termination as a condition subsequent should the firm transportation be subsequently contracted. Under the Gas Law, available capacity is that part of the pipeline's transportation capacity that has not been contracted under a firm transportation service agreement. Idle capacity, on the other hand, is that capacity that has been contracted, but is temporarily not being used.

Access to the natural gas pipeline must primarily make use of the available capacity. Access to the idle capacity, mentioned above, is guaranteed only after all of the available capacity has been contracted.

Access to the available capacity is provided through public invitation by the ANP, in accordance with the guidelines of the Ministry of Mines and Energy. Access to interruptible transportation services, using the idle capacity, and the extraordinary transportation service, using the available capacity, will be provided in accordance with regulations that have yet to be enacted by the ANP. These will ensure the publicity, transparency and guaranteed access of all interested parties.

However, the ANP has not yet enacted the new rules on the regulation of open access to gas transportation pipelines that are set out in the Gas Law. At the moment, open access by third parties is regulated by ANP Ordinance 27/2005, which was issued prior to the Gas Law.

The main rules set out in this resolution are as follows:

- The transporter shall allow non-discriminatory access to its transportation facilities, as well as their connection with other transportation facilities, except when a service order refers to a new transportation facility (ie, pipelines that are less than six years old);
- The transporter will serve interested parties with either interruptible transportation services on idle capacity, or those interested in contracting firm transportation service on available capacity. Gas volumes contracted on the basis of firm transportation will take priority over interruptible ones;
- Contracting any available capacity for firm transportation will be done through a public procurement for capacity allocation (CPAC). This is a public process for offering and allocating transportation capacity;

- The transporter must initiate a CPAC whenever there is a request for firm transportation, or on the first-year anniversary of the last CPAC, in compliance with the principles of transparency, equality and publicity;
- The CPAC will require:
  - the delivery and reception points to be made available;
  - the method used for calculating the tariffs; and
  - when applicable, the criteria used for measuring and re-measuring the capacity of the expansion project; and
- If the sum of the service orders exceeds the capacity, the transporter must expand the capacity and recalculate the tariff according to the new capacity. If the transporter does not have sufficient financial resources to undertake this expansion, the shippers may finance it in proportion to the volumes of gas they have ordered.

Although Resolution 27 is still in force, it is hard to reconcile several of its provisions with the Gas Law. For example, the Gas Law guarantees three forms of access (firm transportation, interruptible transportation and extraordinary transportation services), whereas Resolution 27 provides for only two (firm and interruptible). Moreover, the provisions of the Gas Law regarding the exclusivity period for initial shippers of new transportation pipelines differ from those regarding the exemptions for new transportation facilities established in the resolution. The ANP must therefore put in place new regulations to bring about the open access to future gas pipelines that is established by the Gas Law.

Finally, it is permitted to assign transportation capacity that has been contracted under the firm basis to third parties, as long as the rights of the transporter are preserved.

The ANP's Resolution 28/2005 currently regulates the assignment of contracted transportation capacity. According to this resolution, the shipper may assign all or some of its contracted transportation capacity to a non-transporter third party, and is able to make the necessary changes to the transportation contract already in force, provided the transporter's rights under the contract are observed. The transporter and the ANP must be informed in advance of these assignments of capacity. Within 30 days of the capacity assignment being agreed, the shipper must send the ANP copies of the contract or term that sets out its basis.

1.3 ANP classification

Pipelines are classified as follows:

- oil pipelines (for transporting petroleum and liquid by-products);
- natural gas pipelines (for transporting natural gas); and
- poliducts (for transporting more than one type of product).

The Gas Law identifies three types of gas pipeline, as explained above: transfer, transportation and production flow pipelines.

Natural gas transfer gas pipelines are used to move natural gas within the owner's own production, collection, transfer, storage or processing facility. They are an exclusive interest of their owners.

Natural gas transportation pipelines, on the other hand, transport natural gas from processing and storage facilities, or other natural gas transportation pipelines, to third-party storage facilities, other transportation pipelines or delivery points that belong to the state's natural gas distribution concessionaires.

The Petroleum Law states that the ANP may reclassify transfer pipelines as transportation pipelines if there is a proven third-party interest.

Finally, gas production flow pipelines are used to move natural gas from the producing wells to the processing and treatment facilities or liquefaction units.

Oil pipelines are used to transport petroleum from onshore and offshore production wells to the refineries. They are also used when imported petroleum is unloaded at offshore terminals and transferred to the refineries.

Poliducts are capable of carrying more than one liquid product. This might be petroleum and its by-products, such as gasoline, diesel and kerosene. Poliducts operate under pressure; that is, they are completely filled with liquid. So pumping liquid into one end of the poliduct causes the same amount of liquid to emerge at the other end.

2. Tariffs

The tariffs charged by transporters must not be discriminatory. They should reflect the type of service being rendered, its duration, the products and the volume to be transported, the distance between the delivery and reception points, and any operating and maintenance costs. This is in accordance with Article 24 of ANP Resolution 115, mentioned above.

The ANP has the power to change a tariff if a complaint is presented providing sufficient proof of the transporter's pricing incompatibility.

Pipelines of less than 15 km come under the same rules for defining tariffs. The tax burden and losses and contamination levels of the transported products must also be observed. For these pipelines Resolution 115 contains no right of recourse to the ANP against the transporter's prices.

In relation to natural gas transportation pipelines under concession, the Gas Law sets out that the tariffs to be paid by shippers should be established by the ANP. The agency will apply to the maximum tariff established for the public invitation process a coefficient that corresponds to the ratio between annual revenue established in the bidding process (since the winning offer usually is the one with the smallest annual revenue) and the maximum annual revenue established in the tender protocol.

The criteria for calculating the transportation tariffs of pipelines that were already in operation when the Gas Law was enacted are established in ANP Resolution 29/2005. These tariffs must reflect both the costs of efficiently rendering the services and the bases of those costs, such as the distance between the reception and delivery points, the volume required and the contracted terms. Resolution 29 determines that the tariff for firm transportation should be structured around at least the following charges:

- an entry capacity charge, to cover the fixed costs of the reception capacity, general and administrative expenses, and any fixed operation and maintenance costs;

- a transportation capacity charge, to cover any investment costs related to the transportation capacity;
- an output capacity charge, to cover any fixed costs related to the delivery capacity; and
- a movement charge, to cover any variable costs incurred in the actual transportation of the gas.

The tariffs for an interruptible transportation service will be based solely on the volumetric charge. The value of this will be established according to the probability of interruption and other conditions of such a service, using the firm transportation service as reference.

3. Terminals

Law 8,630/1993 (the Ports Law) generally regulates activities that relate to national ports and port facilities. It gives main scenarios in which a facility can be built and operated: within an organised port area, and outside an organised port area.

The Ports Law defines an 'organised port' as an area designed to meet navigation needs, to allow the transportation of passengers, and to allow the transportation and storage of goods. The federal government is responsible for exploring organised ports directly or by means of concessions. To explore facilities that are within an organised port area, the interested party must bid for the relevant lease agreement with the port authority, which may be either the federal government or the relevant concessionaire.

These processes do not apply to facilities to be built outside the limits of an organised port area. The construction or operation of these facilities is not subject to a bidding process, but is subject to the requirements and regulations of the competent governmental entity. In the case of an oil terminal, this is the ANP.

The ANP recognises a terminal as a group of facilities used for receiving, shipping and storing the products of the petroleum industry. Terminals may be classified as onshore or water terminals. The latter is divided into maritime, fluvial and lacustrine types. All three have the same function; only their location differs. Maritime terminals are located on ocean coasts, fluvial terminals on rivers and lacustrine terminals on lakesides. Fluvial terminals are used mainly in the Amazon region in the north of Brazil, where road access can be precarious.

Water terminals are port facilities for transferring cargo from ships to land (and vice-versa) or between ships. They are therefore important in the logistical chain of oil transportation.

ANP Ordinance 311/2001 classifies a loading terminal as the place in their country of origin where products are loaded, and an unloading terminal as the place in the national territory where imported products are unloaded.

Ordinance 311 also establishes that for the quality control of products such as petroleum, fuel oils and liquefied oil gas, certain processes must be followed. These include hiring an inspection firm that has been accredited by ANP, in accordance with ANP Resolution 45/2010. The inspection firm must issue a certificate at the loading terminal to confirm that the product quality complies with the ANP's specifications.

The construction, expansion and operation of onshore, maritime, fluvial and lacustrine terminals are subject to Ordinance 170, and therefore dependent on the agency's previous authorisation. The authorisation approval and granting process is the same as that for constructing and operating pipelines.

The Gas Law permits any Brazilian company or consortium to receive authorisation from the ANP to construct and operate natural gas liquefaction plants and LNG regasification plants, subject to regulation yet to be enacted by the ANP. Because these regulations have not yet been enacted, it may be concluded these authorisations are still governed by Ordinance 170.

3.1 Licensee rights and third-party access

ANP Ordinance 251/2000 establishes the criteria and compensations for open access to water terminals for petroleum and petroleum by-products. This ordinance covers both public and private water terminals, whether they are maritime, fluvial or lacustrine. The facilities covered include the vessel mooring systems, pipelines within the terminal, and storage and other complementary systems wherever these are essential to the movement of products from or to offshore transport. There is no provision for open access to onshore terminals for petroleum and petroleum by-products.

The following are the main rules set out in Ordinance 251:

- When operated by the port authority or its agents, water terminals are for public use. When operated by legal entities duly authorised by the Ministry of Transport, they are classified as general or private terminals for joint use.
- Exclusive private water terminals are not allowed by the ANP.
- Terminal operators must allow access to any third party according to the availability and general service conditions of the terminal.
- Contracting more than 50% of the terminal's capacity to a single shipper is considered discriminatory.
- The security and operational condition of the pipeline interconnection between the terminals and the third party's facilities must be guaranteed, provided that the rules concerning security and operational safety are observed.
- As well as complying with the provisions of the operational authorisation issued by the ANP, the operators shall maintain, on their websites, information about availability, tariffs, general conditions of service and volumes moved for the last 12 years.
- Owners of private terminals for joint use shall have right of preference for moving their own products.
- The terminal operator must specify a schedule for meeting access orders that have been made before the 20th day of the previous month, keeping in mind the owner's right of preference and any contracts already executed.
- In case there is capacity available, the operator shall prepare an extemporary schedule (ie, a schedule prepared for considering access orders placed after the 20th day of the previous month), according to the sequence in which the orders are presented.
- Any shipper with a confirmed order is obliged to make full payment for any services scheduled but not executed due to a fault of its own.

- The shipper may also assign the confirmed order to a third party, on the same conditions as agreed with the operator.
- The owner of a private terminal may not reserve capacity that it does not use, except in cases of proven acts of God or *force majeure.*
- The operator may refuse to transport products whose quality does not comply with the general service conditions or products that may contaminate those of other shippers.
- The shipper and transporter are responsible for the quality of the products, provided that the transporter use the principle of fungibility, unless otherwise expressly stated.
- Operator tariffs must not be discriminatory and should reflect the service offered, and consider the products and volume involved, and any losses and existing levels of contamination. The current tax burden should also be taken into consideration, as well as any operational and maintenance costs (including investment returns). Subsidies of any kind or costs attributable to other shippers or terminals will not be considered.

3.2 LNG

LNG is natural gas that has been submitted to a process of liquefaction for storage and transportation, subject to regasification later. The value chain of LNG generally includes the following activities: exploration, production and processing, liquefaction, transportation, storage, regasification and distribution.

The Gas Law states that the ANP may authorise Brazilian companies or consortia to construct, expand and operate LNG terminals. Again, because the ANP has not enacted any new regulation on this subject since the Gas Law, it may be concluded that this authorisation process is governed by Ordinance 170.

Furthermore, the ANP establishes the conditions for granting and transferring such authorisations in strict observation of the regulations on safety and environmental protection in facilities.

The Gas Law also states that natural gas pipelines that start at LNG terminals and interconnect with the transportation network that is not part of the terminal shall be considered transportation pipelines. The ANP is responsible for defining which pipelines do or do not integrate with LNG terminals.

ANP Resolution 50/2011 therefore establishes the information that must be provided regarding LNG terminals and the criteria used to define which pipelines are part of those terminals. The resolution defines an 'LNG terminal' as a facility used for the liquefaction of natural gas or for the importation, discharge or regasification of LNG. This includes any ancillary services or temporary storage tanks necessary for regasification and further delivery of the gas to the pipeline network or other means of transportation.

In classifying these pipelines, the ANP will consider technical, regulatory and economic criteria as well as their purpose. In other words, the agency will consider whether the pipelines are dedicated to and used exclusively by the LNG terminal. If a pipeline is classified as part of the LNG terminal, it cannot be reclassified as a gas transportation pipeline.

Resolution 50 also determines that before beginning the operation of an LNG terminal, the authorised party must inform the ANP of the effective costs of construction and the estimated operational costs.

The terminal's operator may use their discretion to grant third parties access to their facilities: the Gas Law does not guarantee such access. In these cases, any services rendered must be formalised by a contract between the terminal's operator and the interested third party, who shall be considered a user of the terminal.

The distribution of liquefied natural gas is regulated by ANP Ordinance 118/2000. This establishes that authorisation for distributing LNG in bulk must be requested from the ANP through an application accompanied by the relevant corporate and technical documents. The ANP has 60 days to reply to such requests.

In accordance with the Petroleum Law and the Gas Law, the prices of LNG are freely negotiated between the relevant parties. The ANP will intervene only when agreement is not reached.

4. Gas storage

The Gas Law establishes that natural gas may be stored by companies or consortia whose head offices are in Brazil and that are incorporated in accordance with Brazilian law. Storage is undertaken at the sole risk of the entrepreneur, and is granted either by means of concession, subject to a previous a bidding process, or authorisation.

The storage of natural gas in hydrocarbon reservoirs that have been returned to the federal government by E&P concessionaires, or in other geological formations, is subject to concession for their use, through a bidding process. The ANP is responsible for elaborating any tender protocols and promoting bidding rounds for such concessions, as well as for establishing the rules regarding third-party access to these facilities. The geological formations that are subject to these bidding processes will be defined by the Ministry of Mines and Energy or the ANP, on the ministry's behalf. Interested parties may also submit geological formations to be considered as storage.

After consultation with the ANP, the Ministry of Mines and Energy will establish the exclusivity period for parties who have made or helped make using the storage facility possible. Any third-party access rules must respect this exclusivity period. It is important to note that the ANP has not yet enacted the rules for third-party access to these facilities.

Decree 7,382 establishes that imported natural gas or natural gas exploited and produced by E&P concessionaires under the applicable concession agreements, may be stored by the E&P concessionaire in natural geologic formations. This decree also establishes that ANP shall provide interested parties with geological data about any areas with potential for natural gas storage, and may authorise those parties to execute non-exclusive exploratory activities in these areas. Any data that arises from such activities will be provided to the ANP at no cost.

The concessionaire is responsible for maintaining the integrity of the geological formations used for storing natural gas, leaving the ANP responsible for defining the processes for supervising such activities. If the formations are not regularly used, the concessionaires will be penalised under the terms of the concession agreement.

Finally, it must be emphasised that storing natural gas outside hydrocarbon reservoirs that have been returned to the federal government, or in other geological formations, is subject to a system of authorisation, without a prior bidding process. There is no obligation to grant third-party access to such facilities.

5. Conclusion

It may be seen that the construction, expansion and operation of gas and petroleum pipelines and terminals in Brazil are subject to an extensive and complex legal and regulatory framework. For regulatory purposes, the market is divided between facilities used for petroleum and its by-products, and those used for natural gas.

The Gas Law and Decree 7,382 were drawn up to stimulate competition and investment in the transportation and storage of natural gas and LNG. However, as described above, certain aspects, such as third-party access to pipelines, are still awaiting definition and regulation from the Ministry of Mines and Energy and the ANP. There is still no date scheduled for the first public invitation to define new natural gas transportation pipelines.

Nonetheless, there is a widespread expectation of large natural gas reserves in the Brazilian pre-salt fields and new exploratory frontiers in the country's interior. If such expectations are confirmed, large investments in natural gas transportation and processing infrastructure will be necessary in order to make these commodities available to Brazilian consumers and for export. It is therefore likely that the Brazilian government will soon have to make efforts to promote the expansion of the gas pipeline network and the construction of LNG terminals.

The authors would like to thank Saulo Padua and Bruno Vignal for their kind assistance in the preparation of this chapter.

Environment

Jorge Tuffi P D Cassab
Elina Cunha
Maria Christina M Gueorguiev
Werner Grau Neto
Pinheiro Neto Advogados

1. General principles and governmental authorities

Until the enactment of Constitutional Amendment 9 of November 9 1995 (EC 9/95) and Law 9,478 of 6 August 1997 (the Petroleum Law), oil and gas exploitation, production, importation and refinement in Brazil remained a strict monopoly of the federal government.

EC 9/95 relaxed the federal government monopoly over oil and natural gas industries that was set out in Article 177 of the 1988 Constitution, and authorised the union to contract oil and gas activities to state or private companies. The amendment also established the legal conditions to be observed in these contracts. These were enacted two years later and became known as the Petroleum Law.

The Petroleum Law sets out the conditions for exploiting and transporting oil, its by-products and natural gas. It contains provisions concerning the national energy policy and activities related to the oil monopoly, and establishes further regulations to these. With regard to environmental protection, Article 1, IV of the law states that "national policies on the rational use of energy sources will pursue the following objectives: ... IV – environmental protection and energy conservation".

The Petroleum Law also created two official entities dedicated to energy policy and regulation. These are the National Council on Energy Policy (CNPE) and the National Petroleum, Natural Gas and Biofuels Agency (ANP).

Article 8, IX of the Petroleum Law also states that:

[The] ANP's main activity will be the regulation, contracting and inspection of the economic activities inherent to the petroleum industry, it being incumbent on ANP: ... IX – to ensure compliance with good conservation practices and the rational use of oil, its byproducts and natural gas and environmental protection.

As per Article 44, the ANP is also entitled to establish contractual obligations with contractors regarding environmental protection:

The contract will establish that the concessionaire will be required to: I) – take, in all its operations, the necessary actions for conservation of the reservoirs and other natural resources, for the safety of persons and equipment and for environmental protection.

The Brazilian Constitution includes a special chapter on environmental protection, which provides that all individuals have the right to an ecologically balanced environment. Among the many constitutional principles that relate to the environmental protection, the following should be highlighted in reference to the upstream oil and gas industry:

- the precaution/prevention principle (Article 225, §1, IV), which considers it a crime not to undertake precautionary measures established by the authorities, as per Article 54 of Law 9,605/97, and Article 225, §1, V; and

- The polluter pays/damage repair principle (Article 225, §§2 and 3), which empowers the federal, state and municipal governments, as well as the government of the federal district, to defend and protect the environment, and to take any necessary steps to protect against damage to Brazilian fauna and flora.

An entire system is dedicated to the enforcement of environmental laws in Brazil. The Brazilian Environmental System (SISNAMA) comprises:

- the Brazilian Environmental Council (CONAMA), which is the senior regulatory, advisory and decision-making agency;
- the Ministry of the Environment, which is charged with the coordination, supervision and control of the Brazilian Environmental Policy; and
- the Brazilian Environmental and Renewable Natural Resources Institute (IBAMA), which is the executive agency.

SISNAMA also comprises other federal agencies, public foundations engaged in environmental protection and entities that fall under both state and municipal jurisdictions (eg, state and municipal offices and state and municipal environmental agencies).

2. Oil and gas regulation

2.1 Criteria for location

Like mining, oil and gas exploration and production are less flexible with respect to location than other industries. Indeed, exploration and production depends on the local availability of oil and gas.

According to Resolution 8, issued by the CNPE on July 21 2003, environmental restrictions allow some areas to be excluded from exploration and production bidding. The decision to protect certain areas from exploitation will be based on a joint recommendation prepared by the ANP, IBAMA and state environmental agencies.

This prior assessment does not exclude the specific environmental licensing of the activity. This involves a detailed analysis of the impact on the environment and the local community, as well as the imposition of mitigation and compensatory measures determined by the Environmental Agency.

2.2 Permits for exploration and production activities

Companies engaged in potentially polluting activities are subject to environmental licensing procedures. In general terms, by establishing that environmental licensing must be performed at one level of environmental authority, CONAMA's Resolution 237/97 empowers state agencies to proceed with environmental licensing.

As a rule, state agencies deal with environmental licensing and IBAMA is permitted to license only those activities that have a national or regional impact.

CONAMA's Resolution 23 of December 7 1994 prescribes the environmental licences that must be obtained by enterprises engaging in the exploration and extraction of liquid fuels and natural gas.

On October 26 2011, Ordinance 422 was issued by the Ministry of the Environment. This outlined the procedure for the environmental licensing of oil and gas exploration and production at sea and in contiguous zones.

The ordinance divides the environmental licensing procedure into three parts:

- the licensing of seismic research, which aims to establish the conditions, restrictions and measures for environmental control with which the entrepreneur is obliged to comply;
- the licensing of well drilling, for obtaining an operation licence for drilling activities; and
- licensing for:
  - the construction of units and systems for the production and pipeline transportation of the fuels;
  - the exploration of the oil and gas wells; and
  - long-term test attainment, with the aim of obtaining data and information regarding reservoirs over more than 72 hours.

The licensing procedure can be completed by either the owner or the operator. The party that applies for the licence from IBAMA assumes responsibility for the activity and will be considered primarily responsible by the administration. However, it will have a right of recourse against those parties who actually give rise to any irregularity.

2.3 Liability

The liability of individuals or legal entities for activities that are harmful to the environment is established in the Brazilian Constitution. Under these provisions, any individual or legal entity responsible for a behaviour or activity that is harmful to the environment will, in theory, be subject to the following three levels of liability:

- the civil level, involving the obligation to repair or remediate any damages caused to the environment and/or to third parties, or meet an indemnity if reparation or remediation is not possible;
- the administrative level, involving the imposition by the environmental control and inspection bodies of warnings and fines, as well as other administrative penalties; and
- the criminal level, involving the imposition of restrictions to liberty or rights.

Administrative, civil and criminal responsibilities are mutually independent and potentially cumulative, so the imposition of an administrative penalty does not exempt the infringing party from additional financial compensation, if the violation should cause any environmental damage. Likewise, the imposition of administrative penalties and the imposition of compensation duty do not exclude the additional imposition of restrictions to liberty or rights should the conduct fall under criminal law.

It is notable that the Brazilian legal system accepts joint liability. Previous decisions handed down by the Superior Court of Justice have held direct and indirect polluters jointly liable for environmental damages.

However, attributing liability depends on demonstrating a causal link between the activity carried out and the damage caused to the environment. Environmental liability in the civil sphere does not depend on proving fault; it is enough to prove the chain of causation between the activity and the damage. Strict liability applies not only to the damage caused to the environment, but also to that caused to third parties (eg, neighbours, employees and service providers) that are in any way affected.

It is important to stress that the international conventions and treaties concerning liability for damages caused by oil pollution have the force of federal law in Brazil.

The Supreme Court has applied the theory of dualism to indicate that the law applicable to such situations may relate to more than one legal system. The court's understanding is that international law is applicable between sovereign states and internal law applies within a state and regulates relations between that state and its citizens.

Where environmental protection is concerned, the more restrictive law will generally be applied. So in reference to the matter in hand, the Brazilian internal environmental rules, rather than the international convention and treaties, will be used to deal with any damages caused by the oil extraction activity. This is because within the Brazilian economic exclusivity zone, the internal rules on environmental protection apply. Rules posed by conventions and treaties will apply should a third state claim for damages deriving from the same activity.

3. Current issues

The main critical issues involved in oil and gas exploration and production activities relate to environmental licensing, the impact on protected areas, climate change policies and the risks of spillage.

Environmental licensing is critical for infrastructure activities in general. In order to expedite and provide clearer criteria for environmental rules, on October 26 2011 the government issued six ordinances for core infrastructure sectors and set out additional guidance for environmental administration. Through Ordinance 422, the Ministry of the Environment outlined the procedure for the environmental licensing of oil and gas exploration and production at sea and in surrounding zones.

The risk of certain activities due to their proximity to protected areas is another point of concern. In these cases the managing entity in charge of conservation unities is consulted in case an exploration and production activity may affect the area. The managing entity is entitled to agree or disagree with the proposed activities and can also recommend the Environment Agency to add additional conditions to the environmental licence.

On December 29 2009 the National Policy for Climate Change was approved under Law 12,187. This commits the Brazilian government to reduce national emissions by between 36.1% and 38.5% before 2020. Although deforestation is considered the main source of greenhouse gas emissions in Brazil the original bill proposed limiting fossil fuel activities. This provision was not approved and oil and gas emissions are expected to be regulated according to the national and state level inventories, specific regulations and environmental licensing.

On the other hand, a greater awareness is growing of oil spillages, especially those at sea. In such instances, the Public Prosecutor's Office and the environmental authorities can take action with respect to the environment and/or third parties that may be affected.

4. Conclusion

Brazilian laws and regulations on oil and gas exploration and production activities are very strict. Control over their risks is enforced by the Brazilian administration through complex licensing procedures. Damage to the environment or third parties is treated under the principle of strict liability. Criminal liability may also apply.

Tax

Camila Galvão Anderi Silva
Fernando Tonanni
Machado, Meyer, Sendacz e Opice Advogados

1. Introduction

In the past decade, Brazil has become one of the most attractive destinations for investing in the oil and gas industry. During this period, the country has achieved economic stability, a consolidated domestic market and sustainable economic growth. Indications of this are the investment-grade status awarded to Brazil's foreign currency debt by the rating agencies Standard & Poor's and Fitch Ratings in 2008, and the maintenance of economic stability during the global financial crises in 2009 and 2011. In addition, the new discoveries in the oil and gas industry, especially in the offshore pre-salt area, have consolidated Brazil as a global player.

As a consequence, the Brazilian oil and gas sector has seen a large increase in investment, targeting exploration and production activities, operations in the supply chain and an increasing number of M&As.

These rapid changes are under the watch of Brazilian lawmakers, regulators and government agencies. It is crucial for investors to understand the current legal framework and developments in this sector. Because the government takes and local taxation deeply affect the viability of projects and the returns from exploration and production, an analysis of these is advisable.

This chapter focuses on Brazil's taxation of foreign investments in its oil and gas industry. It starts with an overview of the legal framework of the industry and the applicable government takes before covering:

- the Brazilian tax system;
- Brazilian corporate income taxes and the peculiarities applicable to companies engaged in exploration and production activities;
- the taxes imposed on sales of crude oil and natural gas;
- those tax aspects to be considered in the pre-operational phase and the tax benefits directed to the oil and gas industry; and
- those international tax aspects that affect foreign investors in the oil and gas industry.

Current trends and potential changes in the tax system will be addressed in the conclusion.

2. Overview of the oil and gas industry in Brazil

Brazil's first oil discovery was not made until 1939. Its first commercial field was only exploited in 1942, onshore in the Reconcavo basin in the northeastern part of the country. Drilling here continued on a small scale until October 3 1953, when, after an intensive public campaign, President Getulio Vargas signed Law 2,004, which created a government monopoly over the production of oil and its by-products. This law also created the state oil company Petrobras.

Since then, Petrobras's work in deep and ultra-deep water exploration technology has placed Brazil in a global leading position across the full production cycle for fields located in waters more than 2,000 metres (m) deep.

Following Constitutional Amendment 9/1997, President Fernando Henrique Cardoso sanctioned Law 9,478 (the Petroleum Law). This abolished Petrobras's legal monopoly and allowed other companies to compete in the production of oil and its by-products. The opening of Brazil's market encouraged a large wave of foreign investments.

The new competitive environment was based on concession contracts for the exploration and production of designated onshore and offshore blocks. These were granted by the government, represented by the National Agency of Petroleum, Natural Gas and Biofuel (ANP), after a transparent bidding procedure in which any company could participate.

Since 1999, the ANP has conducted 10 bidding rounds. These have resulted in the awarding of approximately 730 concessions of oil and gas exploration and production blocks, both onshore and offshore.[1]

Thanks to these concessions, Brazil has recently become self-sustainable: the volume of oil produced – approximately 2 million daily barrels for 2010[2] – exceeds the country's domestic consumption. However, most of this production is of heavy crude oil, which is not the same quality of oil generally consumed in Brazil. Furthermore, Brazil does not have sufficient refinery capacity to refine all its production.

The vast majority of Brazil's reserves are in deep and ultra-deep waters. Promising oil reserves have recently been discovered at depths of between 5,000 and 7,000 metres below the sea surface, in an offshore area of approximately 150,000 km^2 within the Espírito Santo, Campos and Santos Basins in the states of Espírito Santo, Rio de Janeiro and São Paulo. This area and its promising reserves are deemed to constitute a new frontier for the production of oil and gas in Brazil – the pre-salt area.

Approximately 28% of the pre-salt area has already been granted under ordinary concessions, while the rest is yet to be awarded. These concessions (which include the Tupi, Iara and Carioca fields) are expected to double Brazil's daily oil production by 2020,[3] transforming Brazil into a strong net exporter of oil. Official estimates by the Brazilian government are that the full pre-salt area should reveal oil reserves of at least 50 billion of barrels of oil equivalent.[4]

---

1 Information available at the official website of the Brazilian National Agency of Petroleum, Natural Gas and Biofuels – www.anp.gov.br.

2 Federal Government Official Presentation of the New Legal Framework for the Pre-Salt. "Novo Marco Regulatório – Pré-sal e áreas estratégicas" Agosto de 2009.

3 Federal Government Official Presentation of the New Legal Framework for the Pre-Salt. "Novo Marco Regulatório – Pré-sal e áreas estratégicas" Agosto de 2009.

4 Ministry of Mines and Energy and PETROBRAS.

3. Government takes: special participation and royalties

Under the Petroleum Law and Decree 2,705/1998, parties with a concession from the ANP must pay the government (or states and municipalities, as applicable), government takes on the commercial production of oil and natural gas. In particular these are:

- royalties corresponding to 10% of the production of oil and gas; and
- special participations in the event of high profitability of the block or if large amounts of oil and natural gas are produced.

In accordance with the Constitution, all the oil and natural gas reserves located in the Brazilian territory (including the continental shelf, territorial sea and exclusive economic area) are considered publicly owned assets. The member states, the municipalities, the federal district and certain government agencies are entitled to a portion of the results of their exploration, or a corresponding financial compensation.

Based on this provision, Law 7,990/1989 expressly determines that third-party use of any mineral resources will require compensation to be paid to the states and municipalities. The Petroleum Law establishes the guidelines for applying these compensations (which are generally referred to as 'government takes').

All concession contracts are required to pay government takes, which may be divided into four general categories:

- signature bonus;
- royalties;
- special participations; and
- payment for area occupation or retention.

Unlike the signature bonus (which is a lump-sum amount payable on signing the concession contract) and the payment for area occupation or retention (which is based on the size of the area to be exploited), royalties and special participations are based on the actual input of oil and/or natural gas produced by the block. They thus closely reflect the concept of government participation in the results of mineral exploitation.

Decree 2,705/1998, which regulates the Petroleum Law, generally defines a government take as all those payments made by a concessionaire as a result of the exploration and production of crude oil and natural gas. The decree further sets out that royalties and special participations are payable under the following rules:

- Royalties – these are to be paid monthly by concessionaries for each field, beginning in the month in which commercial production begins. They are equivalent to 10% of the total production of crude oil and natural gas of the field during that month, at the relevant reference prices. The government may decide to decrease the amount of royalties to 5% of the monthly production based on the characteristics of the block, geological risks or production expectations.
- Special participations – these are payable when high volumes of oil or natural gas are produced or if a certain field enjoys high profitability. They are payable quarterly, from the start of commercial production of the field, and

are assessed according to the quarterly net revenue from the production of oil and/or natural gas, based on progressive rates and in proportion to the actual production at the field.

We may therefore conclude that:

- the exploitation of oil and natural gas is subject to the payment of government takes, including royalties and special participations; and
- the payment of these is tied to the fact that a private party is being granted a concession to explore a publicly owned asset.

Considering that royalties are imposed by law and are applicable upon certain events, is there a question about their legal nature and whether they may be characterised as tax revenue?

For example, and as described above, the Constitution determines that government takes consist of financial compensation for the exploration of public mineral resources, and are therefore characterised as contractual revenue, as opposed to tax revenue. In other words, the oil and natural gas reserves are a public asset whose use should be compensated in the same way as that of real estate – that is, by the payment of a rental fee to its owner.

Further doubts arise from the definition of taxes in the national tax code. This generally characterises taxes as mandatory and monetary payments that do not result from the violation of a legal provision, are determined by law and collected by the government.

The Federal Supreme Court was able to analyse the nature of this financial compensation when a lawsuit was brought by a mining company that questioned the constitutionality of these charges, under the argument that they were a 'disguised tax'.[5] The court ruled that:

- not all mandatory and monetary payments that are not a sanction to an illegal act, are established by the law and are collected by the direct administration may be considered a tax;
- the Constitution expressly establishes the possibility of such financial compensation for the exploration of mineral resources; and
- this compensation has a contractual nature (ie, it is a payment for the use of a party's assets) and may not be characterised as taxation.

In support of these arguments the Constitution further establishes that no taxes other than those on the distribution of goods and on interstate and intermunicipal transportation and communication services (ICMS), import duty, and export tax may be imposed on oil and its by-products. Considering that the Constitution expressly lists these three taxes, any further charges may not be deemed as taxes.

The payment of royalties and special participations is therefore a financial compensation for the exploration of public goods (oil and gas reserves), and not a taxation.

---

5 Extraordinary Appeal 228.800-5/DF.

4. Overview of the Brazilian tax system

As in most Latin countries, the Brazilian legal system is based on civil law. Accordingly, the rules are established by the current legislation. Precedents do not generally play a significant role since they usually apply only to the litigants themselves. However, it is important to note a recent global trend in both civil and common law, which is to single out relevant elements from the other model and combine them with the elements of the original system. Brazil is also following this trend and has been adapting its civil law system with certain features of common law. These include the repetitive appeal, according to which all matters on the same subject are suspended until the higher courts issue a decision that will apply across all cases.

The general rules of the Brazilian tax system are outlined in the Constitution. This determines precisely which taxes can be imposed by which federal sphere, and what is the taxable event. The Constitution also determines immunities and the main tax principles.

Among the most important principles on which the Brazilian tax system is based is that of strict legality. According to this, with just a few exceptions, no tax can be imposed unless there is a valid law defining its principal aspects: the taxable event, the taxable basis and the applicable tax rate.

Taxes may be imposed by federal, state and municipal governments, as well as by the federal district, which accumulates state and municipal jurisdictions. As a rule, the same tax cannot be imposed by two different federal spheres. Nationwide laws usually present guidelines for the states and municipalities so as to make the imposition of these taxes uniform. Nevertheless, the states and municipalities are still allowed to rule on many aspects of the taxation of their jurisdictions. They may also have their own interpretation of the nationwide guidelines. This creates an almost independent system and makes the overall tax system in Brazil highly complex.

Ruling on tax-related controversies takes place in the administrative and/or judicial sphere. As a rule, the discussion is initiated by the administration. The controversy may be taken to the judiciary either after or before the administration's involvement, or alternatively to it entirely. Disputes may be initiated by the judiciary if they refer to claims by the taxpayer regarding the interpretation or application of certain legal provisions. Additionally, at the administrative level, most jurisdictions allow taxpayers to consult the authorities about the most appropriate tax treatment for their transactions.

Federal taxes are managed by the Brazilian Revenue Service, under the Ministry of Economics and Finance. The states, municipalities and federal district also have similar agencies that manage the taxes attributed to them.

Because oil and gas exploration and production usually require the setting up of a local company (in part a result of the bidding rules to the concession rounds), it is critical for foreign investors to understand the corporate taxes imposed on Brazilian companies, the sales taxes imposed on crude oil and natural gas, and the taxes that apply to the purchase of equipment and services in the pre-operational phase. These aspects are reviewed in Sections 5, 6 and 7 of this chapter.

Moreover, considering that non-resident investors may be subject to Brazilian taxation only whenever they receive income paid by Brazilian sources or gains derived as a result of the disposition of Brazilian assets and rights, Section 8 covers the taxation of various forms of return of investments in Brazil (dividends, interest on equity, interest under debt funding and capital gains) as well as the taxation of royalties, know-how licences, charter fees and other incomes.

Finally, other taxes that may apply to exploration and production in Brazil are:

- import duty;
- tax on manufactured products (IPI);
- contributions to the employees' profit participation programme (PIS) and social security contributions (COFINS);
- state value added tax (ICMS);
- withholding income tax (WHT);
- contribution for intervention in the economic domain (CIDE);
- services tax (ISS); and
- social security contributions.

The main features of each of these are described below.

4.1 Import duty

This is imposed on the import of foreign products. Its taxable basis is the customs value, which generally corresponds to the cost, insurance and freight value of the imported products, plus additional expenses due to wharfage.

Import duty rates vary according to the tax classification code of the imported product under the MERCOSUR Common Nomenclature, which follows the harmonised commodity description and coding system.

Import duty is a cumulative tax, and therefore cannot be recovered by the importer.

4.2 Tax on manufactured products

IPI is a federal tax imposed on transactions involving manufactured products, including imports or domestic sales.

Its rates vary according to the tax code of the product under the MERCOSUR nomenclature, which is used as the basis for the IPI table of rates.

For imports, IPI is imposed once the product has cleared customs based on the customs value plus the amount of import duty due. For domestic sales, the taxable basis is typically the value of the transaction.

IPI is a non-cumulative tax. This means that IPI due on prior transactions (including on imported products), can be offset against the IPI calculated by the taxpayer on their subsequent taxed transactions.

IPI does not apply to exported products.

4.3 PIS and COFINS

PIS and COFINS are federal contributions imposed on a company's gross revenues. They may be assessed under three main regimes: the cumulative, the non-cumulative and the monophasic regime.

As a rule, PIS and COFINS are not imposed on export revenues or on the sale of fixed assets.

The assessment of PIS and COFINS under the cumulative regime results in the application of an aggregate 3.65% rate on gross revenues without the possibility of deduction of credits. This applies to companies that calculate their corporate income tax on the basis of presumed profit (see Section 5 below) and to other companies listed by the law. (This is usually not the case for companies engaged in exploration and production.)

The non-cumulative regime, in turn, results in the application of an aggregate rate of 9.25%. Deductions of credits are only possible where expressly authorised. (This is usually the case for companies engaged in exploration and production.)

PIS and COFINS may also be imposed under the monophasic regime. This applies to certain products, including cosmetics, automobiles, medicine, combustibles and beverages. This system works like a tax substitution regime: the importer or manufacturer is liable for collecting the contributions on the whole commercialisation chain.

PIS and COFINS are also imposed on imported goods and services, typically at the rates of 1.65% and 7.6%, respectively.

4.4 ICMS

ICMS is a state tax similar to a value-added tax. It is imposed on transactions involving sales and other commercial operations with goods (including electricity), the rendering of intermunicipal or interstate transport services, and communication services. It is also imposed on import transactions, including the import of machinery and equipment.

The taxable basis of ICMS due on the sale of products is, as a rule, the value of the transaction, plus insurance, conditional discounts and freight, and is always calculated on a grossed up basis.

The taxation rate depends on the state where the supplier is located. On interstate transactions carried out between taxpayers, the rate is established by the Senate. This is generally 7%, for products from companies located in south and southeast states, except for Espírito Santo, to companies located in the north, northeast and central-west and Espírito Santo. Other interstate transactions between taxpayers are subject to a 12% rate.

On internal transactions, in which the supplier and the acquirer are ICMS taxpayers and are located in the same state, the general rate is usually between 17% and 19%.

If a taxpayer acquires fixed assets and consumable goods on an interstate transaction it must, as a rule, take a differential rate. This corresponds to the difference between the applicable interstate rate and the rate of the state in which the buyer is located.

As established in the Constitution, the ICMS is a non-cumulative tax. This means that, as a rule, the tax paid on each transaction may be offset against that due on upcoming transactions.

ICMS is not imposed on the export of products or services.

ICMS may also be imposed under a tax substitution regime.

4.5 ISS

ISS is a municipal tax imposed on all services, excluding those subject to ICMS taxation. Imported services are also subject to ISS.

The rate of ISS will vary depending on the municipality and the nature of the service, between a minimum and a maximum of 2% and 5%. Civil construction services may benefit from a lower ISS rate. The taxable basis of ISS is the price of the service. In case of services that involve the supply of goods, the law may allow the price of those goods to be deducted from the total price. In these cases, the sales of those goods will be subject to ICMS.

Exported services are not subject to ISS, except if the result of the service is verified in Brazil.

4.6 IOF/exchange

IOF/exchange is a federal tax imposed on foreign exchange agreements.

The taxpayer is the entity executing the foreign exchange transaction and the party liable for collecting the tax is the financial institution or currency broker who performs the transaction.

Foreign exchange transactions for imported services are subject to a 0.38% rate; an exemption is available for imported goods. The 0.38% rate also applies to payments made abroad under rental, charter or lease agreements. Other transactions may be subject to rates of 2% or 6%, or be exempt.

4.7 WHT

As a general rule, payments made by Brazilian sources to non-resident beneficiaries are subject to a WHT, at either a 15% or 25% rate, depending on the nature of the payment and the location of the beneficiary (whether or not it is located in a low tax jurisdiction, as defined by the law).[6] However, in certain situations, a 0% WHT rate applies.

WHT is imposed on the gross amount paid to the foreign beneficiary by the local taxpayer.

4.8 CIDE

CIDE is a federal tax imposed on services rendered by foreign entities to Brazilian residents. These include the supply of technical services, administrative assistance and similar services. It is also imposed on payments for trademark and patent royalties.

It may also be imposed on the import and commercialisation of specific products, such as combustibles.

CIDE is assessed according to the gross amount invoiced, before the deduction of Brazilian WHT, and is payable by the Brazilian resident.

5. Corporate income taxes

Foreign investors engaged in exploration and production in Brazil normally undertake these activities via subsidiaries incorporated in the country. These may

6 Low tax jurisdictions are discussed in Section 7.2 below.

take the form of corporations or limited liability companies. Branches in Brazil of foreign corporations are not an option for the oil and gas industry due to the time consuming process of their creation and the need for them to be authorised by the Ministry of Development, Industry and Commerce.[7]

Exploration and production activities are also usually developed with several players under a consortium agreement. In these cases, the subsidiary of the foreign investor joins a consortium agreement with the other players. Consortia are regulated by Law 6,404/1976 (the Corporate Law). They must be created for a pre-determined period of time for the development of a specific project. One of the parties to the consortium is appointed its leader and is liable for all its accounting records, bookkeeping and supporting documents. The consortium is not normally deemed a taxable unit for the purposes of corporate income taxes (ie, it is tax transparent); each party must recognise its own revenues and expenses and assess its own tax liability.

Companies incorporated in Brazil and branches of foreign companies are deemed to be taxable. Consequently, exploration and production activities developed via local subsidiaries, branches or via a Brazilian subsidiary under a consortium agreement will be subject to Brazilian corporate income taxes.

These comprise the IRPJ corporate tax and the social contribution on net profits (CSLL). Both are imposed on the corporation's taxable profits. For that purpose, the taxable profit must take account of all income that is available to the recipient.

The overall corporate tax is imposed on the income of all taxable Brazilians wherever they are in the world.

Brazilian tax law sets out four basic regimes for imposing corporate income taxes:

- real profit;
- presumed profit;
- profit as determined by the tax authorities; and
- a simplified regime for the collection of federal taxes.

Companies engaged in exploration and production are normally subject to corporate income taxes under the real profits regime. For this reason, the other three regimes will not be reviewed below.

Under the real profits regime, the taxable basis determined from the accounting profit of the corporation taxpayer, adjusted according to the relevant additions and exclusions. Income and expenses must be recognised on an accrual basis (a cash basis is allowed only in certain situations).

IRPJ is imposed at a rate of 15% plus a surtax of 10% on any taxable profits over R240,000 for the year. CSLL is imposed at a rate of 9%.[8] The aggregate rate may therefore be as much as 34% on taxable profits.

The accrual period for determining real profit may be annual or quarterly. If the accrual is annual there is an obligation to anticipate the tax each month.

---

7 The concession bidding rules also normally require the participation of an entity incorporated in Brazil.

8 Corporate taxpayers engaged in financial activities (such as financial institutions) are subject to CSLL at a rate of 15%.

Tax losses may be carried forward indefinitely. However, their actual use in any year is limited to 30% of the year's taxable profit. Non-operational losses may also be carried forward, but they may only be offset against non-operational profits, such as capital gains. Again, the 30% limit applies. Tax losses are eliminated if the company generating them merges with another entity, or if there is a change in the control and business activity of the company.

Law 11,638/2007 introduced changes to Brazilian generally accepted accounting principles, in order to harmonise these with the International Financial Reporting Standards. Changes were made to the criteria usually adopted for recognising of income, expenses and costs, and certain transactions.

The government decided that these changes should not be considered for tax purposes. Brazilian resident companies should therefore rely on the principles prevailing until December 31 2007 with regard to the recognition of revenues, expenses etc. Indeed, Law 11,941/2009 introduced an optional 'transitional tax regime' for 2008 and 2009, which gave tax neutrality to the changes made to the accounting principles. So, the introduction of the International Financial Reporting Standards need not affect the assessment of Brazilian taxes. From 2010, the tax neutrality provided in the transitional tax regime became mandatory for all Brazilian entities, pending a law regulating the new accounting rules. Therefore, the RTT currently specifies that the effects of Law 11,638 apply only for accounting and corporate purposes, and not to the assessment of Brazilian taxes. Under the regulations enacted by the Brazilian tax authorities, all tax adjustments under the transitional regime must be made annually via an electronic system (known as FCONT).

5.1 Deductions allowed under the real profits regime

As a general rule, whether expenses are deductible for corporate tax depends on whether the expense is usual, ordinary and necessary for the development of the company's operations. Only those expenses that are directly related to the development of business activities are therefore deductible for the purposes of corporate income tax. Accounting provisions are in general not deductible, and expenses must be supported by reliable documentary proof.

Special rules apply to certain categories of expenses, including advertising expenses, amortisation, bad debts, gifts and contributions, entertainment expenses, insurance premiums, interest payments, directors' remuneration and research expenses. Deductibility depends on specific conditions being fulfilled, and it is often limited. Below we present examples of specific rules connected with the deductibility of costs and expenses for oil and gas companies:

- In order to claim deductions for cross-border payments of trademark and patent royalties, or fees for technical, administrative or scientific assistance services, the relevant licence or services agreement must be registered before the Brazilian Patent and Trademark Institute. Additionally, the deduction of cross-border payments of royalties and fees for technical, administrative and scientific assistance is limited to 1% to 5% of the net income from the sale of the respective products or services. Trademark royalties are deductible up to

1% of the net income arising from the sale of the products or services. In any case, the aggregate deductible amount of patent and trademark royalties and technical, administrative and scientific assistance services is limited to 5% of the net income;

- Losses from exchange rate fluctuations are treated as financial expenses. They may be deducted provided that certain general requirements are observed. Such gains and losses are recognised on a cash basis, although taxpayers may elect to recognise them on an accruals basis;
- Pre-operating expenses may be amortised over a minimum period of five years. As a general rule, expenses incurred by the company before the concession has been effectively exploited may be amortised once the exploitation begins. If the asset is sold before these expenses have been completely amortised, the balance may be deducted from the taxable basis for corporate income tax for that year; and
- The acquisition of fixed assets is not considered a business expense. However, the depreciation of fixed assets may be a deductible expense.

Below we present a more detailed analysis of the tax depreciation of assets.

5.2 Tax depreciation of assets and the exhaustion of oil wells

Companies that are subject to Brazilian corporate income tax under the real profits regime can deduct any expenses related to the depreciation of assets that are related to their operations. The devaluation of an asset resulting from its use, natural causes and normal obsolescence may therefore be considered an expense incurred by the taxpayer.

The depreciation cost is calculated by applying the annual depreciation rate of each asset to its acquisition cost. In principle, this rate will be calculated using a straight-line method, based on the time for which the asset is expected to have economic use. The Federal Revenue Sevice will, from time to time, publish the admissible useful lifetime of each type of asset, based on its normal use.

Normative Acts 162/1998 and 130/1999 currently determine the annual depreciation rates of assets in general. Under normal circumstances, involving the use of the assets in only one daily shift, with no acceleration on their depreciation from intense use or tax incentives, the depreciation rates listed in these acts must be followed. It is currently accepted that changes in depreciation resulting from the introduction of the International Financial Reporting Standards should not be observed for corporate income tax, due to the tax neutrality that guides the introduction of these standards.

Despite the rates defined by the Federal Revenue Service, Brazilian tax laws allow taxpayers to use a different depreciation rate, provided that they can prove that this is more adequate to their assets.

In case of doubt, the taxpayer or the Federal Revenue Service can draw on an appraisal report from the National Institute of Technology or another official entity of scientific or technical research. In such cases, the useful lifetime recommended by the institute will prevail until it is changed by a higher administrative or judicial decision. This must be supported by another expert report. The rationale for this is that some assets involve very specific and technical knowledge, and their lifetime may only be determined by experts attesting to their use in light of the taxpayer's activity.

Since no rules currently deal with the depreciation of assets for companies engaged in exploration and production, those companies may have difficulties defining the proper depreciation rates for corporate tax purposes.

Indeed, many fixed assets of exploration and production companies have a useful life different from the general ones listed by the Federal Revenue Service. This may be due to a higher degree of obsolescence (eg, support vessels), or difficulties in qualifying the relevant assets under the Federal Revenue Service's lists (the assets that form an oil well, for example). In these cases, obtaining an appraisal from the National Institute of Technology is recommended.

It should also be noted that there is a difference between depreciation and exhaustion. Depreciation applies to the devaluation of the asset resulting from its use, while exhaustion applies to devaluation resulting from the asset's exploitation.

Assets exclusively for use in the exploitation of mines, quarries and forests are subject to exhaustion for Brazilian corporate tax purposes. This is based on the term of concession, the exploitation agreement or the production volume, and their relation with the known production capacity. In other words, in relation to these assets, tax depreciation (in fact, exhaustion) should take place after the term of concession, exploitation agreement or the production volume vis-à-vis the total capacity of the asset. This mitigates any potential mismatches between the asset's depreciation period as defined by the Federal Revenue Service and the actual income generated during that term.

Despite the fact that the specific legal provisions on exhaustion apply only to assets involved in the exploration of mines, quarries and forests, there are arguments that oil wells should also be subject to exhaustion. This is controversial, however, and a definitive position from the administrative or judicial courts has not yet been stated.

Finally, there is a specific provision in the tax laws that applies to Petrobras only. This allows Petrobras to deduct from the basis of its corporate income tax those amounts destined each year to the exploitation and extraction of crude oil.

6. Taxes on the sale of crude oil and natural gas

In addition to corporate income taxes, companies that recognise revenues from sales of crude oil and natural gas are subject to PIS, COFINS and ICMS.

Exports of oil and natural gas are not subject to tax, since the Constitution has established these transactions as immune.

6.1 PIS and COFINS contributions

PIS and COFINS are usually imposed at the 1.65% and a 7.6%, rates, respectively, if the supplier calculates these contributions under the non-cumulative regime.

6.2 ICMS taxation

As a general rule, ICMS is collected on behalf of the state in which the supplier is located. However, the Constitution establishes a different criterion for oil. In these cases, ICMS is due to the state in which the acquirer is located. Therefore, the interstate sale of oil that is destined for industrialisation or commercialisation is not subject to ICMS.

This method was adopted so as to reduce the economic advantage that those states holding exploitable oil fields would have over the others.

Some states also grant ICMS benefits to specific transactions with natural gas. These are usually connected to their destination, such as the generation of electricity.

7. Tax aspects of the pre-operational (CAPEX) phase

7.1 Taxes on the domestic acquisition of goods and services

(a) *Domestic acquisition of goods*

As a general rule, equipment bought in the domestic market is subject to the imposition of IPI, ICMS, PIS and COFINS. The recoverability of each of these taxes is different.

Although IPI is generally recoverable, this does not apply in relation to the acquisition of fixed assets.

In relation to the PIS and COFINS contributions, if the buyer is under the non-cumulative regime it may calculate PIS and COFINS credits by applying 1.65% and 7.6% to the depreciation of the goods. Alternatively, it is possible to calculate these credits in shorter periods, depending on the date of acquisition and according to certain terms and conditions.

ICMS credits on equipment that will be part of the company's fixed assets is generally accrued on a monthly basis for four years, at a ratio of 1/48 per month. However, some state rulings allow the use of the credits in shorter periods.

It is important to stress that ICMS credits must be proportional to the transactions carried out. That is, the law generally disallows credits proportional to the transactions that are not subject to that tax.

(b) *Domestic acquisition of services*

The domestic acquisition of services, in turn, is subject to ISS, PIS and COFINS.

ISS is imposed at a rate between 2% and 5%, depending on the nature of the service and on the municipality to which the tax is due. PIS and COFINS are imposed on the service provider's total revenue at an aggregate rate of 9.25% under the non-cumulative regime or 3.65% under the cumulative regime.

ISS is not recoverable. The recoverability of PIS and COFINS credits depends on the nature of the service and whether the regime adopted is cumulative or non-cumulative.

7.2 Taxes on the import of goods and services

(a) *Import of goods*

Definitive import: As a rule, the import of equipment into Brazil is subject to import duty, IPI, ICMS, PIS-Import and COFINS-Import. The rates for import duty and IPI depend on the tariff code of the equipment.

Import duty and IPI on the import of fixed assets are not recoverable. The other taxes are normally recoverable, in general, under the same rules as the domestic acquisition of assets summarised above.

Temporary import: For goods that will remain in Brazil for a determined period of time, the importer may choose a temporary admission regime. For certain situations in which the goods will not be economically used in Brazil, the taxes are totally suspended.

The temporary admission regime may also apply to goods that will remain in Brazil under rental/lease/charter agreements to manufacture products or render services. In these situations, import duty, IPI, PIS and COFINS are partially suspended. These taxes will be imposed at the rate of 1% for each month the good is in Brazil. This regime is useful for Brazilian companies engaged in the exploration and production of oil and gas, as it allows the temporary use of foreign equipment and vessels under leasing or charter arrangements.

When the total or partial suspension of taxes under the temporary admission regime is granted, typically similar ICMS benefits are also granted.

(b) Import of services

Imported services are subject to WHT, CIDE, ISS, PIS and COFINS.

WHT is imposed at a rate of 15%. This increases to 25% if the beneficiary is located in a low tax jurisdiction. CIDE is imposed on the import of technical services at a rate of 10%. ISS is imposed on the price of the service. Its rates vary from 2% to 5% depending on the nature of the service and on the municipality to which the tax is due. Finally, PIS and COFINS are imposed at an aggregate rate of 9.25%.

These last may be recovered, depending on the assessment regime being used and the nature of the services.

7.3 Tax benefits in the oil and gas industry

(a) Special customs regime for goods used for research and exploration

Since the Petroleum Law opened the market for the exploration of oil and natural gas, there has been a growing need for new tax rules to reduce the import costs of equipment. In 1999 a special customs regime for goods used for the research and exploration of oil and gas (REPETRO) was created, to sit alongside the existing rules and benefits.

Federal tax benefits: REPETRO comprises a set of special customs regimes which may be combined as required. Their rules apply to the following taxes: import duty, IPI, and PIS and COFINS contributions on import transactions.

The special customs regimes that comprise REPETRO are as follows:

- Presumed export – as a general rule, tax incentives on the export of products apply only if those goods physically leave the Brazilian territory. However, the presumed export regime may apply to the sale of equipment manufactured in Brazil to a company located abroad, even if it does not leave the Brazilian territory.

  Therefore, the REPETRO regime may be applied to equipment delivered directly to a foreign company within the domestic territory, so long as that company pays for it in a convertible currency.

In this situation, the pieces of equipment are purchased and owned by a foreign company, which later rents them either to a Brazilian company holding an exploration and production concession or another service provider. REPETRO gives the foreign entity an efficient tax burden for acquiring the equipment from a Brazilian manufacturer, without the need to export and re-import the equipment into Brazil.

The equipment rental is performed under another customs regime comprised within REPETRO, the temporary admission regime. Under REPETRO, the temporary admission regime grants total suspension of the federal taxes.

- Drawback regime – this is a special customs regime that allows federal taxes to be suspended for the import or domestic purchase of resources, provided that these are used to manufacture products that will be exported.

  Under REPETRO, this customs regime grants relief to national manufacturers of equipment for the oil and gas industry.

  Exports may be carried out as a presumed export to fulfill the terms of the drawback regime.

Goods admitted under REPETRO: Federal legislation does not detail which goods may be admitted under REPETRO, but it does give some general descriptions:

- vessels to be used in the exploration and production of oil and natural gas fields, or for related support and storage activities;
- equipment to be used in exploration and production;
- drilling and production platforms, including supporting platforms;
- vehicles fitted with tools and other equipment to be used in exploration and production; and
- structures designed to support platforms.

Operational aspects: The use of REPETRO must be approved by the Federal Revenue Service.

The following entities may adopt the regime:

- those authorised to perform exploration and production activities in Brazil;
- those contracted by the concessionary or authorised entity under a time charter arrangement, including subcontracted entities; or
- those contracted to render services to the concessionary or authorised entity, including subcontracted entities.

Companies that wish to choose REPETRO must comply with several obligations, including having a system that enables the Federal Revenue Service to inspect its application and verify those goods that have been admitted under it. Other specific requirements apply to companies contracted by the concessionary.

State tax benefits in connection with REPETRO: In order to reduce the ICMS burden, the states agreed on a special tax treatment for goods to be used in the oil and gas sector under the REPETRO regime. This agreement is currently ruled by ICMS Covenant 130/2007.

According to this covenant, transactions involving goods for exploration and production are subject to the following reductions and exemptions to ICMS:

- reductions on goods imported for oil and gas production to an effective rate of 7.5%. In this situation credits may be recognised (non-cumulative regime). Alternatively, the taxpayer may choose to apply a 3% rate without credits;
- exemption or reduction on goods imported for oil and gas exploration platforms to an effective rate of 1.5% rate, without the recognition of credits; and
- exemption or reduction on the domestic acquisitions of resources by a Brazilian manufacturer who will export these products under REPETRO. This results in an effective rate of 7.5%. In this situation credits may be recognised (non-cumulative regime). Alternatively, the taxpayer may choose to apply a 3% rate without credits.

Covenant 130 includes a detailed list of goods that may be admitted under this regime.

However, each state issues its own specific rulings regarding the benefits authorised by Covenant 130. As a result, the benefits may vary from state to state.

Tax	With REPETRO	Without REPETRO
Import duty	0% (suspended)	14%
IPI	0% (suspended)	0%
PIS	0% (suspended)	1.65%
COFINS	0% (suspended)	7.6%
ICMS (oil and gas production – São Paulo or Rio de Janeiro)	3% (without recognition of credits) or 7.5% (with recognition of credits)	14% to 18%

Comparison of the tax burden, with and without REPETRO: The table above compares the tax burden for importing equipment at the CAPEX stage with and without REPETRO benefits. For the sake of illustration we are presenting those taxes levied on transactions involving a floating production, storage and offloading unit, classified under tariff code 8905.20.00 (MERCOSUR Nomenclature).

(b) ***Bonded warehouse customs regime for platforms contracted by foreign companies***

This special customs regime suspends federal taxes on the import or domestic acquisition of materials, parts, pieces and components to be used in the construction or conversion of oil and gas related platforms or modules. It may apply to:

- the platform under construction or conversion;
- a shipyard; or
- other seaside industrial facilities, to be used in the construction of offshore structures, oil platforms and platform modules.

The beneficiary is the Brazilian company that is hired by a foreign company to construct or convert of oil and gas platforms.

Several other customs regimes may apply to the industry and to the production of equipment destined for the oil and gas industry.

8. International tax aspects

This section focuses on Brazilian taxation on income derived by foreign investors in the Brazilian oil and gas industry, as well as on potential limits imposed by double tax treaties between Brazil and other jurisdictions. There is then a review of Brazil's international anti-avoidance rules.

8.1 Taxation of foreign investors in the oil and gas industry

Foreign investors are subject to Brazilian tax only if they:

- have a branch formally created in Brazil or have a corporate taxable unit in the country;
- receive income from Brazilian sources; or
- recognise gains from the disposition of Brazilian assets and rights.

Bearing in mind that foreign investors rarely use branches in Brazil to develop exploration and production activities, it is relevant to analyse the specific situations that may result in the qualification of a taxable unit of a foreign investor in Brazil.

(a) ***Permanent establishment***

Unlike many other jurisdictions, there is no concept of permanent establishment in Brazil. Nevertheless, Brazilian tax law presents two situations under which a non-resident taxpayer may have a corporate taxable unit in Brazil, even without being formally registered in the country.

The first situation is non-resident businesses that conduct their activities in Brazil. Although this is not automatically the case, non-residents may be deemed as having a taxable unit in the country. Non-residents may then be subject to taxation in Brazil for their local business or professional unit. Although there is no legal definition, a business unit may be construed as a separate unit of an enterprise or centre of activity for trading and performing services. An example would be *'de facto'* company, which is an entity that has failed to register its by-laws with the board of trade or any other authority, but is nevertheless regarded as a regular company for tax purposes. Doing business through a non-incorporated Brazilian legal entity can lead to a *'de facto'* company. However, since exploration and production under the concession regime are performed by companies incorporated in Brazil, this sort of taxable unit for non-resident investors would not occur in the oil and gas industry.

As to the second situation, Brazilian tax law establishes that non-residents are subject to income tax on profits derived from the sale of imported goods through a number of different agents. These include individuals acting on behalf of the non-resident via a mandate, individuals acting under the name of a non-resident, local agents or representatives who are able to conclude contracts on behalf of the non-resident. This situation would be unlikely to apply to foreign investors in the Brazilian oil and gas industry.

Because there is no concept of permanent establishment and there are few instances when a non-resident might hold a taxable unit in Brazil, there is little precedent for dealing with taxation in this circumstance. Non-residents are usually subject to taxation on income received from Brazilian sources from assets or rights located in Brazil. As reviewed below, this may be more burdensome than regular corporate taxation in Brazil.

(b) Tax treatment applicable to cross-border payments made to foreign investors

Payment of dividends: Dividends paid by Brazilian legal entities to shareholders out of after-tax profits are currently not subject to WHT. This applies to dividends related to profits generated since January 1 1996. Dividends paid from profits generated before that date may be subject to WHT. The rates of this will vary according to the legislation applicable to each year.

Payment of interest on equity: In addition to dividends, legal entities may distribute interest on equity to their shareholders. This is a hybrid form of capital remuneration provided by Brazilian tax law.

For tax purposes, interest on equity is limited to the daily variation of the Brazilian long-term interest rate, as determined by the Central Bank of Brazil. The amount deducted may not exceed the greater of:

- 50% of net income (after social contribution on net profits has been deducted and before the provision for IRPJ and the amounts attributable to investors as interest on equity) in respect of the period in which the payment is made; or
- 50% of the total retained earnings and profit reserves from the beginning of the period in which the payment is made.

If the taxpayer is subject to the real profits regime, then the total interest on equity is deductable from the taxable basis of corporate income tax.

Interest on equity is subject to WHT at a rate of 15%, or 25% if the investor is located in a low tax jurisdiction.

Payment of interest under debt funding: WHT is imposed on interest payments at a rate of 15%, or 25% if the beneficiary is located in a low tax jurisdiction. Thin capitalisation and transfer pricing rules apply with regard to the deduction of interest expenses by the Brazilian legal entity.

Brazilian exporters may, under certain conditions, use export finance facilities, for which an advance payment is made for the exports and the interest is paid by the exporter. In these cases, the WHT rate may be reduced to 0%, on condition that the beneficiary is not located in a low tax jurisdiction. This 0% rate applies to interest payments made by Brazilian companies that export crude oil and are funded by export finance agreements.

Payment of trademark and patent royalties and compensation for transfer of know-how: Royalty payments and payments made as compensation for technical and administrative services and the transfer of know-how are subject to WHT at a general rate of 15% rate. This increases to 25% when the beneficiary is located in a low tax jurisdiction.

Cross-border charter payments: Charter fees paid by Brazilian companies to use vessels benefit from a 0% WHT rate, as long as the beneficiary is not located in a low tax jurisdiction. If this is the case, WHT is imposed at 25%.

Capital gains derived by non-residents: Capital gains made by non-residents through capital reduction or the disposition of Brazilian assets, including quotas or company shares, are normally subject to WHT.

If the buyer is a non-resident, its legal representative in Brazil is liable for collecting WHT. However, if the buyer is a Brazilian resident, it is liable itself.

Only transactions that effectively involve the disposition of assets and rights may give rise to taxable capital gains for non-resident investors (ie, when there is no WHT imposition on unrealised gains).

Capital gains recognised by foreign investors from shares registered as direct foreign investments are generally subject to WHT at a 15% general tax rate (or 25% rate if the investor is located in a low tax jurisdiction).[9] The taxable capital gain is the positive difference between the sales price of the asset or right (or the price paid upon the capital reduction) and the cost of its acquisition. This cost must be supported by the appropriate documentation. If this documentation does not exist, the amount registered with the Central Bank of Brazil as direct foreign investment may be used.

Due to an increase in M&A activity in the Brazilian oil and gas industry, many foreign players are considering the impact of WHT on the income from sales of shares of Brazilian concessionaires.

(c) *Limitations imposed by the double tax treaties*

Brazil currently has double tax treaties with 29 jurisdictions.[10] The majority of these were signed during or before 1980.

---

9 A specific tax exemption applies to gains recognised by foreign investors from the sale of shares of Brazilian companies publicly traded either on the stock exchange or the organised over-the-counter markets.

10 These are the following jurisdictions: Argentina, Austria, Belgium, Canada, Chile, China, Czech Republic, Denmark, Ecuador, Finland, France, Hungary, India, Israel, Italy, Japan, Korea, Luxembourg, Mexico, the Netherlands, Norway, Peru, the Philippines, Portugal, Slovakia, South Africa, Spain, Sweden and Ukraine.

Although Brazil is not a member of the Organisation for Economic Cooperation and Development (OECD), these treaties to a great extent follow the OECD Model Convention in force at the time they were signed. They are also influenced to some extent by the United Nations Model Convention, mainly with respect to attracting taxing rights to the source state. Recent precedents indicate that the Brazilian courts intend to rely on the official OECD commentaries in their interpretation of double tax treaties.

Brazilian law does not fully regulate the interaction between double tax treaties and domestic law. However, it is generally understood that double tax treaties are an agreement between two states, and may not be revoked by one of those states.

A distinct aspect of Brazilian policy, which deviates from the OECD Model Convention, is the inclusion of matching credit clauses in double tax treaties signed with developed countries. This is especially true in respect of payment of dividends, interest and royalties. Because Brazil was primarily a capital-importer at the time it signed many of its double tax treaties, they tend to privilege taxation at source rather than grant exclusive taxing rights to the beneficiary's home nation.

As a general rule, Brazil's double tax treaties do not place limitations on Brazilian taxing rights. Nevertheless, some specific provisions may limit these rights for oil and gas multinationals:

- a limited WHT rate of 12.5% on interest payments made by Brazilian sources to Japanese residents under cross-border debt funding (as per the treaty with Japan);
- a limited WHT rate of 10% in relation to the payment of royalties – which may include compensation for the transfer of know-how (excluding trademark royalties) – under the treaties signed with Spain, Austria, Israel and Mexico;
- the general definition of royalties as payments made for the rent or right to use equipment, which may result in tax matching credits for beneficiaries in a treaty jurisdiction (eg, the treaties signed with Spain and Italy); and
- restrictions on Brazilian taxing rights in relation to WHT on gains derived by Japanese residents from the sale of Brazilian shares (as per the treaty with Japan).

8.2 International anti-avoidance rules

Brazilian international anti-avoidance rules comprise transfer pricing rules, the recently introduced thin capitalisation rules, rules resulting in the more burdensome taxation of entities located in low tax jurisdictions, and the Brazilian controlled foreign corporation rules. These may all affect the structures commonly adopted by multinational groups engaged in exploration and production in Brazil.

(a) Brazilian transfer pricing rules

Transfer pricing rules were adopted in Brazil in 1996. The conciliation of these with internationally accepted methods was a challenge to multinational enterprises in Brazil. The difficulties arose from the deviations of the Brazilian rules from the standards of the OECD transfer pricing guidelines. It should be mentioned in reference to these deviations that advance pricing agreements are not available under the Brazilian rules, and that Brazilian law has adopted fixed margins (ranging from 15% to 60%) for the various methods, regardless of the taxpayer's business or industry. In this sense, the concept of functional analysis does not exist under Brazilian transfer pricing rules. However, the minister of finance may establish other statutory margins for each industry in order to determine the parameter price in controlled transactions.

All cross-border transactions performed between a legal entity incorporated in Brazil and a related party outside of Brazil or in a low tax jurisdiction or privileged tax regime[11] come under the scope of the Brazilian transfer pricing rules.[12]

Legal entities incorporated in Brazil are deemed to refer to:

- a parent company located abroad;
- a branch or subsidiary located abroad;
- an individual or a legal entity resident or incorporated outside Brazil that holds more than 10% of the share capital of a Brazilian legal entity;
- a legal entity incorporated abroad that is controlled by a Brazilian legal entity or that receives investments from one equivalent to more than 10% of its share capital;
- a legal entity incorporated abroad for which the same persons participate in the management, control or capital of both it and the Brazilian company, or hold at least 10% of the share capital of those companies;
- an individual or legal entity resident or incorporated abroad that, together with a Brazilian company, holds more than 10% of the share capital of a third entity;
- an individual or legal entity that is associated with the Brazilian company under a consortium or a condominium agreement;
- an individual resident abroad who is a relative or spouse of the director of the Brazilian company or of its controlling quota holder or shareholder;
- an individual or legal entity that has exclusive rights to distribute as an agent, dealer or concessionaire the Brazilian company's goods, services or rights; and
- an individual or legal entity that grants the Brazilian company exclusive rights to distribute the non-resident's goods, services or rights.

Transfer pricing rules for imports: Brazilian transfer pricing rules provide three methods for determining the guide price for products, services or rights imported by Brazilian companies:

- Comparable uncontrolled price method – here the guide price is based on the average price of identical or similar products or services;
- Resale price less margin method – here the guide price is based on the average resale price of the goods applied by the importer, minus unconditional discounts, taxes, brokerage fees and a profit margin of either 60% of the

11 Privileged tax regimes are discussed further below.
12 Exception made for situations in which other specific rules apply.

resale price of the final product, minus deductions and costs accrued by the importer, for imported goods used in the production process; or 20% of the resale price of the imported good; and
- Cost-plus method – here the guide price is based on the average production cost of identical or similar products, services or rights in the jurisdiction in which they were originally produced, increased by the taxes paid in that jurisdiction and with a fixed profit margin of 20% of the cost after taxes.

If more than one method applies, the Brazilian company may choose the one that gives the highest guide price in proving its compliance with Brazilian transfer pricing rules.

If the average price paid by the Brazilian importer exceeds the average price determined under these methods, a transfer pricing adjustment is required. As a consequence, the amount deemed to be paid in excess for the import will be added to the taxable base of the corporate income taxes due. On the other hand, if the average price is lower than the guide price, no adjustment is required.

Transfer pricing rules for exports: If the average sales price of exports by a Brazilian company in a year is less than than 90% of the average price of the same goods sold domestically, their price will be determined by the tax authorities under one of the following four methods:

- CUP method for export transactions – here the guide price is based on the average price of similar products practiced by a Brazilian company with foreign independent parties;
- Wholesale price in the country of destination, minus profit margin – here the guide price is based on the average sales price applied in the wholesale market to which they are being exported, less local taxes and a 15% fixed profit margin;
- Retail price in the country of destination, minus profit margin – here the guide price is based on the average sales price applied in the retail market to which they are being exported, less taxes and less a 30% fixed profit margin; or
- Acquisition or production cost, plus taxes and profit margin – here the guide price is based on the average acquisition or production cost, with the addition of Brazilian taxes and a 15% fixed profit margin.

If more than one method applies, the company may adopt that which gives the lowest export price. If the average export price applied by the Brazilian company is greater than the guide price reached by one of these methods, no adjustment is required. On the other hand, if the average price is lower than the guide price, an adjustment is required, with the difference added to the taxable base.

Brazilian law uses safe harbour rules for transfer pricing in controlled export transactions. Under the first of these, a taxpayer is deemed to have applied an appropriate transfer price when the average export price is at least 90% of the average domestic price. A second safe harbour rule allows a difference of up to 5% either way between the guide price and the transaction price.

Two other safe harbours aim to simplify the application of the transfer pricing rules. However, they are not considered true safe harbours, because the tax authorities are still required to observe the methods of transfer pricing. For the first, if the exporter is able to prove that the net commercial profit from the export is at least 5% of the average export income, the exporter may support its transfer pricing with just the export transaction documents. The same applies if the exporter is able to prove that the net export income is not more than 5% of the total net income for that year.

Brazilian transfer pricing rules do not currently apply to cross-border payments of trademark or patent royalties, nor to fees payable as compensation for the transfer of technology or the rendering of services. Brazilian companies may treat these payments as deductible expenses when assessing the taxable basis of the corporate income tax, up to the specific limits covered above.

Transfer pricing rules for interest payments: Under Brazilian transfer pricing rules, the amount of interest paid to related parties abroad (or parties located in low tax jurisdictions or under privileged tax regimes) may not exceed the equivalent of the London interbank offered rate plus 3% per year. Amounts paid in excess will be treated as non-deductible items for the purposes of corporate income tax. However, if the loan agreement is submitted to be registered with the Central Bank of Brazil – which is the usual procedure – this restriction will not apply. The rate that has been registered will then be acceptable for tax purposes.

(b) ***Thin capitalisation rules***

The interest paid by Brazilian corporate taxpayers to foreign related parties is only deductible for corporate income tax purposes provided that:

- the expense is necessary to the company's activities; and
- the interest rate complies with Brazilian transfer pricing rules.

For foreign parties not located in low tax jurisdictions or under privileged tax regimes, two further conditions must be met:

- The amount of the Brazilian entity's indebtness must be less than twice the value of the stake held by the related party in the Brazilian borrower; or
- The Brazilian entity's total indebtness must be less than twice the value of the stake held by all related parties. If the foreign beneficiary is located in a low tax jurisdiction or under a privileged tax regime, the entity's indebtness must not exceed 30% of the equity of the Brazilian borrower.

(c) ***Controlled foreign corporation rules***

Brazilian controlled foreign corporation rules are currently regulated by Section 74 of Provisional Measure 2,158-35/2001. This requires Brazilian corporate taxpayers to add their profits to those of any foreign controlled or affiliated companies at the end of each year. The combined profits must be taxed whether or not they arise from active or passive activities, regardless of the jurisdiction in which the company is located, and regardless of whether the profits are available to the Brazilian company.

These rules may affect players in the oil and gas industry with foreign subsidiaries, or affiliated companies who are profitable outside of Brazil (such as those whose entities are involved in charter transactions).

(d) Low tax jurisdictions and privileged tax regimes

Brazilian tax laws define a 'low tax jurisdiction' as a country or jurisdiction which does not impose any income tax, or which imposes it at a maximum rate of less than 20%, or which does not permit access to information on shareholding structure, the ownership of quotas or shares and beneficial ownership of the income.

In addition the concept of a privileged tax regime was introduced by Law 11,727/2008. This is a tax regime which:

- does not tax income, or taxes it at a maximum rate of less than 20%;
- grants tax benefits to non-resident entities or individuals without requiring them to carry out substantial economic activity in the country, or makes them contingent on the non-exercise of substantial economic activity;
- does not tax foreign income, or taxes it at a maximum rate of less than 20%; or
- does not permit access to information on shareholding composition, the ownership of assets and rights, or economic transactions.

The most appropriate interpretation of this law is that the new concept of a privileged tax regime will apply solely for transfer pricing rules in export and import transactions and the recently introduced thin capitalisation rules. This concept should not therefore affect the definition of low tax jurisdiction used for WHT in connection with capital gains, interests and other income.

In 2010, a new list was enacted by the Federal Revenue Service via Normative Instruction 1,037/2010. This included countries considered as low tax jurisdictions[13] and locations considered as having privileged tax regimes.[14]

---

13 Normative Ruling 1,037/2010 lists the following jurisdictions as low tax jurisdictions: American French Polynesia, American Samoa, Andorra, Anguilla, Antigua and Barbuda, Aruba, Ascension Islands, Bahamas, Bahrain, Barbados, Belize, Bermudas, British Virgin Islands, Brunei, Campione D'Italia, Cayman Islands, Channel Islands, Cyprus, Singapore, Cook Islands, Costa Rica, Djibouti, Dominica, Dutch Antilles, Gibraltar, Grenada, Hong Kong, Kiribati, Labuan, Lebanon, Liberia, Liechtenstein, Macau, Madeira, Maldives, Isle of Man, Marshall Islands, Mauritius, Monaco, Montserrat, Nauru, Niue, Norfolk Island, Sultanate of Oman, Panama, Pitcairn Islands, Qeshm Island, St. Helena Island, St. Kitts and Nevis, St. Pierre and Miquelon, Saint Vincent, San Marino, Santa Lucia, Seychelles, Solomon Islands, Swaziland, Switzerland (which is currently suspended), Tonga, Tristan da Cunha, Turks and Caicos Islands, United Arab Emirates, US Virgin Islands, Vanuatu, Western Samoa.

14 The rormative Ruling considers the following as privileged tax regimes:
- holding companies incorporated under Danish law that do not develop substantive economic activities;
- holding companies incorporated under Dutch law that do not develop substantive economic activities (this is currently suspended);
- international trading companies incorporated under Icelandic law;
- offshore companies incorporated under Hungarian law;
- LLCs incorporated under US state law, in which the equity interest is held by nonresidents not subject to US federal income tax;
- *Entidad de Tenencia de Valores Extranjeros* incorporated under Spanish law (currently suspended);
- international trading companies and holding companies incorporated under Maltese law; and
- *Sociedad Anonima Financiera de Inversion* incorporated under Uruguayan law until December 2010.

9. Conclusion: trends in Brazilian taxation of the oil and gas industry

Brazil is known to have a complex tax system, with burdensome taxes imposed at various levels of the production and commercial chain. As reviewed in this chapter, this reality may also affect the oil and gas industry.

Specific provisions of Brazilian tax legislation and the format under which certain benefits are granted may adversely affect the competitiveness of Brazilian players in the oil and gas supply chain.

All these factors mean that a careful analysis of Brazilian taxes applicable to developing exploration and production activities is required to ensure the viability of projects and appropriate returns.

The exponential growth of the Brazilian oil and gas industry, and the challenges arising from the discoveries in the pre-salt area, will certainly result in higher industry pressures for a more appropriate tax framework.

These demands may affect the REPETRO regulations. Changes to adapt the Brazilian transfer pricing legislation to internationally adopted standards would also be welcomed by multinational investors. More generally, developments to simplify and reorganise the Brazilian tax system, such as unifying the state and federal value added taxes, would also help Brazilian competitiveness.

In light of all this, Brazilian government agencies, lawmakers and actors in the oil and gas industry not only face challenges in exploring oil between 5,000 and 7,000 metres below the sea surface. They also face challenges from the Brazilian tax system and future fiscal policies for the sector. Brazil is often referred to as the country of the future. With the pre-salt area the future of the oil and gas industry is not distant, and its planning should start now.

Decommissioning

Eduardo Pereira
Petra Energia

1. Introduction

Oil and gas are non-renewable commodities. Every oil or gas field has its own lifecycle. This begins with the commercial discovery of a field. Then a large amount of infrastructure is required for development. The production facilities involved commonly include platforms, drilling rigs and storage facilities. Once oil or gas has been extracted, they need to be raised to a pipeline or a terminal for their final destination. When production has ceased, all installations and structures must be decommissioned; they cannot stay on site. There are two main reason for this. The first is the safety of users of the sea: derelict structures may impair safe navigation. The second is the prevention of pollution and protection of the environment.

Decommissioning therefore means disposing of any infrastructure used to explore, produce or raise oil and/or gas.[1] Decommissioning was originally referred to as 'abandonment', simply because most of the infrastructure was dumped in situ. However, the current definition of 'decommissioning' is now deemed more suitable, even though some countries still maintain the traditional reference to abandonment.[2]

This chapter analyses the Brazilian regulations that apply to decommissioning. It assesses on two levels whether the government has adopted the best international practice. The first level refers to the maturity of oil and gas provinces. Brazilian basins are relatively young compared to those in the United Kingdom and Norway. This comparison illustrates the best practices from countries that currently face decommissioning challenges. The second level refers to the length of standing of the production sharing agreement (PSA). The new Brazilian PSA regime is relatively young in comparison to those in Africa and Asia, which have been in place for decades. This comparison draws on a large number of international practices so as to provide guidance on some different approaches for the Brazilian model. The international practices in either or PSA regimes are compared to the Brazilian approach below.

1 The PSA established for the JDZ in Timor Sea states that: "Decommission means, in respect of the Contract Area or a part of it, as the case may be, to abandon, decommission, transfer, remove and/or dispose of structures, facilities, installations, equipment and other property, and other works, used in Petroleum Operations in the area, to clean up the area and make it good and safe, and to protect the environment."

2 For the purposes of this chapter 'decommissioning' and 'abandonment' are used interchangeably.

2. Petroleum title

The proprietary rights of oil and gas commonly belong to the relevant host government. (One exception is private property in the United States.) Host governments have several options for exploiting these natural resources,[3] but mainly refer to three different types of arrangements:

- licence;[4]
- PSA;[5] and
- service contract.

In the first arrangement the government is relying on returns from tax, and assigns all proprietary rights of any production to the licensee. In the second arrangement part of the production is assigned to the contractor (subject to tax), with the majority usually remaining government property. In the third arrangement (a pure service agreement) no rights of oil and gas are assigned, and only a service fee is charged. However, hybrid models are possible. A hybrid regime adopts more than one of these arrangements, or a combination of features, in its jurisdiction. A good example of a hybrid model is a service contract that allows a premium in kind if certain criteria are satisfied.

Distinguishing such arrangements is relevant to decommissioning because who owns the infrastructure will vary between them. In a licence regime the infrastructure is likely to belong to the licensee as this person is going to bear all the costs and risks involved in its implementation. In a PSA regime the infrastructure should revert to the government: the costs of its implementation are likely to be deducted as cost recovery. In a service agreement the infrastructure is likely to belong to the government as this entity, not the contractor, will be responsible for implementing it.

Host governments should be aware of these distinctions before deciding on their legal arrangement. Oil and gas companies should also be aware of them before investing in any province, as decommissioning is a critical factor in determining the economics of any projects.

3. International regulation

Decommissioning may be governed by international, regional or national legislation, but its application will vary from country to country. International treaties will affect only those parties who have signed and ratified that treaty. Regional treaties tend to exist between countries with shared maritime boundaries. National legislation on decommissioning is often not well regulated (or sometimes

3 For further information see: Bernard G Taverne, *Petroleum, Industry and Governments: A study of the Involvement of Industry and Government with the Production and use of Petroleum* (2nd edn, Kluwer Law International, Alphen aan den Rijn 2008); Bernard Taverne, *An introduction to the regulation of the petroleum industry: Law, Contracts and Conventions* (Graham & Trotman, London 1994); Eugene V Rostow, *A National Policy for the Oil Industry* (Yale University Press, London 1948), 3–26; Danièle Barberis, *Negotiating Mining Agreements: Past, Present and Future Trends* (Klumer Law International, London 1998), 4–60.

4 A licence is also referred to as a concession agreement or lease. These terms are used interchangeably in the petroleum industry but have the same meaning.

5 PSAs are also referred to as petroleum sharing contracts.

does not exist) in new or young oil and gas provinces as these issues arise towards the end of a field's production, which may last up to 40 years.[6]

The United Kingdom is a good example of the above matrix. It is a signatory party to international[7] and regional treaties,[8] and has also implemented national legislation regarding decommissioning.[9] Brazil does not have the same matrix, as no regional treaty affects Brazil with respect to decommissioning obligations. Nevertheless, Brazil is a signatory party to international treaties, which are the basis for the country's own decommissioning regulations. As a result, it is important to understand the international obligations that affect Brazil before analysing its national regulation.

3.1 Geneva Convention

The first international law to govern the laws of the sea was the Convention for the Continental Shelf, signed in Geneva in 1958. As its title suggests, this convention aimed to establish a basis for an international law of the sea that paid particular attention to maritime boundaries. However, it also addressed decommissioning issues, as may be seen in its Article 5.5:

Due notice must be given of the construction of any such installations, and permanent means for giving warning of their presence must be maintained. Any installations which are abandoned or disused must be entirely removed.

At first sight this appears a radical and somewhat draconian article for host governments and oil and gas companies to follow. It clearly requires that all and any installation must ultimately be removed from the seabed. Although this nowadays seems unrealistic, it was quite feasible at that time. Most offshore operations when the convention was drawn up did not exceed shallow waters (in particular in the Gulf of Mexico).

As technology improved, oil and gas companies began to operate in deeper waters. This was not only a real technical challenge but also proved incompatible with Article 5.5. Completely removing an offshore platform that was 300 kilometres (km) away from the coast and in waters 3,000 metres (m) deep was not only a technical challenge but also a very expensive operation. Consequently, a new international approach to decommissioning was called for.

3.2 United Nations Law of the Sea

Although a new international regime was necessary to make regulation adequate to the practical reality it took nearly three decades for this to be achieved. The United Nations Law of the Sea (UNCLOS) of 1982 provided more flexibility for its signatory parties. Article 60 (3) sets out the following standards for removing installations or structures:

Due notice must be given of the construction of such artificial islands, installations or

---

6 Charez Golvala, 'Upstream joint ventures – bidding and operating agreements', in Geoffrey Picton-Turbervill (ed.), *Oil and Gas: A practical handbook* (Globe Law and Business, London 2009), 45–6.

7 Eg United Nations Law of the Sea (1982).

8 Eg Oslo and Paris Convention for the Protection of the Marine Environment of the North East Atlantic (1992).

9 Petroleum Act 1998.

> *structures, and permanent means for giving warning of their presence must be maintained. Any installations or structures which are abandoned or disused shall be removed to ensure safety of navigation, taking into account any generally accepted international standards established in this regard by the competent international organization. Such removal shall also have due regard to fishing, the protection of the marine environment and the rights and duties of other States. Appropriate publicity shall be given to the depth, position and dimensions of any installations or structures not entirely removed.*

The 'competent international organisation' created for maintaining these standards is the International Maritime Organisation (IMO), established under the umbrella of the United Nations. It issued its guidelines in 1989. In short, these required the following:

- the complete removal of all structures in water depths of less than 75 m and weighing less than 4,000 tonnes;
- the partial removal of all structures in a water depths above 100 m and weighing more than 4,000 tonnes, leaving a minimum depth of 55 m of clear water for safe navigation;
- the determination of position, depth and dimensions of any installation or structure not entirely removed;
- an indication on nautical charts of any remaining structures; and
- an indication of liabilities for future claims.

It is clear that the safety of navigation was a critical concern for the international authority. It must always be secured even if some flexibility might be allowed with regard to the removal of installations.[10]

After 1998 the allowances were restricted further. The depth at which complete removal was required was increased from 75 m to 100 m. More significantly, any installation was now required to be designed and constructed in a way that allowed for its complete removal.

Although the IMO guidelines have further reduced in flexibility in the last few years, a less draconian approach exist in practice, as not all installations have been required to be removed. This new approach became far more acceptable internationally. But it is important to stress that the IMO's guidelines are just that; they are not obligatory. Their implementation and effectiveness is more an act of the goodwill of each signatory than a compulsory obligation.

Regional conventions might add further restrictions on decommissioning to the IMO's guidelines. The Oslo and Paris Convention for the Protection of the Marine Environment of the North East Atlantic (OSPAR) is a good example. This requires the removal of all installations of less than 10,000 tonnes rather than the 4,000 tonnes noted in the IMO guidelines.[11] However, this chapter will not cover any regional treaties as Brazil is not a signatory party to any of these.

---

10 See also UNCLOS sections 60 (1), (2), (4), (5), (6), (7) and (8).
11 For more information about OSPAR see: www.ospar.org/.

It is important to distinguish between the removal of an installation and its disposal. As John Paterson suggests, "It is one thing to remove an installation or structure, whether wholly or partly; what happens to it thereafter is quite another."[12] It is therefore important to consider the London (Dumping) Convention, which sets out the international basis for disposing of waste.

3.3 London (Dumping) Convention[13]

The Convention on the Prevention of Marine Pollution by Dumping of Waste and Other Matter 1972 (the London Dumping Convention) has been described as:

> *one of the first global conventions to protect the marine environment from human activities and has been in force since 1975. Its objective is to promote the effective control of all sources of marine pollution and to take all practicable steps to prevent pollution of the sea by dumping of wastes and other matter.*[14]

More than 80 states are currently parties to this convention.[15] Brazil became a signatory on July 26 1982 and became an effective member to its jurisdiction on August 25 1982.[16] According to Article III of the convention, 'dumping' is defined as follows:

- any deliberate disposal at sea of wastes or other matter from vessels, aircraft, platforms or other man-made structures at sea; and
- any deliberate disposal at sea of vessels, aircraft, platforms or other manmade structures at sea.

However, it is also relevant to note that the same provision also provides for the exclusion of certain issues from its definition of 'dumping', as follows:

- the disposal at sea of wastes or other matter incidental to, or derived from the normal operations of vessels, aircraft, platforms or other man-made structures at sea and their equipment, other than wastes or other matter transported by or to vessels, aircraft, platforms or other man-made structures at sea, operating for the purpose of disposal of such matter or derived from the treatment of such wastes or other matter on such vessels, aircraft, platforms or structures;
- the placement of matter for a purpose other than the mere disposal thereof, provided that such placement is not contrary to the aims of the convention; and
- the disposal of wastes or other matter directly arising from, or related to the

12 For further information see: John Paterson, Decommissioning of Offshore Oil and Gas Installations` in Greg Gordon, John Paterson, Emre Usenmez (eds), *Oil and Gas Law: Current Practice and Emerging Trends* (2nd edn, Dundee University Press, Dundee 2011), 292–301.

13 www.imo.org/OurWork/Environment/SpecialProgrammesAndInitiatives/Pages/London-Convention-and-Protocol.aspx

14 www.imo.org/OurWork/Environment/SpecialProgrammesAndInitiatives/Pages/London-Convention-and-Protocol.aspx.

15 www.imo.org/OurWork/Environment/SpecialProgrammesAndInitiatives/Pages/London-Convention-and-Protocol.aspx.

16 www.imo.org/OurWork/Environment/SpecialProgrammesAndInitiatives/Pages/London-Convention-and-Protocol.aspx.

> exploration, exploitation and associated off-shore processing of sea-bed mineral resources will not be covered by the provisions of the convention.

Oil and gas infrastructure is clearly included under the definition of 'dumping'. However, some flexibility is provided within the exclusions clause otherwise it would not be feasible to operate offshore.

But the most relevant part of this convention is the categorisation of waste. Three categories are used:

- waste whose disposal is forbidden;
- waste whose disposal requires a special consent; and
- waste whose disposal requires a general consent.

Consequently, offshore installations might be disposed of at sea, but only to the extent that this does not fall foul of the legislation. Nevertheless, prior consent will always be required, and this must be carefully considered before it is given.

A 1996 protocol aimed to "further modernize the [London Dumping] Convention and, eventually, replace it".[17] This has been signed by 40 countries, although not all have ratified it. Under this protocol all dumping is prohibited, except for specific situations known as the "reverse list." However Brazil, like most other nations, is not a signatory party.[18] Consequently, this chapter does not cover the 1996 protocol.

4. Brazilian law and regulation

The concepts and international regulations mentioned above need to be considered, but it is more important to verify Brazilian regulations and practice for decommissioning.

4.1 Concession agreements

As previously described, oil and gas are natural resources that commonly belong to the host government. Brazil is no exception; under its Constitution oil and gas belong to the government.[19] However, Article 177 of the Constitution authorises private parties to search for and exploit natural oil and gas.[20] Law 9,478/97 determined the licensing regime for exploring and exploiting these resources in Brazil.

Until 2010, when the new PSA regime was implemented, this was the only legal recourse available for searching for and exploiting oil and gas. The concession agreement has seen minor changes since its first inception in the late 1990s. The latest agreement, which originates from the 10th licence round, regulates decommissioning in the following terms:[21]

---

17 www.imo.org/OurWork/Environment/SpecialProgrammesAndInitiatives/Pages/London-Convention-and-Protocol.aspx.

18 www.imo.org/OurWork/Environment/SpecialProgrammesAndInitiatives/Pages/London-Convention-and-Protocol.aspx.

19 See Article 176 of the Constitution.

20 See Article 177 of the Constitution.

21 www.anp.gov.br/brasil-rounds/round10/index_e.asp

(a) ***Compliance with applicable regulation and industry best practices:***

13.19 The Concessionaire may interrupt the drilling of a well and abandon it before reaching the expected geological goal, in accordance with the applicable Brazilian laws and the Best Practices of the Oil Industry. If the well represents part of the Minimum Exploration Program and it does not reach the expected goal, the well shall not take into account in the compliance with the Minimum Exploration Program unless the ANP [Brazilian Petroleum Agency], at its sole discretion, determines otherwise.

18.8 When performing all and any relinquishment of the Blocks within the Concession Area, the Concessionaire shall rigorously comply, not only with the provisions of paragraphs 3.5, 18.11 to 18.19 and Clause Twenty-One, but also with all other legal provisions and instructions of the ANP, in accordance with the Best Practices of the Oil Industry, regarding the relinquishment and abandonment of areas and removal and reversion of assets.

18.11 The planning and performance of any Inactivation and Abandonment Operations, including areas, wells, structures, fields, transfer lines, parts or units of surface or sub-surface facilities, offshore or onshore, shall be made in accordance with the applicable Brazilian legislation and the Best Practices of the Oil Industry and also according to Clause Twenty-One.

(b) ***Allocation of responsibilities and liabilities for decommissioning obligations:***

18.9 In accordance with the applicable Brazilian legislation, the relinquishment mentioned herein shall not exempt the Concessionaire from the fulfilment of all outstanding obligations, nor for any liabilities, irregularities or infractions occurring at a later date.

18.10 In the event of a pre-existing well or production infrastructure in the Concession Area that the Concessionaire may, at any time during the life of this Agreement, use or dispose of for any purpose, the Concessionaire shall assume the responsibilities of the obligations and has no right to waiver or any kind of indemnification in relation to the ANP or Union, pursuant to Clause Eighteen and Twenty-One.

(c) ***Allocation of costs and guarantees***

18.12 When it refers to a field, the inactivation planning and abandonment and the organization to provide the necessary funds shall be contemplated in the respective Development Plan, pursuant to paragraph 9.1 and periodically reviewed, during the Production Phase. Such revisions will be subject to paragraph 9.8.

18.13 The costs of the Inactivation and abandonment Operations in a field shall be established, in order to cover the activities of definitive well abandonment, the inactivation and removal of lines and facilities and the recovery of areas, pursuant to the applicable Brazilian legislation.

18.14 Upon request by the ANP, the Concessionaire shall deliver an inactivation and abandonment guarantee, by means of insurance, letter of credit, provisional guarantee fund, or other form of acceptable guarantee to the ANP, in conformance with the applicable Brazilian legislation;

18.15 The value of the inactivation and abandonment guarantee for a Field will be revised if there are approved revisions to the Development Plan of this Field that will alter the cost of inactivation and abandonment operations.

18.16 *If the inactivation and abandonment guarantee is constituted by a provisional guarantee fund, the calculated balance after the completion of all the necessary operations to inactivate and abandon the Field will revert exclusively to the Concessionaire.*

18.17 *The presentation of the inactivation and abandonment guarantee does not discharge the Concessionaire's obligation to complete, at its own cost and risk, all of the Operations necessary to inactivate and abandon the Field.*

These provisions are no different from the majority of licence regimes. Firstly, they require compliance with applicable law (including environmental law) and international best practice. Secondly, they allocate all liability and costs related to decommissioning to the licensee. Thirdly, they require certain guarantees at the planning stage to ensure that the decommissioning obligations can be carried out. However, provisions 18.18 and 18.19 differ from a licence regime. Both refer to the reversion of ownership and the recovery of costs:

18.18 *As a result of and by applying Article 28, paragraphs 1 and 2, and Article 43, item VI of the Petroleum Law, all and any assets, real estate or not, main or ancillary, existing in the Concession Area, whose acquisition costs are deductible in accordance with the applicable rules for calculating the Special Participation and which, at the sole discretion of the ANP, are necessary to allow the continuance of the Operations or are object of the public interest, shall revert to the possession and ownership of the Federal Government, and to the administration of the ANP, by the time of the exclusion of the Block(s) from the Concession Area or by the termination of this Agreement, if the Concession Area comprises of only one Block. However, if the Concessionaire is sharing assets for the Operations of two or more Fields in the same Concession Area, it shall have the right to retain such assets until all such Operations are completed. To fulfill the obligations established in this and in paragraph 18.9, the Concessionaire is obliged to observe the applicable Brazilian legislation, as well as adopting and executing, at its own account and risk, all legal, operational and administrative actions which may be necessary, also according to paragraphs 3.5, 18.8 and 18.11 and Clause Twenty-One.*

18.19 *The assets which shall not be reverted, under paragraph 18.18, including the unserviceable ones, shall be removed and disposed of by the Concessionaire, at its own cost and risk, pursuant to the provisions of this Agreement and the applicable Brazilian legislation.*

As previously mentioned, PSAs deal with cost recovery, and so the reversion of ownership is a common feature. Provisions 18.18 and 18.19 similarly maintain the licensee's liabilities for decommissioning, but they are fairly unusual for a licence regime.[22]

---

22 This obligation is also imposed in Article 28 of the Petroleum Law: "In any event of termination of the concession agreement, the Concessionaire shall execute, at its own costs, the removal of the equipment and goods that shall not be object of reversion, being liable to recover or indemnify the damages originated from its activities and to practice the environmental recovery acts determined by the governmental authorities."

Therefore, we can say that the Brazilian licence regime requires decommissioning obligations that most oil and gas players in the petroleum industry are used to dealing with.[23] However, the following paragraphs analyse the obligations required by the new petroleum regulations encompassed in Law 12,351/2010.

4.2 The PSA regime

The PSA regime is regulated by Law 12,351/2010. Although there is currently no model for such an arrangement, Law 12,351/2010 determines the general clauses that must be covered. Item XV of Article 29 addresses decommissioning in the following terms:

> *the criteria to relinquish and vacate the areas by the contractor, including the removal of equipment and installations and for reversion of goods.*

The PSA model therefore clearly requires the regulation of decommissioning obligations. However, it does not provide any detail about those obligations. It only calls for criteria by which to relinquish areas and to remove equipment and installation. In other words, the decommissioning obligations are left uncertain. Everything is left to the PSA model rather than a legislative approach. Nevertheless, a cost recovery provision might be expected since it refers to the reversion of goods.

Financial guarantees for the costs and liabilities of decommissioning are similarly uncertain. Article 29 also states that "the indication of the guarantees [is] to be issued by the contractor". Although this requirement is fairly broad it is likely to require a similar approach to the licence regime. In other words, the PSA model should secure the payment of the decommissioning obligations, but it does not refer to a reserve fund as is often provided in a PSA.

Brazil's PSA law might be criticised for being vague on the details of several critical issues. However, the process of modifying any law can be complicated and bureaucratic. Because technology and other matters are constantly changing, the best approach may be to establish the specific details of decommissioning in another, less bureaucratic layer of regulation. It is better to provide flexibility to adjust future PSA models as required.

4.3 ANP Ordinance 25/2002

The ANP regulates abandonment through its Ordinance 25/2002. However, for the sake of completion, ANP Ordinance 13/2011, which regulates the surrender of acreage, also includes certain specific regulations relating to abandonment within the exploration phase.

The main substance of Ordinance 25/2002 is the technical requirements involved in the process of abandonment.[24] This section does not cover the technical details of Ordinance 25/2002, but analyses the general obligations it implies.

The overall goal of the ordinance is to prevent fluids leaking, in particular to the

---

23 Although several countries refer to abandonment rather than decommissioning it is possible to suggest that international practices tend to avoid such terminology. See note 2.

24 The fact that ordinance 25/2002 refers to "abandonment" rather than "decommissioning" indicates the lack of public sensitivity about this issue in comparison to mature provinces like the UK and Norway.

surface or seabed.[25] Its general obligations might be described in the following terms:

- the ANP must be notified before any abandonment; [26]
- the ANP must approve the abandonment of any production well;[27]
- wells cannot be abandoned while they can jeopardise neighbouring wells, except for safety or environmental reasons;[28]
- API specifications;[29]
- testing equipment;[30]
- the clearance of structures;[31]
- adjustments to navigation charts;[32] and
- emergency plans.[33]

It may be argued that Ordinance 25/2002 provides engineering guidance more than anything else. It provides extensive details about procedures but does not deal fully with costs and liabilities. The reason for this is simple: this ordinance relies on the statutory provisions of the decommissioning process. Nevertheless, it is possible to verify the implications of international obligations on clearance and navigation with regard to the disposal of infrastructure on the seabed.[34] The next section compares international practices with the Brazilian regulations.

5. International practice

Oil and gas are relatively old commodities. Their first operation dates to that of Colonel Drake in Pennsylvania in 1856. Since then, governments and oil and gas companies have gained experience not only in the United States, but across the globe.[35] Modern legislation tends to require compliance with industry best practices.

Brazil is a good example. Its licence and PSA regimes both refer to international industry best practices. The Petroleum Law of 1997 determines that the concession agreement imposes an obligation "to adopt the industry international best practices". The PSA law refers twice to a similar necessity. Firstly, it determines that the ANP shall enforce industry best practices within Brazilian operations.[36] Secondly, it requires that all operations under the PSA shall be performed in accordance with industry best practices.[37] In the second case, the obligations are directly imposed on Petrobras, as by law this will be the only entity allowed to operate under the PSA.[38]

As previously mentioned, Brazil is a young province in comparison to the United Kingdom or Norway, for example. It has also only recently adopted a new PSA

---

25 See Article 1.
26 See Article 4.
27 See Article 5.
28 See Article 6.
29 See Article 7.
30 See Article 8.
31 See Article 6.
32 See Article 27.
33 See Articles 19, 20 and 21.
34 See notes 30 and 31.
35 Daniel Yergin, *The Prize: The Epic Quest for Oil, Money & Power* (2nd edn, Free Press, New York 2008).
36 See Article 11.
37 See Article 15.
38 See Article 4.

regime. In order to establish industry best practice with regard to decommissioning for future PSA models in Brazil it is therefore important to pay particular attention to:

- mature provinces, which face real challenges in dealing with decommissioning; and
- countries and regions that have used PSA models for a long period.

The following sections therefore analyse the British experience and international PSA models in order to establish what might be a positive approach and what should be avoided in Brazilian decommissioning regulations.

5.1 Lessons learnt from the UK licence[39]

The UK Continental Shelf (UKCS) is a mature province. Offshore installations were first constructed there in the 1960s, and widespread decommissioning is now a reality for the UK oil and gas industry. The UK government, fearing the insolvency of licensees and potential liabilities falling on taxpayers, has passed several statutory rights to deal with decommissioning.

The most notorious powers are contained within Sections 29 and 30 of the Petroleum Act of 1998. Section 29 (1) authorises the secretary of state to request the submission of the decommissioning plan:

(1) The Secretary of State may by written notice require –

(a) the person to whom the notice is given; or

(b) where notices are given to more than one person, those persons jointly,

to submit to the Secretary of State a programme setting out the measures proposed to be taken in connection with the abandonment of an offshore installation or submarine pipeline (an "abandonment programme").

Most jurisdictions grant similar powers. But the following Section 30 goes further in determining those persons who might qualify under Section 29:

Persons who may be required to submit programmes

(1) A notice under section 29(1) shall not be given to a person in relation to the abandonment of an offshore installation unless at the time when the notice is given he is within any of the following paragraphs—

(a) the person having the management of the installation or of its main structure;

(b) a person to whom subsection (5) applies in relation to the installation;

(c) a person outside paragraphs (a) and (b) who is a party to a joint operating agreement or similar agreement relating to rights by virtue of which a person is within paragraph (b);

(d) a person outside paragraphs (a) to (c) who owns any interest in the installation otherwise than as security for a loan;

39 See also: Flávia Kaczelnik Altit and Mark Osa Igiehon, "Decommissioning of upstream oil and gas facilities" in Geoffrey Picton-Turbervill (ed.), *Oil and Gas: A practical handbook* (Globe Law and Business, London 2009), 257–80, A. T. Martin, "Decommissioning of International Petroleum Facilities: Evolving Standards and Key Issues", OGEL, 1/5 (2003); John Paterson, Emre Usenmez (eds), *Oil and Gas Law: Current Practice and Emerging Trends* (2nd edn, Dundee University Press, Dundee 2011), 292–301.

(e) a company which is outside paragraphs (a) to (d) but is associated with a company within any of those paragraphs.

The list of people that may be liable for decommissioning costs is therefore broad, and includes any party that holds an interest at any time in the applicable licence or installation.

The idea behind this approach was to protect the taxpayer at all costs. However, it creates several uncertainties. The life of an asset might extend for several decades and its ownership might change several times. Consequently, several parties might be liable, and there is no rule about the selection or order of parties on which the secretary of state might call for the decommissioning costs. Norway takes a similar approach, but it differs in providing a list of parties that might be called before others in bearing the decommissioning obligations.[40]

Although the UK approach tends to protect the taxpayer, it also affects the tax regime. Holding any party that has held a participating interest in a particular licence potentially liable for the costs of decommissioning creates instability and insecurity. This in turn affects the level of transactions in a mature province. It will reflect most obviously on M&A activities. Sellers will require some or all of the indemnities, parent companies' guarantees and letters of credit from reputable banks to cover the buyer's decommissioning liabilities. However, in a mature province it is unlikely that a major company will be interested in acquiring such asset, and smaller companies will be unlikely to be able to afford such a burden.

However, a licensee might request the exemption of its decommissioning obligations under Section 35 of the act:

(1) The Secretary of State may at the request of one or more of the persons who submitted an abandonment programme withdraw his approval of the programme.

(2) If a request under subsection (1) is made by some but not all of the persons who submitted the programme, the Secretary of State shall give the others an opportunity to make written representations as to whether his approval should be withdrawn.

(3) The Secretary of State shall after determining whether to withdraw his approval of an abandonment programme give notice of his determination to each of the persons who submitted the programme.

Although the secretary of state could provide such exemption this is not irrevocable, as Section 34 shows:

(1) Where the Secretary of State has approved a programme submitted to him under section 29 –

(a) either he or the persons who submitted it acting together may propose an alteration to the programme or to any condition to which it is subject; and

(b) either he or any of those persons may propose that any person who by virtue of section 36 has a duty to secure that the programme is carried out shall cease to have that duty, or that a person who does not already have that duty shall have it (either in addition to or in substitution for another person).

---

40 For further information see: www.npd.no/en/Publications/Facts/Facts-2010/Chapter-7/ and www.olf.no.

> *(7) The Secretary of State shall determine whether a change proposed under subsection (1) is to be made and shall then give notice of his determination, and of his reasons for it, to –*
>
> *(a) every person who, before the determination was made, had a duty to secure the carrying out of the programme; and*
>
> *(b) any person who has that duty as a result of the determination.*
>
> *(8) Where the Secretary of State determines that a change proposed in accordance with this section shall be made, this Part of this Act shall thereafter have effect as if the programme had been approved by the Secretary of State after being submitted under section 29 with the alterations, or as the case may be by the persons, specified in the determination.*

Consequently, there is no security or certainty for any of the persons referred to in Section 30 of this act.

Another lesson learnt by the UK government was the importance of public participation in the decommissioning process. The Brent Spar[41] incident demonstrated that a wide number of stakeholders should participate in any decommissioning process, as it is ultimately likely to affect the environment and public concerns. As a result, several public debates should be held during the creation of a decommissioning plan.[42]

The statutory provisions mentioned above secure the positions of the UK government and the UK taxpayer. However, they seriously harm M&A and development activities. Decommissioning obligations are therefore an additional hurdle for new entrants to the UKCS. The UK approach is likely to decrease the number of operations and ultimately the amount of tax that will be paid by this industry. Thus, a system like this should not be reproduced without the inclusion of mitigating factors, such as clarity about the order in which a government will pursue shareholders or the availability of tax reliefs to offset the costs of decommissioning.

5.2 PSAs in international practice[43]

The Brazilian PSA regime has only recently been approved by the Brazilian Congress, and is still relatively new. It does not yet have a PSA model in place. For this reason it is important to compare models in countries or regions that have used PSA for a longer time in order to determine best industry practices. This section refers to the relevant clauses of PSA models in Africa, Asia and the Middle East, and elsewhere.

---

41 Brent Spar is the leading example involving the disposal of an oil and gas store facility. Shell and the British government agreed on a disposal plan but it suffered several modifications because of the actions of Greenpeace and ultimately the public's opposition. For further information see: www.scotland.gov.uk/Uploads/Documents/AE07Brent2004.pdf

42 See sections 5.3, 5.4, 6.1, 6.27 and 11 of the Guidance Notes for Decommissioning of Offshore Oil and Gas Installations and Pipelines under the Petroleum Act 1998 produced by the Offshore Decommissioning Unit, Department of Energy and Climate Change. Available at www. og.decc.gov.uk/regulation/guidance/decommission.htm

43 See also: A. Konoplianik, "The fight against PSA in Russia, Who is to Benefit and why not the State?", OGEL, 1/3 (2003); Ian Rutledge, "The Sakhalin II PSA – a Production "Non-Sharing" Agreement, Analysis of Revenue Distribution", SERIS (2004); O. O. Rewane, "Creating a Comprehensive and Investor-Friendly PSA Regime: Where does Russia keep going wrong?", OGEL, 3/1 (2005); Mike Bunter, "The Iranian Buy Back Agreement", OGEL, 1/2 (2003).

(a) Africa

Africa is an important continent for the oil and gas industry as it encompasses major producers such as Libya, Nigeria and Angola. It also has the potential to increase its reserves through the prospects of young provinces like Kenya, Tanzania and Uganda. This section analyses a combination of those scenarios as well as present PSAs from Nigeria, São Tomé and Principe, and Tanzania.

Nigeria, São Tomé and Principe: The following is taken from the Joint Development Authority Model Production Sharing Contract of 2005.[44]

13.6 Decommissioning

The expenditure for Decommissioning will be estimated on the basis of technical studies by the CONTRACTOR to be agreed by the Management Committee as part of each Field Development Programme and revised as necessary.

13.7 Unless otherwise agreed by the JDA, the procedure for providing funds to meet the Decommissioning obligation shall be as follows:

(a) an amount shall be established on a Development Area basis, commencing at the start of production, on a unit of production basis as follows:

*DP = (PVDC – DF) * (P / RP), where:*

DP = Decommissioning provision for the period (millions of US Dollars)

PVDC = Present Value of Decommissioning costs (millions of US Dollars)

DF = Balance of Decommissioning fund at the start of the period (millions of US Dollars)

P = Crude Oil production in the period (millions of barrels)

RP = Estimated remaining Crude Oil (millions of barrels)

(b) All Decommissioning provisions shall be held in a Decommissioning fund, which shall be an interest bearing escrow account jointly established by the Parties at a first class commercial bank or other financial institution. The bank or financial institution shall have a long term rating of not less than "AA" by Standard and Poor's Corporation or an "Aa2" rating by Moody's Investor Service or a comparable rating by another mutually agreed rating service.

(c) For the purposes of calculating the Present Value of Decommissioning Costs, the following formula shall be used:

PVDC = EDC / (1 + i) n, where:

PVDC = Present Value of Decommissioning Costs

EDC = Estimated Value of Decommissioning Costs in nominal terms at the expected date of Decommissioning

i = interest rate applicable to the escrow account in the current period

n = number of years between current period and expected date of Decommissioning

13.9 The CONTRACTOR shall annually meet any shortfall between the actual Decommissioning costs and the Decommissioning fund for any Development Area by increasing the amount of security or the amount of the Decommissioning Fund.

---

44 This model can be found at: www.ogel.org/legal-and-regulatory-detail.asp?key=1008

Tanzania: The following is taken from Article 20 of the Model Production Sharing Agreement of 2008:[45]

(g) Contractor shall effect and, at all times during the terms of this Agreement, maintain for Petroleum Operations hereunder insurance of such type and in such amount as is customary in accordance with Good Oilfield Practices. The said insurance shall, without prejudice to the generality of the foregoing, cover:

(i) any loss or damage to all assets used in Petroleum Operations;

(ii) pollution caused in the course of Petroleum Operations for which Contractor or the Operator may be held responsible;

(iii) property loss or damage or bodily injury suffered by any third party in the course of Petroleum Operations for which Contractor, Operator, Government or TPDC may be liable or Contractor may be liable to indemnify the Government and TPDC;

(iv) the cost of removing wrecks and cleaning up operations following an accident in the course of petroleum Operations; and

(v) Contractor's and/or Operator's liability to its employees engaged in the Petroleum Operations.

(h) Contractor shall require its sub-contractors to carry insurance of such type and in such amount as is customary applicable in accordance with Good Oilfield Practices.

(i) Prior to relinquishment of any area, Contractor shall perform all necessary abandonment activities to restore the area as nearly as possible, to the condition in which it existed on the Effective Date including removal of such facilities, equipment or installations as Minister may instruct, and shall take action necessary to prevent hazards to human life, property and the environment which may be caused by its facilities, equipment or installations. In carrying such abandonment activities the Contractor shall observe Good Oilfield Practices.

(j) In order to discharge its obligations for site cleaning and abandonment, the Contractor, Government and TPDC shall, within two (2) years of the commencement of commercial production, enter into an agreement to establish an Abandonment Cost Reserve Fund. Such agreement shall address the administration and utilization of funds deducted from Cost Oil and/or Cost Gas in accordance with the following:

(i) TPDC and Contractor shall estimate the cost for site cleaning and abandonment in good faith, on the basis of industry average costs in accordance with generally acceptable petroleum industry practice;

(ii) the payments deposited into the fund shall be placed in a US Dollar, long term, interest bearing account in a commercial bank located within the United Republic of Tanzania to be designated by TPDC and Contractor. The bank so designated shall have a long term rating of not less than "AA" by Standard and Poor's Corporation or "P-1" by Moody's Investor Service or a comparable rating by another mutually agreed rating service;

45 This model can be found at: www.tpdc-tz.com/tpdc/

(iii) *if, upon expiration or other termination of this Agreement, TPDC determines to conduct the site cleanup and abandonment operations, such funds, plus all accrued interest, shall be paid to TPDC whereupon Contractor shall be released from any further obligation and liability with respect to such site cleanup and abandonment;*

(iv) *if, within sixty (60) days prior to the expiration or other termination of this Agreement, TPDC has failed to advise Contractor of TPDC's determination to conduct the site cleanup and abandonment operations, such funds, plus all accrued interest, shall be paid to Contractor and Contractor shall thereupon conduct all such operations in accordance with generally accepted petroleum industry practices;*

(v) *if the reserve fund in (iii) and (iv) above is insufficient to pay the costs of cleanup and abandonment, such shortfall shall be paid by Contractor. Where the reserve fund exceeds the costs incurred such excess shall revert back to TPDC.*

(b) Middle East and Asia

This region contains the largest oil and gas reserves. It must be noted that most countries in the Middle East prefer service contracts so as to avoid issues of sovereignty and politics related to the ownership of natural resources. However, in many cases the service contract has several of the features of a PSA. Asian countries, however, are more interested in attracting external investors and for this reason tend to prefer a PSA regime. This section analyses the following mix of young and well-developed oil and gas provinces: Kurdistan, Cyprus and India.

Kurdistan: The following is taken from the Kurdistan Region Model Production Contract of 2007:[46]

38.1 To enable the CONTRACTOR to recover the costs associated with future Petroleum Field decommissioning and site restoration and any other similar expenditure to be borne by the CONTRACTOR under this Contract, the CONTRACTOR shall have the right to establish a reserve fund for future decommissioning and site restoration (a "Decommissioning Reserve Fund"). The Decommissioning Reserve Fund may be established at any time during the final ten (10) Calendar Years of the term of the Production Operations of a Petroleum Field but, upon the reasonable request by the CONTRACTOR, the GOVERNMENT shall allow the CONTRACTOR to establish such fund over a longer period. Once established, the CONTRACTOR shall make regular contributions to the Decommissioning Reserve Fund based upon estimated Petroleum Field decommissioning and site restoration costs in accordance with standard principles and technical norms generally accepted in the international petroleum industry, and taking into account interest received and future interest expected to be earned on the Decommissioning Reserve Fund. Any contributions by the CONTRACTOR to the Decommissioning Reserve Fund shall be made in

46 This model can be found at: www.krg.org/articles/detail.asp?smap=02010100&lngnr=12&anr=18746&rnr=223

Dollars and shall be deemed Petroleum Costs when paid into the reserve fund, and shall be recovered by the CONTRACTOR in accordance with the provisions of Articles 1 and 25. Contributions to the Decommissioning Reserve Fund shall be placed with a first rate bank approved by the Management Committee in accordance with Article 8.5.

38.2 *If, at the end of the term of the Production Operations of the Petroleum Field, the GOVERNMENT decides to take over production operations in the Petroleum Field:*

(i) the GOVERNMENT shall become liable for its future decommissioning and site resoration;

(ii) the contributions and any interest accumulated in the Decommissioning Reserve Fund, to the extent that such contributions have been recovered as Petroleum Costs, shall be paid to the GOVERNMENT; and

(iii) the GOVERNMENT shall release the CONTRACTOR from any obligations relating to decommissioning and site restoration and shall indemnify the CONTRACTOR for any costs, liabilities, expenses, claims or obligations associated therewith.

38.3 *If the CONTRACTOR undertakes the Petroleum Field decommissioning and site restoration, the contributions and any interest accumulated in the Decommissioning Reserve Fund shall be paid to the CONTRACTOR and shall be used for the Petroleum Field Decommissioning Operations. The CONTRACTOR shall undertake any such Decommissioning Operations in accordance with standard practice in the international petroleum industry.*

38.4 *If the Decommissioning Reserve Fund is not sufficient to cover all Decommissioning Costs for the Petroleum Field, the balance shall be paid by the CONTRACTOR and may be recovered as Petroleum Costs from any other Production Areas or, if applicable, from any other area which is the subject of another Petroleum Contract (as defined by the Kurdistan Region Petroleum Act) of the CONTRACTOR or any of its Affiliates anywhere in the Kurdistan Region and, to the extent the balance is not recoverable as aforesaid, such remaining balance shall be paid by the GOVERNMENT.*

38.5 *If the Decommissioning Reserve Fund exceeds all Decommissioning Costs for the Petroleum Field, the balance shall be transferred to the GOVERNMENT.*

38.6 *Any expenditure incurred by the CONTRACTOR in relation with this Article 38, including but not limted to any contributions to the Decommissioning Reserve Fund, shall be deemed Petroleum Costs and shall be recovered by the CONTRACTOR in accordance with the provisions of Articles 1 and 25.*

38.7 *The CONTRACTOR shall submit to the Management Committee for approval in accordance with Article 8.5 a detailed plan for decommissioning the Production Area facilities and site restoration (the "Decommissioning Plan"), such Decommissioning Plan to be submitted no later than twenty four (24) Months prior to the date estimated by the CONTRACTOR for the end of Commercial Production from the Production Area.*

Cyprus: The following is extracted from the Model Production Sharing Contract of 2007:[47]

18.1. *The Contractor shall be the owner of the assets, whether movable or immovable, which it has acquired for purposes of Hydrocarbons Operations, subject to the following provisions.*

18.2. *Upon termination, relinquishment or cancellation of this Contract, whatever the reason therefor, with respect to all or part of the Contract Area, the assets belonging to the Contractor and necessary for Hydrocarbons Operations in the relinquished area shall become the ownership of the Republic, free of charge, unless it is the intent that they shall be used by the Contractor for purposes of exploitation of other Fields located in the Republic of Cyprus. Such transfer of ownership shall cause, as the case may be, the automatic cancellation of any surety or security concerning those assets or which those assets constitute.*

If the Minister decides not to use said assets, he shall have the right to require the Contractor to remove them at the latter's expense, it being understood that the abandonment operations shall be carried out by the Contractor in accordance with good international petroleum industry practice, and in accordance with the time schedule and conditions defined in the abandonment plan which will have been approved pursuant to Article 18.3.

The Contractor shall take all necessary measures in order to free the said assets from any charge and liability and settle any VAT that may become due under the provisions of the VAT legislation in force.

18.3 *No later than six (6) years prior to the anticipated date of abandonment of a Field or termination of, or relinquishment of part of, any Exploitation Area, the Contractor shall submit to the Minister for its approval the relevant abandonment plan including the estimated abandonment costs, pursuant to Regulation 16.*

The Minister may propose amendments or modifications to the above-mentioned abandonment plan, by notice to the Contractor including all the justifications deemed necessary, within ninety (90) days following receipt of said plan. In such a case, the Minister and the Contractor shall meet as soon as possible to review the requested amendments or modifications and establish by mutual agreement the plan in final form, in accordance with good international petroleum industry practice. The date of approval of the plan shall be the date of the above-mentioned mutual agreement.

In order to secure the implementation of the abandonment plan, the Contractor shall be required to establish a reserve fund, as from the approval of the abandonment plan. Such fund shall be deposited in an escrow account in a bank acceptable to the Minister. The total amount and the annual provisions shall be mutually agreed and included in the approved abandonment plan. Such annual provisions shall be deemed to be Hydrocarbons Costs and recoverable pursuant to Article 8.2. In the event that the actual abandonment costs exceed the total accumulated provisions, the remaining balance of the abandonment costs shall be borne exclusively by the Contractor.

---

47 This model can be found at: www.mcit.gov.cy/mcit/mcit.nsf/0/FE3EB5707ADA0E6EC225771B00 35B0D2/$file/PSC_Model_Production_Sharing_Contract.pdf

In the event that actual abandonment costs are lower than the total accumulated provisions, the remaining balance of the reserve fund shall be shared between the Republic and the Contractor pursuant to Article 8.3.

India: The following is taken from India's Model Production Sharing Contract of 2010:[48]

14.9 On expiry or termination of this Contract or relinquishment of part of the Contract Area, the Contractor shall:

(a) subject to Article 27, remove all equipment and installations from the relinquished area or former Contract Area in a manner agreed with the Government pursuant to an abandonment plan; and

(b) perform all necessary Site Restoration in accordance with modern oilfield and petroleum industry practices and take all other action necessary to prevent hazards to human life or to the property of others or the environment.

14.10 The Contractor shall prepare a proposal for the restoration of site including abandonment plan and requirement of funds for this and the annual contribution. This will be submitted along with the annual Budget for the consideration and approval of the Management Committee. The annual contribution shall be deposited by the Contractor in the Site Restoration fund which will be established, in accordance with the scheme notified by the Government. For this purpose, the annual contribution to Scheme shall be calculated based on unit of production method i.e. Reserve to Production Ratio.

14.11 Subject to Section 3.2 of Accounting Procedure, any Site Restoration fund scheme formulated by Government and subject to provisions of this Contract, any and all costs incurred by the Contractor pursuant to this Article shall be cost recoverable including but not limited to sinking funds established for abandonment and restoration of the Contract Area.

14.12 In this Article, a reference to Government includes the State Government.

14.13 Where the Contract Area is partly located in areas forming part of certain national parks, sanctuaries, mangroves, wetlands of national importance, biosphere reserves and other biologically sensitive areas passage through these areas shall generally not be permitted. However, if there is no passage, other than through these areas to reach a particular point beyond these areas, permission of the appropriate authorities shall be obtained.

(c) Elsewhere

Several other oil and gas regions might be examined in this context. But for the sake of brevity two more PSAs are presented – on for the Caribbean and another for the Timor Sea.

Timor Sea: The following extracts are taken from the Production Sharing Agreement for the Joint Development Area between Timor-Leste and Australia:[49]

48 This model can be found at: petroleum.nic.in/nelp9.htm
49 This model can be found at: www.ogel.org/legal-and-regulatory-detail.asp?key=1751

4.14 *Decommissioning*

(a) The Contractor shall submit to the Designated Authority, for its approval, pursuant to sub-paragraph 4.11(d)(v), a Decommissioning Plan for the Development Area and a schedule of provisions for the Decommissioning Costs Reserve.

(b) The Decommissioning Plan shall be revised and resubmitted to the Designated Authority for its approval at such times as are reasonable having regard to the likelihood that the Decommissioning Plan (including cost estimates thereunder) may need to be revised.

(c) The Contractor shall carry out the Decommissioning Plan substantially in accordance with its terms.

(d) Estimates of the monies required for the funding of the Decommissioning Plan shall be charged as Recoverable Costs beginning in the Calendar Year following the Calendar Year in which Commercial Production first occurs. The amount charged in each Calendar Year shall be calculated as follows:

(i) The total Decommissioning costs at the expected date of Decommissioning shall first be calculated;

(ii) There shall be deducted from such total Decommissioning costs the additions made to the Decommissioning Costs Reserve made, and taken as Recoverable Costs, in all previous Calendar Years together with interest on such Recoverable Costs calculated to the approved date of Decommissioning at the actual or forecast rate of Uplift (whichever is applicable);

(iii) The residual Decommissioning costs, resulting from the calculations under sub-paragraph 4.14(d)(i) and (ii), shall then be discounted to the Calendar Year in question at the forecast rate of Uplift for each Calendar Year remaining until the Calendar Year of Decommissioning;

(iv) The discounted total of residual Decommissioning costs shall then be divided by the total number of Calendar Years remaining prior to the Calendar Year of Decommissioning itself, including the Calendar Year in question;

(v) The resultant amount shall be the addition to the Decommissioning Costs Reserve for the Calendar Year in question;

(vi) It is the intention of this provision that the total accumulated provision allowed, including interest calculated to the Calendar Year of Decommissioning at the rate of Uplift, will equal the total Decommissioning costs;

(vii) If the amount in sub-paragraph 4.14(d)(v) is a negative amount, then such amount shall be treated as a reduction of Recoverable Costs for the Calendar Year in question.

4.15 *Decommissioning Security*

(a) Prior to Decommissioning, Security pursuant to the Decommissioning Security Agreement shall be provided by the Contractor in an amount equal to the sum of provisions made to the Decommissioning Costs Reserve, and taken as Recoverable Costs, in all previous years together with interest on such Recoverable Costs calculated to the end of the previous Calendar Year at the actual rate of Uplift.

(b) After Decommissioning commences, the Designated Authority shall at the end of each Calendar Year review the amount of Security required for the outstanding Decommissioning and shall take into consideration any Decommissioning costs that have already been incurred.

(c) Failure of the Contractor to provide Security and otherwise to fulfill its obligations under the Decommissioning Security Agreement, shall be a breach of this Agreement.

Trinidad and Tobago: The following articles have been taken from the Revised Deep Water Model Production Sharing Contract of 2010:[50]

37.1 Within sixty (60) days after cessation of production or the sooner relinquishment of some or all of the Contract Area, Contractor shall carry out to Minister's satisfaction an abandonment programme agreed with Minister for all installations and pipelines provided by Contractor under this Contract that Minister elects not to have delivered up to him in accordance with Article 24.1. With respect to the area being relinquished and/or facilities thereon, such abandonment programme shall comply with sound and current international Petroleum industry practices.

37.2 Contractor shall establish an interest bearing escrow account in the name of Minister at a financial institution approved by Minister to accumulate cash reserves for use as a contingency fund against possible pollution and eventual abandonment of wells and decommissioning of facilities related to Petroleum Operations in the Contract Area.

37.3 Contractor shall pay twenty five (25) cents in the currency of the United States of America per barrel of oil equivalent produced into said escrow account. All amounts paid into such escrow account by the Contractor shall be cost recoverable subject to the Accounting Procedure and the auditing provisions of the Contract.

37.4 Minister may at his sole discretion access funds from the escrow account in the event that Contractor fails to effect environmental clean-up during the term of this Contract, or properly abandon wells, or decommission facilities to the satisfaction of Minister upon termination of this Contract. Where Minister accesses the escrow account as aforementioned Contractor shall be required to pay into the account the sum used for said purposes within sixty (60) days.

37.5 Not later than five (5) years before the earlier of:

(a) the scheduled expiry of the term of the Contract; or

(b) Contractor's anticipated termination of Production of a Field or of operation of a pipeline; Contractor shall submit for Minister's approval a proposed abandonment programme and budget covering all such installations and pipelines provided by Contractor under this Contract.

37.6 Minister shall act without unreasonable delay in reaching a decision on Contractor's proposal under Article 37.5 and may approve or modify or impose conditions thereon. Before modifying or imposing conditions on the proposal, Minister shall notify Contractor of the proposed modification or conditions and give Contractor the opportunity to make written representations within sixty (60) days thereafter about

50 This model can be found at: www.energy.gov.tt/business_and_investing.php?mid=55

the proposed modifications or conditions. After taking into consideration such representations Minister and Contractor shall make their best efforts to mutually agree on the proposed modifications or conditions of the abandonment programme and budget. In the event that Minister and Contractor cannot mutually agree on the proposed abandonment programme and budget, either Party may by written notice to the other Party propose that the dispute be referred for determination in accordance with the provisions of Article 33. Until such time that the determination has been made, Contractor shall make payments into the escrow account referred to in Article 37.2, based on its proposed abandonment programme and budget. After the determination is made, Contractor shall adjust the payments to such escrow account to reflect the abandonment programme and budget so determined.

37.7 In the event that Contractor does not present a timely proposal to Minister under Article 37.5 Minister, after giving thirty (30) days notice to Contractor of his intention to do so, may prepare an abandonment programme and budget for the Contract Area if Contractor does not present a proposal by the end of the thirty (30) day period. When Minister has so prepared the abandonment programme and budget, it shall have the same effect as if it had been submitted by Contractor and approved by Minister.

37.8 The approved budget for carrying out the approved abandonment programme shall be provided for by monies paid into the escrow account established under Article 37.2. In addition to the payments made under Articles 37.3 and 37.4 Contractor shall also pay into the account a per unit of production assessment. If the approved budget is less than the value of the escrow account, Contractor shall pay the difference based on a per unit of production assessment. The assessment shall be calculated dividing the difference between the approved budget and the value in the escrow account by the estimated units of production to be produced and saved by Contractor between the date of Minister's approval and the anticipated date of the abandonment.

37.9 Upon determination of the Contract, where Contractor fulfils all obligations in respect of environmental remediation, abandonment of wells and decommissioning of facilities to the satisfaction of Minister, all existing funds in the escrow account shall remain with Minister. If the escrow amount is insufficient to complete the approved programme, Contractor shall pay all such additional required costs. In the event Minister elects to have the facility delivered up to him, the escrow account shall be transferred to Minister, who shall assume all responsibility for the facility, its abandonment and hold Contractor harmless against any liability with respect thereto accruing after the date of such transfer to Minister.

(d) Analyses of PSAs

It is important to stress that different countries take different approaches to PSAs. For example, Bangladesh and Tanzania provide detailed provision on the different stages of the decommissioning process. India and Cyprus, on the other hand, address the same issue through a relatively short and simple provision. However, all the models employ a reserve fund that the host government may use to cover decommissioning costs whenever necessary. Brazilian stakeholders who want to follow international practices are likely to expect there to be provision for a reserve fund in the PSA model. The extracts above provide several examples of how to construct a such a provision, from a simple reference to a complex calculation.

6. Conclusion

Although the decommissioning obligations in Brazil are clearly laid out, it is difficult to predict their efficacy. This is because the first licence round occurred in the late 1990s and most operations are still at a relatively early stage for assessing the risks and costs of decommissioning. Under the PSA regime, decommissioning is likely to be become an obligation of the contractor, but there is no clear guidance as to how the necessary finances will be secured and/or implemented.

It is therefore difficult to analyse the success of Brazil's decommissioning regulations at this stage. However, international experience shows the importance of securing decommissioning costs through reserve funds, as well as holding a wider debate among stakeholders on all stages of the decommissioning plan. Tax reliefs and liability for any installations that remain on the seabed may critically affect decommissioning activities.

Finance, part I

Luiz Claudio Campos
Ernst & Young Terco

1. Sector overview

1.1 Present scenario and data

(a) *Production*

According to the National Agency of Petroleum, Natural Gas and Biofuel (ANP), in 2010 Brazil produced approximately 750 million barrels of petroleum, including condensed and crude. This was an increase of 5.3% and placed Brazil 12th in the world ranking of petroleum producers. In 2011 Brazil produced approximately 635 million barrels of petroleum; the average daily production in 2011, as of October, was approximately 2.086 in thousand barrels per day, an increase of 5.4% compared to the same month in the previous year. The diagram below shows oil and gas production before and after the discovery of the pre-salt area.

Figure 1. Petrobras total production (thousand boe/d)

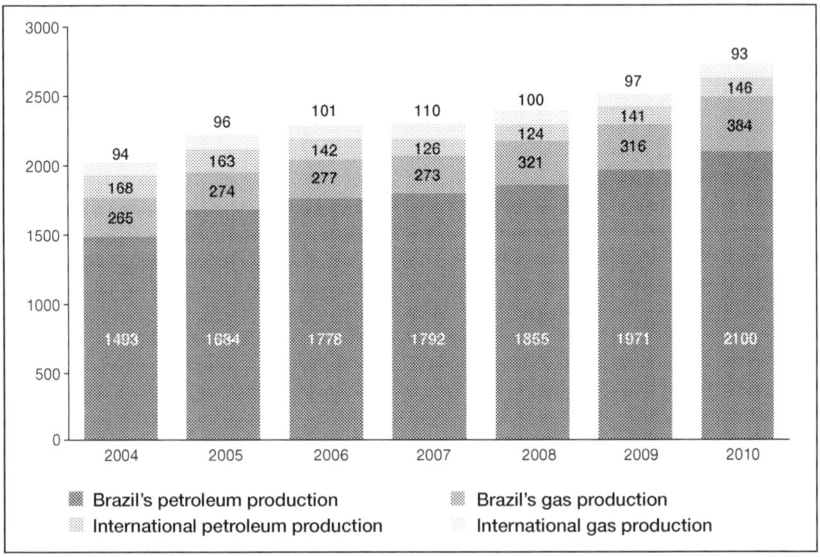

Source: Indústria Nacional: o Pré-Sal como propulsor da indústria Brasileira (Gabrielli, Petrobras President) – edited by author using publicly available information

A significant number of oil wells are located in the state of Rio de Janeiro; the state is responsible for 74.09% of the entire country's production and in 2010 produced 79.31% of the national total. The marine fields represent 684 billion barrels of oil or 91.2% of Brazil's total production for 2010. As of October 2011, the marine fields represented 579 billion barrels. Rio de Janeiro was responsible for 81.2% of the total marine production, with an average annual growth rate of 5.1% for the past 10 years. The reserve to production ratio (R/P) indicates the remaining lifespan of a natural resource and is expressed in terms of years. In Brazil this ratio was 19 years in 2010, representing an increase of 0.6% in 10 years.

With regard to natural gas, Brazil produced 19.8 million cubic metres (m^3) by October 2011, with an average growth of 5.6% per year over the past 10 years. About 1.4 billion m^3, or 7.2% of the total annual production, was burned and lost, while 3.4 billion m^3, or 17.22%, were reinjected. Once again Rio de Janeiro was the major producer, with 7.7 million m^3, representing 39% of the country's production. Espírito Santo was ranked second, with 3.6 million m^3, 18.33% of the national total.

Until October 2011, the marine fields were responsible for 14.9 million m^3, or 74.11%, of natural gas produced in Brazil. Onshore production accounted for 25.89% of the total in 2011 or 5 million m^3.

The R/P ratio for natural gas reserves increased from 15.9 to 18.4 years between 2001 and 2010, with a growth rate of 1.7% per year. In 2010 Brazil was ranked 35th of natural gas producers in the world.

(b) *Reserves*

At the end of 2010 Brazil had a reserve of 28.5 billion barrels, between proved reserves and those not formally recognised by the ANP; this was an increase of 34.7% compared to the previous year. Part of this rise was because of the inclusion of pre-salt reserves. The proven oil reserve was estimated to be 14.2 billion barrels, an increase of 10.7%, during the same period. This figure represents 50% of the total reserve (93.6% of it being offshore). Rio de Janeiro was responsible for 87.8% of this figure and for 82.2% of the total annual production.

Brazil was ranked 15th in the world in terms of major proved oil reserves in that year.

The country's proven reserves of natural gas increased by 15.2% to reach 423 billion m^3 in this year, which represents 51.3% of the total reserve (estimated to be 824.7 billion m^3). As will oil reserves, the majority of natural gas reserves – 85.7% – are offshore. Rio de Janeiro is also responsible for a significant proportion of these reserves, with 220.5 billion m^3 offshore or 52.1% of the national volume.

(c) *Foreign trade*

In 2010 Brazil imported 123.6 million barrels of oil. In 2011, until October, the amount of imported oil had been falling by an average of 2.3% per year, although there was an increase between 2004 and 2007. During the 10-year period beginning in 2000 the price of imported oil peaked at $141.08 in July 2008. In 2011 until October the average price of imported oil was 41.58% higher than in the previous year.

Brazil's most important oil supplier is Africa, which sold 80.7 million barrels of

Table 1. Summary

	2001	2002	2003	2004	2005	2006	2007	2008	2009	2010
Oil production (thousand bbl)										
Brazil	471,862	530,855	546,080	540,717	596,255	628,797	638,018	663,275	711,883	749,954
Onshore	77,170	78,952	79,738	78,632	74,962	70,841	69,893	66,337	65,465	78,952
Offshore	394,692	451,902	466,342	462,085	521,292	557,957	568,126	596,938	646,418	683,981
Natural gas production (million m³)										
Brazil	13,999	15,525	15,792	16,971	17,699	17,699	18,152	21,593	21,142	22,938
Onshore	5,828	6,169	6,709	7,766	7,375	6,657	6,283	6,273	6,045	6,024
Offshore	8,171	9,357	9,083	9,206	10,324	11,042	11,869	15,320	15,096	16,914
Burning and loss of natural gas (million m³)										
Brazil	2,621	2,136	1,626	1,469	2,474	1,852	1,948	2,187	3,424	2,418
Onshore	263	209	232	334	1,021	306	299	290	298	309
Offshore	2,358	1,927	1,394	1,135	1,453	1,545	1,649	1,897	3,126	2,109
Total oil reseves (million bbl)										
Brazil	12,993	13,076	13,494	14,768	16,132	18,175	20,380	20,855	21,134	28,467
Onshore	1,215	1,371	1,361	1,299	1,355	1,569	1,458	1,456	1,469	1,492
Offshore	11,778	11,705	12,133	13,469	14,778	16,606	18,922	19,398	19,666	26,975
Proven Reseves of Natural Gas (million m³)										
Brazil	222,731	530,855	546,080	540,717	596,255	628,797	638,018	663,275	711,883	423,003
Onshore	77,159	76,070	76,597	73,730	71,752	74,522	68,131	66,305	65,489	68,803
Offshore	145,572	168,477	168,743	252,354	234,643	273,381	296,860	297,931	301,606	354,200

Source: ANP Brazilian Statistic Annuary – compiled by author using publicly available information

oil to Brazil in 2010, 65.2% of all oil imported into the country. Other important trading partners include the Middle East (which accounts for 27.9% of imports) and Central and South America (1.6% of imports, 2 million barrels), with Argentina accounting for 0.2%.

Figure 2. The evolution of imported oil volume and oil expenditure imports: 2001-2011

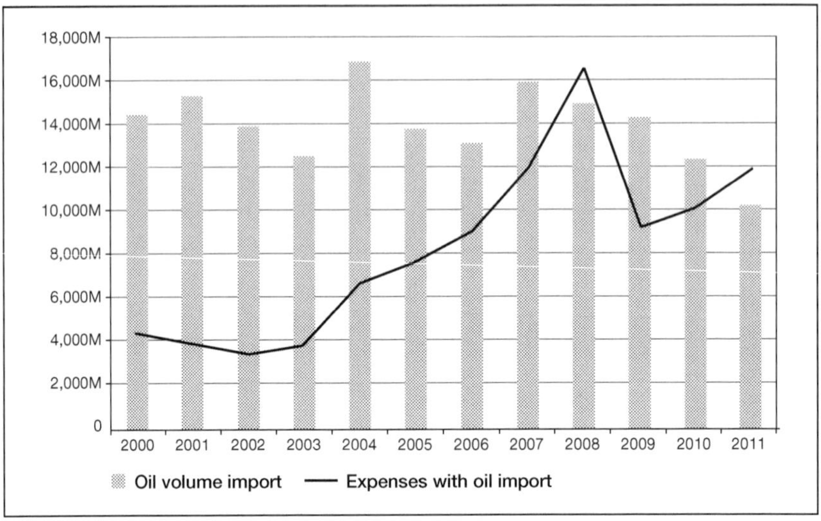

Source: ANP – compiled by author using publicly available information

Brazil's oil exports reached 230.5 million barrels in 2010. As of October 2011, the country had exported 180.7 million barrels. The main destination for these exports was China (25.5%), followed by the United States (23.8%) and Santa Lúcia in the Caribbean (17%).

Natural gas imports amounted to 12.6 million m^3 in the same year, 77.7% of which came from Bolivia. As of October 2011, imports of natural gas amounted to 8.8 million m^3 at a cost of approximately \$2.6 billion. Trinidad and Tobago, Nigeria and Qatar sold most of this liquefied natural gas in a gaseous state. The cost of imports amounted to \$3.1 billion, approximately \$249.50 per m^3 on average.

In 2011 until October, Brazil's imports of oil by-products reached approximately 25.1 million m^3. In the previous year, imports of by-products amounted to 27.4 million m^3, an average growth of 5.36% from 2000. The most significant import was diesel oil, approximately 7.6 million m^3, with the second most significant in terms of volume being Nafta, which accounted for nearly 6.2 million m^3.

Figure 3. Evolution of exported oil volume and revenue from oil exports: 2001-2011

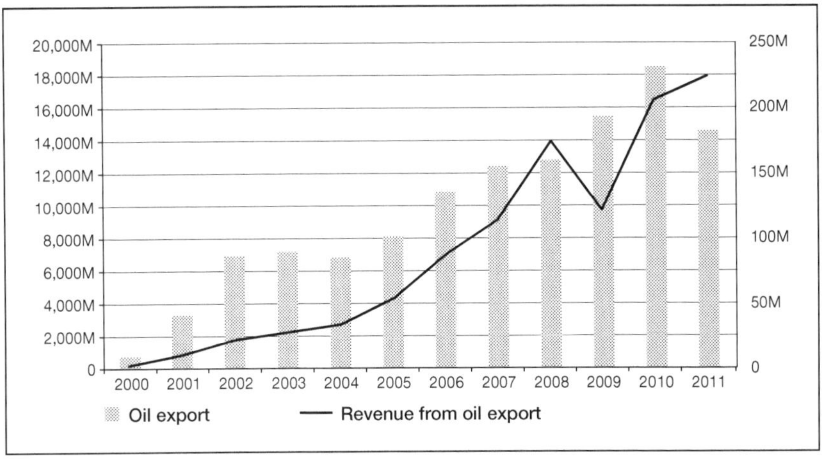

Source: ANP – compiled by author using publicly available information

In the last five years, as at October 2011, exports of oil by-products fell significantly, by almost 35%.

Brazil achieved a total positive result on foreign trade in oil and by-products. This bolstered the country's self-sufficiency in providing oil and by-products, which it achieved in 2006.

Figure 4. The evolution of exported and imported by-products volume and costs, and revenues from oil exports: 2001-2011

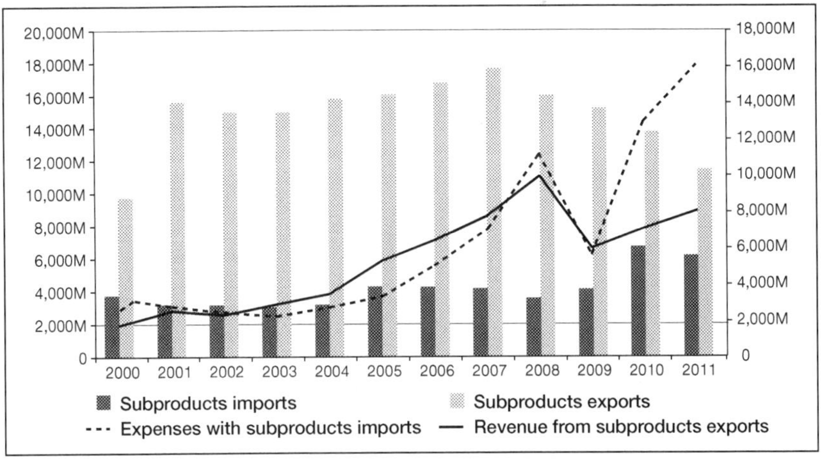

Source: ANP – compiled by author using publicly available information

(d) Investments

According to ANP, between 2001 and 2010 investments by oil and natural gas companies in research and development (R&D) exceeded R5.1 billion, putting Brazil's capital goods and oil supplies industry in a unique position. These investments have made a significant contribution to the renaissance of Brazilian engineering, as can be seen in universities around the country. As a result, the expectations for the next decade in both Brazil and the oil industry are very high.

Law 9,478/1997 is designed to stimulate research and the adoption of new technologies in the exploration, production, transportation and refining of oil. The law determines that ANP must encourage the adoption of those practices.

In order to meet these obligations, in 1998 ANP introduced a clause to the Concession Agreements for Exploration, Development and Production of Oil and Natural Gas. This states that if any special participation is due to a field in any calendar quarter, the dealer must invest an amount equivalent to 1% of gross production in that field in R&D. The law establishes that at least half of this amount should be invested in institutions accredited by the ANP.

According to Elias Ramos de Souza, superintendent of planning and research at ANP, this clause has caused investments to rise to R700 million by 2010. In the last 13 years, total growth was R5 billion. However, this is still small compared to the United States, because Brazil does not yet have the broad support of private companies.

In 2010 1% investments by Petrobras, Shell, Repsol, Manati, Brasoil Manati and Rio das Contas amounted to R743.7 million, almost 16.4% higher than in 2009. Petrobras was responsible for 98.9% of the total invested, while the value of investments grew to R5.1 billion during the period from 2001 to 2010.

The government is a potential partner for companies that intend to invest in R&D in order to promote innovation. This is underlined by the fact that R&D investments are tax deductible and also by the reduced rates that apply to the import of materials required for research. These actions demonstrate that despite being a developing country, Brazil is looking for appropriate ways to encourage and manage technology.

As well as government incentives to promote R&D, there is also a sector fund for oil and natural gas known as CT-PETRO. The main goal of this fund is to:

- encourage innovation in the production chain for oil and gas;
- promote training and qualifications for human resources; and
- develop partner projects between companies and universities.
- CT-PETRO is funded by 25% of the royalties that exceed 5% of oil and natural gas production.

1.2 Pre-salt

The pre-salt layer is a zone below the sea in Brazil that starts in the state of Espirito Santo and continues for 800 kilometres (km), ending in Santa Catarina. It encompasses three sedimentary basins: Espirito Santo, Campos and Santos.

Reserves of oil have been found over 7,000m deep under a salt layer, which, according to geologists, helps to maintain the quality of the petroleum.

Many oil fields and wells have been identified on the pre-salt layer, including

Tupi, with estimated reserves of between 5 and 8 billion barrels, which is considered one of the greatest discoveries of the last seven years. Other fields include Guara, Bem-Te-Vi, Carioca, Iara and Jupiter.

The ANP's forecast indicates that the pre-salt layer may hold reserves of up to 100 billion barrels of oil equivalent (boe). This would put Brazil sixth in the world in terms of oil reserves, behind Saudi Arabia, Iran, Iraq, Kuwait and United Arab Emirates.

The Pre-salt Area Law was approved in 2010, but the model clauses are yet to be finalised. Therefore, it has been decided that the next concession auctions for oil exploration will only be for areas located on land or in shallow water only. The entire region around the pre-salt will not be auctioned until new rules for petroleum exploration and production have been finalised. Those rules are currently being discussed at the federal level and will become part of the new regulatory framework for Brazilian oil. Also ongoing is a process of review and improvement for regulatory frameworks. The recent discoveries in the ultra-deep pre-salt area more than justify the decision to re-examine the current regime.

The current framework was designed for a scenario where oil production was relatively low, the price of a barrel being around $20/bbl, and the risk of exploitation was very high. Although the union has maintained a monopoly on prospecting and mining deposits, it has established concessions as a way of leasing out these activities; under this regime ownership of the oil and gas extracted is transferred to the dealer. Only a portion of the resulting income is paid to the grantor as financial compensation (eg, for signing bonuses, royalties and special participation), which depends on the volume of production.

The discovery of the pre-salt reserves has changed the baseline of oil reserves in Brazil, reducing the risk of exploration at a time that the international price of oil was relatively high (around $60/bbl), which compensates for the costs of exploration and production in ultra-deep water, thus ensuring profitability. Coupled with this is the projection that the international price of oil will rise by 43.1% by 2020 according to the study *Sustainable Brazil – Prospects of Oil, Ethanol and Natural Gas* prepared by Ernst & Young Terco in partnership with the Getulio Vargas Foundation.

Once the volumes are confirmed, the pre-salt discoveries will require the reorientation of energy policy guidelines in Brazil. This is so as to ensure the supply of energy necessary to the country's economic development and general wellbeing. A country's energy policies must not only respond to the critical issues, but also help to shape its future.

Recent discoveries and the prospect of exploitation in the pre-salt area have already placed Brazil in a remarkable position on the world stage. According to the government, the pre-salt reserves already granted in Tupi, Iara and Parque das Baleias have already added 23.5 billion boe to Brazil's reserve levels.

Due to the significant increase in international oil prices, the oil industry has contributed significantly to the budgets of states and municipals that receive royalties from oil. This in turn is likely to have a positive knock-on effect on tax revenues, providing an exceptional opportunity for the government to develop structural programmes in order to supply national requirements for sanitation, health, education and infrastructure.

2. Financing upstream projects

As described in the preceding chapters, the upstream portion feeds the entire oil supply chain – a fact that highlights its importance to the development of the sector in a country with significant reserves of hydrocarbons, such as Brazil. Investment in exploration and production, therefore, is fundamental.

Booz & Company carried out a study of Brazilian goods and services related to oil exploration and production offshore and estimated a domestic demand of $400 billion between 2010 and 2020. Petrobras predicts that it will invest $127.5 billion in the upstream stage, which represents 57% of the company's total investment. Some foreign corporations intend to invest a total of $42 billion over the next 10 years.

Combining this data with the analysis in the previous section, it becomes clear that there are many opportunities in the oil and gas sector. In addition, the size of the investments is unlike anything the industry has seen before. Therefore, there is a strong need for sources of capital to finance such growth. In addition, these sources ought to be adapted to the specifics of the industry, in terms of both project feasibility and risk profile.

The funding mechanisms for the energy and petroleum field available in the local market can be distinguished by whether the funds are based on equity or debt emission. The first group involves initial public offerings (IPOs) and private equity funds, while loans (both long and short term) and project finance are examples of the second.

2.1 Equity

(a) *Private equity*

Banks and private equity funds play an important role in the development of the oil and gas sector. The main objective of such funds is to offer financial and technical support so that companies can become even more competitive.

In the first semester of 2011, investments from these funds represented over 40% of M&A transactions. In 2010, there were 80 transactions by 50 different management companies, with the total invested value amounting to $6 billion. Leonardo Ribeiro, partner ar Ocroma Alternative Investments, confirms that this is the first time since 2004 that the amount invested in private equity exceeded the amount raised through IPOs.

The purpose of private equity funds directed at the oil and gas sector is to leverage companies with the potential for growth and increased competitiveness. Such funds will achieve higher maturing grades only when they receive investments and guidance from experts.

Funds help to buy stakes in companies, whether through direct investment – in a closed capital firm – or buy-outs of open ones, closing the capital. Resources are raised from institutional and private investors. Depending on the strategy adopted, the funds may take an active role in managing the company. Such funds are estimated to provide return on investment within seven years.

Over the years, the amount of investment made by these funds has been rising significantly, especially in the United States. In Brazil, on the other hand, this mechanism is still not common. Two examples of private equity focused on the oil and gas chain are laid out in the following table.

Table 2. Examples of oil and gas funds

	Óleo e Gás FIP	**Fundo Brascan de Pretróleo Gás e Energia**
Manager	BancoModal	BancoBrascan
Equity	R500 million	R100 million
Constitution	2010	2002
Shareholders	Bndespar, Petros, Funcef Fundação Banrisul among others	Bndespar, Petros, Funcef, Banco Brascan, Fundação Atlânticom GP Investimentos, Fapes
Investments	Enesca Engenharia investimentos, R90 million	Brasoildo Brasil Exploração Petrolifera S/A stocks Jaguari Energética S/A convertible debentures

Source: Compiled by author using publicly available information

Other funds that are currently in the process of structuring and funding include:

- Banco Santander do Brasil S/A and Mare Investimentos, which are setting up two private equity funds to invest in the oil and gas sector. Both funds will initially manage assets of R2 billion. One fund is directed at national investors and the other at foreign investors. The two funds will invest in the same projects and develop projects of their own; and
- Plural Capital/GPS/Cultinvest, which aims to raise over R4 billion to invest in Petrobras suppliers.

Despite being developed by private companies, this new method of investment is being encouraged by BNDES (the National Bank for Economic and Social Development), which has created a department specifically to handle chain suppliers of oil and gas. One example was the investment of R20 million through Bndespar, in a fund managed by Banco Modal. The deal involved the application of resources at Enesa, which intends to increase its participation in the sector; it currently accounts for 15% of company revenues.

The oil arm of Eike Batista's group's (EBX), OGX, first capital injection occurred through private investors. In November 2007 the company raised $1.3 billion in a private equity placement, generating capital to purchase concession rights in the ninth bidding round held by the ANP. In this round, OGX acquired concession rights to 21 exploratory blocks in the Campos, Santos, Espírito Santo and Parnaíba basins, comprising a total area of 6,400km^2.

The year after this first injection, the company proceeded with its IPO. Further information about this mechanism is presented below.

The raising of funds in the oil and gas industry results from increased demand. Brazil has around 1 million companies that supply pieces of equipment, parts and services. Most of these are looking to participate in the huge volume of orders being demanded by the industry.

(b) *IPOs*

The structure of an IPO or stock market launch consists of opening the capital of the firm by releasing shares on the stock exchange. IPOs can be used by both small and large companies to raise expansion capital and to trade publicly. Such operations increase a company's liquidity and improve its debt/equity ratio, since an IPO is not a debt emission. Thus, the total amount of a company's fixed costs or interests is reduced. Another advantage of this type of funding is that it allows those managing the company to remain flexible.

One example of the process is OGX, which launched its IPO back in 2008. At the time, the offer was the biggest on the Brazilian market, amounting to R6.7 billion – surpassed only by the IPOs of Santander Brasil and Cielo, which took place in 2009 and were worth R14.1 billion and R8.4 billion, respectively. Analysts estimate that the demand for shares in OGX was 10 times higher than supply; but not all IPOs are this successful.

In 2010 another one of EBX's subsidiaries, the chartering and shipbuilding company OSX, listed its shares on BM&FBovespa. The company expected to raise almost R10 billion, but could reach only R2.8 billion.

The disadvantage of IPOs is that the result cannot be predicted, meaning that there is a risk that the required funding will not be raised. Besides that, there is a lot of necessary bureaucracy, as well as steep implementation costs. The procedure also requires the full and public dissemination of information, which may be useful to competitors, suppliers and customers.

Recently, two other companies in the sector have launched IPOs in Brazil. HRT Participações em Petróleo SA – an independent oil and natural gas exploration and production holding company, formed by a group of senior geoscientists and engineers who previously held key positions at Petrobras and ANP – generated R2.5 billion with its IPO in October 2010. Even though the demand for shares was about three times higher than the supply, as occurred in the OGX offer, the price was fixed at the centre of the interval defined by the company. The resources raised will be allocated to the exploration, development and infrastructure programme in the Solimões and Namíbia basins.

At the beginning of 2011 Queiroz Galvão Exploração e Produção, part of the Queiroz Galvão Group, also joined the listed companies group with a R1.5 billion IPO. After the book building the stock price was set below the range initially offered.

2.2 Debt

(a) *Short-term loans*

Short-term debt can help to provide companies with working capital. The most common way of acquiring this kind of debt is by using funding from commercial banks, due to the low levels of bureaucracy needed. However, despite being an easy way to acquire funds, this can involve high interest rates.

Other classic examples of short-term funding are receivable discounts in commercial banks and asset-backed securities (ABS).

Receivable discounts: This is an advance resources operation designed to anticipate cash flow and assure working capital. It allows the beneficiary to obtain cash for the services it provides or the products it sells, guaranteeing the immediate receipt of recourses that would otherwise be available only in the future.

The bank discount operation is unique. Usually, interest applies to the present value in bank operations. However, in discount operations, the rate applies to the future value or the face amount. The discount rate is proportional to the period of time left until the product matures.

This product offers two options,

- where the service has been provided or the product delivered and the charge has been made by trade note; and
- when the service has not yet been provided or the product delivered. In that case, a future contract is made and the sales payment is received in an agreed period. Then an advanced payment of the credit sale is made, and there is less concern about controlling the bond's maturity.

ABS: This is a fund backed by credit rights. When a company needs to raise capital, it has the option of selling its credit rights to these kinds of funds, using a discount rate applied by the market. The great advantage is that interest rates are lower than those of traditional bank loans. This is because once the fund receives the credit right, the risk of the operation is transferred to the other firm, which then has to honour the credit contract. However, the performance is also lower.

As this transaction is not a loan, it does not affect the company's balance sheet. There are some others characteristics, such as that the firm has the right to request different ABSs for each contract, which is given as a guarantee. There are no charges in this kind of transaction and it has no incidence of IOF (tax on financial operations).

Prominp (Oil and Natural Gas Industry Mobilisation Programme) released the Prominp Receivable in 2004 to provide innovative solutions to financing working capital from oil and natural gas suppliers through ABS. The programme offers attractive conditions for the companies, which helps to raise competitiveness between national firms, especially small and medium-sized firms.

Nowadays, there are a lot of credit rights funds in the Brazilian market and these are frequently used to raise resources. A few examples of ABS in Brazil are given in the table below.

Table 3. ABS

ABS		
Manager	**Fund name**	**Net equity (R million)**
Rio de Janeiro Investimentos	FIDC AGN Fornecedores Petrobras	26.3
BI Invest	FIDC BI Invest Fornecedores Petrobras	19.6
BTG Pactual	FIDC Fornecedores Petrobras – Industrial e Serviços	15.6
Petra e Red Factor	FIDC Red Fornecedores Petrobras	0.5
Plural Capital	FIDC Plural Capital Fornecedores Petrobras	33.9
Silverado	FIDC Multisetorial Silverado – Fornecedores do Sistema Petrobras	116.2
Total	**6 Funds**	**212.1**

Source: Compiled by author using publicly available information

The FIDC (Funds for Investments in Credit Rights) BI Invest Fornecedores Petrobras is said to be the most efficient advance resource instrument to fulfil the needs of Petrobras Providers' short-term cash flow. The fund offers an advance of 75% of the contract.

Progress Programme – Petrobras: The Petrobras Progress Programme was launched in September 2010 in order to help finance Petrobras' supply chain. The programme intends to achieve 34,000 direct suppliers and 216,000 indirect suppliers from the chain and mitigate the risks of implementing projects in the chain. It was also designed to provide a R3 billion resource.

One of the most interesting features of this programme is that the supplier can advance up to 50% of non-performing receivables of the contract with Petrobras. The remaining 50% are maintained to ensure credit to subcontractor suppliers. This allows the growth and development of the companies that form the Petrobras supply chain.

The figure below explains the process.

Figure 5. The financing process of the Progress Programme

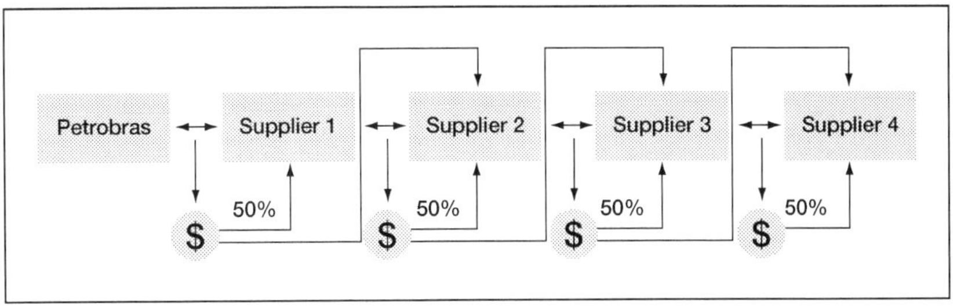

Source: Prominp – edited by author using publicly available information

(b) ***Long-term loans***

Such loans are characterised mainly by funding from CAPEX and are usually available through public institutions for development, such as BNDES, the Federal Savings Bank, the Merchant Marine Fund and multilateral agencies, such as the Inter-American Development Bank and the International Finance Corporation.

This type of financing offers low costs and there are oriented lines for specific purposes, including for the oil and gas sector.

BNDES Programme – oil and gas: This is a support programme for the oil and gas chain from BNDES designed for companies established in Brazil (whether domestic or foreign controlled) under Brazilian law. It was set up with the following objectives:

- to contribute to the development of competitiveness and sustainability in the Brazilian oil and gas industry;
- to provide long-term financing to the sector, thus increasing its capacity to invest in projects up, mid and downstream;
- to stimulate domestic industry on projects from the oil sector;
- to introduce global competitiveness to Brazil; and
- to improve the supply chain of goods and services, in particular by:
    - focusing on innovation and basic engineering;
    - progressively increasing participation by higher value-added services; and
    - paying special attention to production and technology problems that have already been identified.

The programme focuses on micro, small and medium-sized companies with revenues of up to R90 million. It provides them with the flexibility to obtain credit and allows them greater exposure to credit risk (guaranteed contracts) at a reduced cost.

Case – Atlântico Sul SA Shipyard: The project involved the construction of a shipyard in the port and industrial complex of Suape in Pernambuco state. It had total funding of R513.4 million, which covered 77% of the total investment needed of R667.4 million.

The financing was structured with funds from the Merchant Marine Fund, with an interest rate of TJLP (interest long-term rate – currently 6% per annum) plus 3.6% per annum, with a maturity of 20 years.

Table 4. Fees for the BNDES Programme

BNDES Program – Oil & Gas						
Type of investment	Implementation, expansion and modernisation	Strengthening the chain	Turning to the production of goods and services	INNOVATION		
				Innovative capital	Production	Technological
Financial cost	TJLP*			5% PSI	7% PSI	4% PSI
BNDES fees	0.5% / 0.9% / 1.3%	0.9% to 1.3%	2.0% to 2.5%			
Rate of Credit Risk	0.46% up to 2.54%					
Total	6.96% to 9.84%	7.36% to .84%	8.46% to 11.04%	PSI**: 4.0% up to 7.0% fixed Without PSI: 4.5% up to 10.47%		
Amortisation	Up to 10 years	Up to 10 years	Up to 5 years	Up to 8 years	Up to 8 ears	Up to 10 years
Maximum participation	80% to 90%	80% to 90%	80% to 90%	Up to 90%	Up to 90%	Up to 90%

*Interest long term rate **Conditions valid until December 31 2012

Source: BNDES – compiled by author using publicly available information

The particular financing structure meant that there was no need for personal guarantees from the drivers of the project after its completion, which it is atypical of project finance configurations.

(c) ***Project finance***

Under this financing method, future cash-flow generation is the main source of loan repayment; the need to adjust the loan terms for each deal results in a high degree of customisation. Projects with solid expectations of future cash-flow generation, combined with well-designed contracts and collateral structure, are key to a successful deal.

An accurate evaluation of the management and financing methods makes customisation and deal structuring possible, but it also implies that there may be interference from creditors in the borrower's corporate governance, which would reduce the management's flexibility. This is a trade-off that needs to be evaluated by investors.

Another key feature of this financing method is its unique structure. Project finance deals require a wide range of financial, legal, and commercial instruments for risk mitigation, as well as a strict control on financial flows, including the creation of escrow accounts to cover the liabilities and operational flows.

One clear implication of the features of this type of financing is that it is not suitable everywhere. Project finance is best suited to financing industrial and infrastructure projects because of the predictable nature of their revenue stream – which results in lower risks to creditors – and large-scale investment, requiring a higher level of leverage and participation from a higher number of partners, sponsors and lenders.

This methodology keeps the same criteria of project viability analysis as a traditional loan. However, the operation structure is based on the projected cash flow rather than the balance sheets of the project sponsors. Project finance deals are characterised by long-term debt. This method has a high cost structure, but a low cost financing; it also involves the need to create a special purpose entity (SPE).

Generally, an SPE is created for each project, thereby separating other assets owned by a project sponsor from the effects of failure. The assets, contracts and cash flow are isolated from the sponsor's economic group. It also provides an acceptable risk allocation between the involved agents, making the business acceptable for creditors and debtors.

A project may be subject to a high number of risks, such as economic, environmental or political. Usually, the sponsors assume the risk of completion in conjunction with the lenders. It means that lenders regularly require a guarantee from sponsors until the enterprise's conclusion related to the following aspects:

- overruns or budget deviations for more money;
- measures of the rate of production;
- product specifications;
- performance according to the goals set in the viability study; and
- commitment to the schedule.

There are other risks that are usually mitigated or assumed by the lenders, such as:

- risks related to the product's price – if the price falls, there will be insufficient cash generated;
- risks related to a rise in costs, usually due to an increase in the price of raw materials;
- market risks, which can be partially or totally eliminated by so-called 'off-taker agreements', containing take or pay clauses with fluctuating or fixed prices; and
- environmental risks, although these can be mitigated by local government guarantees related to the enterprise's acceptance. If the project's end is intended for export, environmental guarantees can be made by international organisations.

All these risks are higher in developing countries, such as Brazil, and emerging markets. Identifying and allocating those risks is an important element of project finance; in certain projects, the inherent risks may prove unacceptable to the sponsors and financial institutions.

Project finance offers three basic types of guarantee system: full recourse, limited recourse and non-recourse. The first model requires a traditional guarantee system as the risks are considered inherent to the enterprise. It also requires real guarantees beyond the personal commitment of the controllers. The non-recourse and limited recourse models are commonly used for contracts for the purchase of raw materials and long-term selling contracts (off-take). In the non-recourse system the assurances given to lenders are usually the assets of the project itself, as well as the certainty of the expected cash flow, the quality of the contracts and the collateral structure (eg, waterfall mechanisms). In case of failure the lender has no alternative to recover the funding other than through revenue obtained by the project.

Limited recourse is an intermediate system between the full and the non-recourse model. To obtain this type of financing, the sponsor offers stocks, assets and contracts as guarantees. Added to that, the SPE should guarantee the cash flow and comply with the clauses of the contract signed between lender and borrower. The percentage amount that corresponds to the guarantee is usually 120% of the financing value, although in some projects it may be as high as 400%.

Project finance has some facilities not found in traditional financing, including that:

- projects are self-financing and self-paying;
- fewer resources are needed from stakeholders;
- there is greater transparency about project results; and
- there are liquidity guarantees for lenders.

All these factors suggest that project finance models may become even more popular in the future.

Case – ODN I and ODN II drill ships, Odebrecht Oil & Gas: Odebrecht closed a $1.05 billion debt facility for two drill ships, composed of a $890 million debt facility and $160 million export credit agency (ECA) package. This deal will cover 77% of the total investment of $1.3 billion. The loan term will also be used to repay the bridge loan and to support payments for two enhanced capability port contracts.

The financing was structured by international commercial banks and the ECA, with an interest rate of the London interbank offered rate (LIBOR) plus 2.55% per year for the remaining construction period and first two years of operation, rising to LIBOR plus 2.8% per year for the final 10, with a maturity of 12 years and a six-month grace period. Fees on the deal are between 1.75% and 2% per year.

3. Conclusion

In the last few years, the oil and gas sector has become increasingly important to the Brazilian economy. The sector investments represent over 10% of all gross fixed capital formation and look set to reach 15% by 2014.

The oil and gas industry is already strongly tied to foreign markets and the new pre-salt discoveries mean that investments are likely to increase from the middle of the next decade. This in turn will grow exploration and production, the upstream stage, helping to make the sector independent of the rest of the economy. Its growth represents an important support for increasing investment in Brazil and the country's gross domestic product.

The next few years are likely to see an additional demand for qualified human resources and capital goods. Therefore, polices are being developed to help identify points that are limiting the capacity of production. These are essential to help Brazil to make the most of the long investment cycle due to happen in the next decade.

The financial mechanisms discussed in this chapter are extremely important for developing the upstream stage. The historical process of funding for most national companies was based on debt, both short and long term. It is not a cultural norm for Brazilian businesses to capture resources through equity. This is a recent development for the country's economy, including the oil and gas sector.

Recently, Brazil has witnessed the launch of many IPOs from national companies, including oil companies, to raise capital on Bovespa, the Brazilian stock exchange, especially between 2006 and 2010. However, this process has slowed due to the world economic crises. The majority of the projects related to the oil sector have been financed by debt through BNDES programmes.

Brazil is still developing its oil and gas sector. However, the recent opening process and the discovery of the pre-salt layer have placed the country in a leading position in the market. Examples of financing programmes, other than historical government credit lines, are becoming more frequent, supporting the challenges to come in this sector.

Finance, part II

Andrew Duncan
Bank of America Merrill Lynch

---

1. Introduction

Reserve-based lending (RBL), in various forms, has been a consistent feature of oil and gas financing for over 30 years and examples of its use can now be found in every continent around the world. From its initial use in funding the growth of onshore producers in Texas, RBL later played a key role in promoting the development of the UK North Sea as a major hydrocarbon-producing province. More recently, RBL has been applied to assets across West Africa, Asia and Latin America. There are some notable differences (positive and negative) between the RBL structures used in North America and those used around the rest of the world (international RBL). However, the underlying constructs and the requirements from lenders are similar. This chapter will provide background on the structure of international RBL, its practical application in the upstream market in Brazil and some of the reasons why it is the financing structure of choice for many exploration and production companies. It will also provide guidance on the steps a potential borrower might take in order to increase its chances of a successful financing.

2. RBL – the essentials

2.1 The proposition

The basic premise of RBL is that lenders provide leverage, through loans or letters of credit, to borrowers relative to the value contained within the borrower's reserves. Significantly, RBL lenders look to the cash generated from the production and sale of those reserves as the primary source of repayment. Lenders therefore must be able to satisfy themselves that:

- the borrower is fully entitled to those reserves;
- the reserves can be produced in the forecast timeframe;
- the operator has the technical capability to produce the reserves;
- the reserves are capable of reaching a market and being sold (ie, not stranded); and
- the fiscal and regulatory environment is known and acceptable.

Potential lenders will undertake considerable legal, technical and commercial due diligence in order to establish that these criteria are met for each asset intended for leverage. An RBL can be supported by one or multiple assets, which can be located in one or several countries. A key benefit of the RBL structure is that a portfolio of assets of differing maturity and spread across a variety of countries/regions can be aggregated together in terms of their net financeable value. This gives rise to significant advantages to the borrower in terms of diversification, through financing simplification and lower borrowing costs.

2.2 The product

An RBL is commonly structured as a senior secured amortising revolving credit facility, which is provided through funding commitments from one or more lender. Lenders are traditionally banks, but other financial institutions (eg, hedge funds and financing subsidiaries of major corporations) have been known to participate in RBL from time to time. The loans generally rank senior to all other financial indebtedness of the borrower and take shares pledges and (where permitted under law) security over licences, insurance proceeds, assets and proceeds accounts. A bespoke facility agreement documents the relationship between the borrower and the lenders, defining the procedures and responsibilities for drawdown, interest payment, principal repayment, representations and warranties, events of default and numerous other matters. An RBL is a complex structured financing that can take considerable time to structure, negotiate and document; typically it would take a first-time borrower three to six months to complete a financing.

2.3 The model

RBL utilises two key financial covenants to regulate the amount of leverage a borrower can achieve (the available amount):

- the field life cover ratio (FLCR); and
- the loan life cover ratio (LLCR)

In order to calculate the available amount, the borrower and lender will populate a cash-flow model, which will contain asset-specific technical assumptions, such as forecast production rates, operating cost estimates and capital expenditure programmes (including any relevant abandonment costs), as well as a number of economic assumptions, such as commodity prices, interest rates, inflation and foreign exchange forecasts. Any tax or royalties payable by the borrower would also be included at this point, either on an asset-specific basis or ring fenced to a region as appropriate. Also, the applicable commodity price may differ between assets, depending on whether the production is sold at a fixed price or at a price relative to a market benchmark (eg, Brent or WTI). RBL applies equally to licence concession assets and to assets owned through a production-sharing contract. The key output is the resulting stream of forecast-free net cash flows for the life of the assets, which the borrower is entitled to and that the lenders are comfortable as being valid as a primary source of debt repayment.

The above calculated cash-flow stream is then discounted to give a net present value (NPV) (often at the cost of debt) and divided by the FLCR, giving the FLCR-derived available amount. The FLCR is therefore equivalent to a 'loan to value' measure, which ensures that borrowers never leverage their assets for more than a fixed percentage of their notional value. A commonly used value for an FLCR for a portfolio of producing assets would be 1.5 times. This means that borrowers would be effectively able to borrow up to 66.7% of the aggregate modelled value of their assets.

The LLCR-derived available amount is calculated using the NPV of the cash flows during the life of the debt facility only. So this effectively gives a measure of leverage relative to the cash flows that are available to repay the loan principal during the duration of the loan. No consideration is given to any value remaining in the assets after the debt has matured. It is therefore entirely normal for an RBL to amortise fully over the life of the loan, and for the absence of refinancing risk to be seen as a real risk mitigant for these kinds of facilities. RBL lenders use a construct called the 'reserve tail', which reduces their exposure to late-life assets (ie, assets that are nearing the end of their economic producing life) where there is a perceived increase in production risk. The final maturity date for a facility can be brought forward to the date that the reserve tail is breached, usually 25% of the original reserves remaining. In certain circumstances, this can reduce the facility tenor and correspondingly lower the LLCR-derived available amount.

The actual available amount is then usually the lesser of the FLCR and LLCR-derived available amounts and the facility amount (subject to amortisation). The model is therefore important in that it sets the initial available amount that a borrower can achieve at the beginning of a loan, but, just as importantly, it is regularly updated (generally semi-annually) to reset the available amount and in latter years drive repayment of the principal.

The model is therefore a very transparent and dynamic medium for assessing the leveragability of assets and is notably forward-looking. This approach clearly differentiates RBL from other forms of corporate borrowing, in that the majority of corporate debt facilities tend to have backward-looking balance sheet and profit and loss-based financial covenants (eg, net debt/EBITDA or minimum net worth).

2.4 The assumptions

Figure 1. The assumptions

Technical assumptions	**Economic assumptions**
Production profile	Commodity prices
Operating costs	Foreign exchange rates
Capital expenditure	Interest rates
G&A costs	Inflation
Royalites	Taxes
Asset specific	*Typically generic*

Any model is only as good as the assumptions contained within it. As mentioned previously, there are two classifications of assumptions: technical and economic.

The technical assumptions are provided by the borrower to the lenders, who assess their suitability and completeness for inclusion in the model. It is essential that the technical assumptions (production profile, operating costs and capital expenditure) have been previously reviewed and audited by a recognised third-party technical consultant. It is common for financial institutions that regularly participate in the RBL market to employ their own in-house technical expertise, often referred to as the 'bank engineer', although many choose to hire a third-party consultant on an ad hoc basis. The bank engineer's review is critical to the due diligence process as the technical assumptions provide the foundations for every RBL and often drive any required borrower-specific structuring discussions.

The economic assumptions (ie, commodity price, foreign exchange rates, interest rates and inflation) are proposed by the lenders and are normally consistent with other RBL facilities in the market. Particular mention should be made of the commodity price assumptions. In instances where hydrocarbons are sold to a creditworthy counterparty under a long-term off-take agreement, banks will generally honour in full the pricing mechanism reflected in this agreement. Commodity price assumptions for hydrocarbons that are sold into an established spot market (eg, Brent Crude or Henry Hub) are referred to as the 'price deck'. More detail is given below with regard to the risk mitigation of commodity price. However, in summary the price deck is essentially a view on future commodity prices that is generally acceptable to lenders as being appropriate for lending senior debt. It is important to remember that RBL lenders are receiving a fixed return or margin on their loans, with no upside. A view of future commodity prices that is commensurate with equity risk and its potential upside is likely to be much more optimistic than that considered appropriate for lending. Price decks may vary slightly from bank to bank, but as many of the larger RBL facilities will require syndication among a number of lenders, it is vital for a consensus view to be taken that is acceptable to all.

2.4 The asset portfolio spectrum

As mentioned previously, RBL is a particularly flexible product for potential borrowers. It can be structured to provide finance for assets under development, and can also provide funds for the acquisition of further oil and gas assets or just release equity capital locked in existing producing assets that can be redeployed elsewhere in the business. This means that a wide spectrum of asset portfolios can be considered, with a single development asset at one end and a diverse portfolio of producing assets at the other. The structure and pricing of an RBL will tend to reflect where in this spectrum the asset portfolio under consideration is. Single development asset financings will contain strict covenants around the use of funds, with onerous information undertakings reporting on development progress and tight restrictions on distributions. Whereas borrowers that have the benefit of an established producing portfolio can enjoy more freedom around how they use their cash and lighter touch covenants.

Figure 2. The asset portfolio spectrum

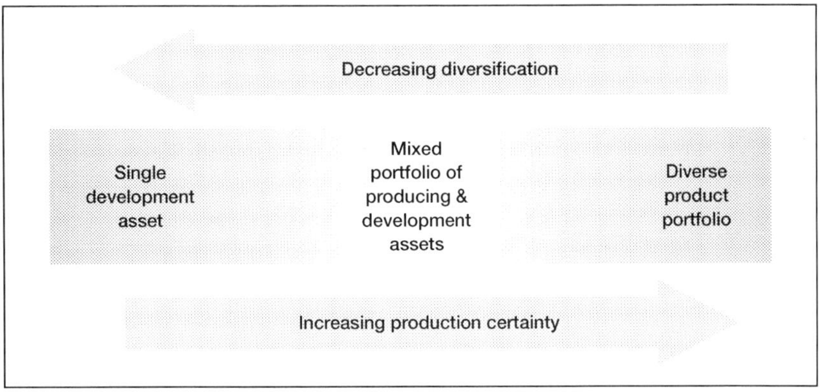

In order for an asset to be considered eligible for inclusion in an RBL, it is usual for it to have the following characteristics:

- reserves (1P and 2P) confirmed by an independent technical consultant;
- full regulatory consent (eg, a valid exploitation licence, approved plan of development or similar);
- a clearly identified off-take route and market;
- if under development, a completed front-end engineering design (FEED) study with a detailed contracting strategy; and
- undisputed documentary evidence of licence ownership or entitlements under a production-sharing contract.

These are not hard and fast rules for asset eligibility, and exceptions are occasionally made in specific circumstances.

One feature of RBL that causes more confusion and misapplication between lenders and borrowers than any other is capital expenditure add-back (CapEx Add-back). Below is an explanation of the fundamentals of CapEx Add-back and details about the specific circumstances in which it may be applied.

When a business looks at the overall economics of a particular project it will often calculate the NPV – that is, take the aggregate of the investments made and the cash flows received over the life of the project and discount them at a defined rate. This gives the business a clear view of the project's overall cash return and provides the business with an objective way of comparing one project with another. However, lenders are looking for something different. Since they are repaid from positive cash flow, they are simply looking to leverage the net cash flows from a project. Therefore the initial investment or capital expenditure costs may not be relevant to them and can be added back to the NPV that is then used to calculate the available amount. Another way of looking at this is that if lenders are leveraging the net cash flows from an asset or portfolio of assets, any capital expenditure that is funded from outside sources (eg, equity, cash in hand or the RBL itself), is not part of this net cash flow and so should be excluded. A simplified example of this is set out below.

Figure 3. A simplified CapEx add-back example (all amounts discounted)

	Year 1	Year 2	Year 3	Year 4
Capital expenditure	($50m)	–	–	–
Project revenues	–	$40m	$30m	$20m
Project costs	–	($10m)	($10m)	($10m)
Project net cash flows	($50m)	$30m	$20m	$10m
Project NPV is $10m, but cash flow for debt service is $60m				

In this example the project NPV is $10 million. However, lenders that provide funding for the project have recourse to $60 million of cash flow in years two to four. Therefore the amount of funding that the lender should be able to provide should be based on the $60 million of positive cash flow once the project is up and running and not the overall $10 million NPV. This is entirely logical and notably positive for the borrower, as it means it should be able to borrow more. This is the fundamental principle behind CapEx add-back.

The above example is particularly easy to analyse because the capital expenditure occurs prior to any positive project cash flows, and the funding for the expenditure must have come from some external source. More complexity comes when the cash flow from a portfolio of assets is aggregated. One would naturally assume that the cash flow from cash-generating assets would fund the capital expenditure on assets under development. Operationally this may be appropriate. However, lenders must take care when assessing the suitability of expenditure for CapEx add-back as the cash flow required to fund development costs is no longer available to service debt. If the borrower has cash in hand plus debt availability, this could be used to fund the capital expenditure, then the principles of CapEx add-back could be applied. It is not important whether the borrower actually uses the cash/debt or the cash flow to fund the CapEx, as the funds are fungible, but their presence within the security net of the facility is key. Notably, if the cash/debt is insufficient to meet the full capital expenditure then the add-back should be scaled back accordingly.

2.5 Facility amount and amortisation

As mentioned above, the available amount that borrowers can access is calculated at the beginning of the loan and recalculated or redetermined every six months thereafter. It is normal therefore for the facility amount (ie, the total amounts of commitments received from the lenders) to be set with this in mind. Generally the facility amount will be set at a level that is consistent with the available amount, enabling the borrower to utilise its full debt availability. Alternatively, the facility amount may be set lower than the available amount if the borrower wants to minimise upfront costs and there is a clear understanding of how much it might wish to borrow over the short term. A far more common situation is that a borrower may wish to oversize the facility amount at a level substantially above the initial available amount, based on its business forecast. This oversizing may be intended for existing assets that are to be brought into the RBL at a later date (eg, an early development asset that has declared commerciality and imminent approval for a plan of development). Alternatively, the headroom in the RBL may be intended to support an acquisition. The oversized facility involves a higher up front cost to the borrower, but this is often a price worth paying, as the borrower:

- is able to move quickly to demonstrate financing capability should an acquisition/development opportunity appear; and
- secures commitments upfront that may not be readily available when it needs them.

The current fragility of the financing markets demonstrates that borrowers should plan ahead and access the funding markets when they are open, because it is not always clear how long they will remain so.

Figure 4. Facility amount and amortisation

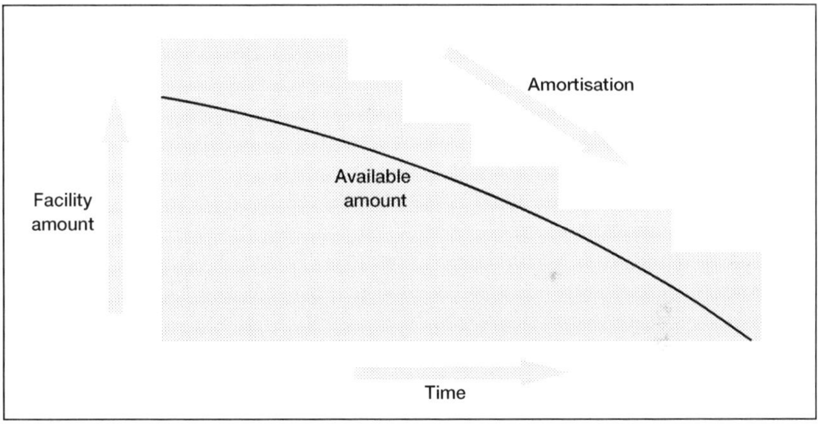

Whatever the facility amount at the start of the loan period, it is common practice for RBL facilities to amortise in the last few years of the facility (ie, the facility amount decreases at a pre-agreed rate at each semi-annual redetermination in a step-wise fashion as the loan approaches final maturity). This amortisation is consistent with the characteristic decline in production of the assets included in the RBL, as well as the desire of lenders to eliminate refinancing risk. A grace period of approximately two years is normal before the start of any amortisation and, in the case of a development finance facility, is essential as no repayments can be expected until cash flow has been established. The actual available amount will continue to vary in accordance with the calculation of FLCR and LLCR.

3. Covenants, information undertakings and representations

The classic RBL structure also contains various covenants, information undertakings and representations and warranties all of which act to ensure that the lenders are kept informed of the borrower's operations and that the borrower does not behave in a way that might impair the asset value against which the loan is secured. A brief summary of the most commonly used clauses is below.

3.1 Covenants

A borrower should ensure that its assets comply with all applicable laws and have all the appropriate licences and authorisations in place. It will also be expected to operate its assets in accordance with good industry practice, including complying with existing contracts, obtaining appropriate insurance cover and meeting all relevant environmental standards.

The value in the borrower's operations and assets is protected through a negative pledge and restrictions on disposals or reorganisations. A change of control through an outright sale of the business or takeover is generally a trigger for a mandatory repayment.

Lenders will look for a senior secured ranking for the RBL debt. Even so, for smaller borrowers, there is usually a prohibition on further financial indebtedness. Larger borrowers, which are more likely to have other debt on the balance sheet, will normally have an agreed carve-out. In practice, lenders will be wary of debt overhang (ie, other indebtedness needing to be repaid before the RBL's final maturity). Borrowers should be aware that lenders will focus on any existing debt and the timing of any principal repayments. RBL lenders are averse to taking on refinancing risk for their own debt and generally will not accept refinancing risk of any subordinated or unsecured liabilities during the tenor of the RBL facility.

All hydrocarbon sales revenues from assets included in the RBL must be deposited in a secured proceeds account that is held by one of the lenders (generally called the account bank). The lenders will take a charge over this account and the priority of payments (or cash-flow waterfall) from this account is documented in the RBL facility agreement. Generally the borrower will have access to the account to meet the operating costs, capital expenditure, tax liabilities and general and administrative expenditure associated with the RBL assets. Next the borrower can use the account to pay fees and interest associated with the RBL facility, any hedging liabilities and principal repayments. At the bottom of the waterfall are the requirements necessary for distributions from the account. These may include development completion, a fully funded debt service reserve account, or a limitation on the timing of distributions until just after an RBL redetermination has occurred. In general, the less production and less diversification in the borrower's assets, the tighter the controls on distributions.

3.2 Information undertakings

In common with other forms of corporate borrowing, lenders will want to see regular copies of audited accounts, unaudited management accounts and all other information that is circulated to shareholders. A reserve report prepared by an independent technical consultant, that is acceptable to the lenders, must also be submitted annually. This is normally a requirement for all exploration and production (E&P) companies that are listed on recognised stock exchanges and so is not usually onerous. However, it is particularly helpful if the lenders are able to define the scope of the reserve report to ensure that it meets the requirements of lenders for an assessment of the RBL assets.

If the RBL contains assets currently under development, then the borrower must provide a regularly updated progress report on these, detailing performance progress and budgets against plan. Specifically if the RBL is a single asset development of a particularly complex nature, then the lenders will often appoint a technical consultant to provide an initial review of it, as well as regular updates through site visits.

It has become common practice for lenders to require the regular submission from the borrower of a 12-month lookahead consolidated cash flow that includes all the activities (eg, operating and capital expenditure, exploration, appraisal and general and administrative) of the group, and not just the borrower and the RBL assets. Lenders are focused on the group's overall liquidity position and want to see that the corporate cash-flow model clearly demonstrates that all near-term committed liabilities can be funded as and when they due. This is often referred to as the 'corporate liquidity test' and failure can trigger an event of default.

3.3 Representations

The representations required of the borrower again are consistent with standard corporate facilities in that they seek confirmation from the board that the borrower:

- is entitled to own its assets and operate its business;
- has the power and authority to carry out its business; and
- is not aware of any default at the time of the representation.

It is common for all obligors to make these representations at the time of signing the facility documentation as well as to repeat them from time to time.

4. Security

RBL lenders require a comprehensive security package; in fact it is a key feature of the product. The security package will normally include some or all of the following:

- cross-guarantees between all obligors;
- a fixed and floating charge over the borrowers' assets;
- a pledge over the shares of the borrowers' asset-owning subsidiaries;
- a pledge over the revenue accounts;
- assignment as loss payee on insurance contracts; and
- assignment of the rights and benefits under any hedging agreements.

All of the above are subject to the applicable legal jurisdiction for the company and its assets. Occasionally the charge over assets is problematic for a borrower as either it is very difficult to achieve under the applicable jurisdiction or it may require the consent of a particular government agency, which may take time to achieve.

Lenders are usually pragmatic in these circumstances; as the asset charge is primarily defensive in nature it is not unusual to see this security requirement dropped. In Brazil, it is understood that a pledge or an assignment of credit rights/receivables and contractual rights in relation to oil and gas assets is achievable with the prior consent of the National Petroleum Agency (ANP). However, the consent will require further reconfirmation upon enforcement.

It is also understood that a pledge over the shares of a Brazilian E&P company will require the prior consent of the ANP as the taking/enforcing of such security would constitute a change of control under the terms of a concession agreement. Therefore it would appear that the legal framework in Brazil does enable lenders to perfect appropriate security, equivalent to that available in other jurisdictions.

5. Events of default

Events of default (eg, failure to satisfy the corporate liquidity test) are there to provide lenders with protection, as well as a measure of control in the event that something goes wrong. They are usually constructed to promote early discussions between the lenders and the borrower, and to allow the parties to act (hopefully in a positive way) before matters escalate.

Conversely, it is also important that the default triggers are not so sensitive as to cause issues for the borrower in circumstances that can be readily remedied. The application of grace periods for specific circumstances is a common feature to allow borrowers time to resolve minor transgressions. That said, a failure to pay any amount due under the facility or cross-defaults with other indebtedness are normally automatic defaults.

6. RBL advantages

RBL is a popular form of financing for E&P independents, giving them access to funds that can have a significantly lower overall cost than equity and, in the majority of cases, lower costs than other forms of debt capital. In common with other forms of debt, RBL facilities can be priced cheaper than equity because they rank superior (ie, they have first claim over the cash flows). Equity holders have to be compensated for their increased risk through higher returns. The introduction of debt into a company's capital structure will benefit its weighted average cost of capital (WACC). This is desirable because if a project or group of projects has a fixed return, then the effect of debt reducing the WACC will consequently increase the equity return – something that every management team should be keen to achieve.

Through development financing, RBL can provide E&P companies with early access to debt. Such a company attempting to fund its first development has very few financing options as it will have no track record of profit generation and will consequently have a very low credit rating. RBL looks beyond the historical balance sheet and profit and loss performance directly at the asset. If this can satisfy the lender's scrutiny of economic profitability within acceptable risk parameters then why should a prior history of losses matter? It is this ability to look forward rather than back that differentiates RBL from other forms of corporate lending and enables E&P companies successfully to raise finance earlier than they may otherwise be able to.

Other significant advantages of RBL are flexibility and scalability. A borrower may fund its first development using an RBL facility; once that asset is producing, the borrower may seek to bring further assets into the facility. The new assets may be producing, obtained through an acquisition or further developments from within a borrower's existing asset portfolio. As long as each asset is suitable for leverage and acceptable to the lenders then its value may be aggregated into the RBL and further funds made available accordingly. If there is insufficient headroom in the existing facility amount, then the borrower can seek to increase this through sourcing further commitments from its existing lenders or by bringing new lenders into the facility. The facility documentation allows for either process, although it is normal for existing lenders to be given first right of refusal for increased commitments before approaching new lenders. So RBL has the flexibility to allow borrowers to bring in new assets and also the scalability to increase the commitments as the borrower grows. The international RBL market has historically shown considerable depth to RBL borrowers, with facilities of up to $2 billion not being unusual.

However, flexibility for the borrower does not end with asset additions. Many E&P companies will review their asset portfolio on a regular basis and a borrower may decide that it wishes to dispose of part or all of its investment in a particular asset. Again RBL is flexible enough to cater for this, with part of the disposal proceeds being used to pay down the RBL facility to the lower available amount commensurate with the remaining asset portfolio.

As part of an E&P company's capital structure, RBL can be used on its own or in conjunction with other forms of debt. RBL will always rank senior but can be structured to work with corporate bonds, convertibles, mezzanine and other unsecured or subordinated debt products. Risks around potential debt overhang and the appropriate amount of overall total leverage would need to be resolved, but in principle there is no reason why multiple debt products cannot be structured to work together. RBL should be seen by finance directors as one, probably essential, part of their company's capital structure that accesses a different pool of liquidity to the others.

The structure of RBL involves regular communication and interaction between borrowers and lenders; not just through the provision of regular corporate information such as annual accounts, but notably through the semi-annual redetermination process. This interaction engenders a close relationship between the two parties, which is desirable for borrowers as it creates a basis for reasonable discussions to be held when circumstances demand. A borrower may, for example, seek a waiver due to an unexpected event or require financial support for a company-making acquisition. These conversations are much easier to have when lenders are knowledgeable about and supportive of a borrower's business.

Another attractive feature of RBL is that their tenors are relatively long (generally five years). Borrowers with good track records and established lending syndicates can even push their tenors out to seven years. These tenors give the borrower committed funding over a relatively longer period and also allow for a reasonable repayment profile. Notably, since the available amount is dictated by asset cash-flow cover ratios, the repayment profile is always aligned with the remaining value of the RBL assets. Many borrowers appreciate that they have no major bullet repayments to make. The recent turmoil in the global financial markets has shown that both borrowers and incumbent lenders should not be completely comfortable with refinancing risk.

7. Risks

Both borrowers and lenders are concerned with risk: lenders because they may lose their money; borrowers because they may lose their company. However, as mentioned earlier, each party's appetite for risk is different and is generally consistent with the benefit received. Lenders have no upside apart from receiving their money back with agreed interest and so are understandably more risk averse than borrowers. Hence, the identification and analysis of risk is a major part of every lender's due diligence when considering the structure of an RBL.

Figure 5. The three Ms of risk control

M **itigation**
anagement
onitoring

Once each risk has been identified, it should be analysed in terms of likelihood of occurrence, magnitude of effect and consequent considerations. Actions to reduce or control risk can be divided into three types:

- Mitigation – risk is completely removed. This is rarely possible and generally involves the creation of another source of risk, albeit probably more acceptable. For example, hedging the interest rate risk can remove all exposure to floating rates but will introduce counterparty risks with the hedging provider. However, as the hedging provider is likely to be a well-rated financial institution, this risk is more palatable.
- Management – risk is reduced to an acceptable level. For example, an E&P company may hedge 30% of its production over a two-year period. Thus commodity price exposure is reduced but not eliminated.
- Monitoring – risk is observed only. Where a risk cannot be mitigated or managed or if it is agreed that the underlying risk is acceptable, then controls may be put into place to monitor the risk only. Actual or potential occurrence may cause other triggers or actions to occur, but no direct risk control is utilised. For example, development cost risk is often uncontrolled through variable contracts. However, frequent budgetary reporting may be adequate for lenders.

The RBL structure contains, through the use of cover ratio-driven availability, an inherent measure of risk management. By lending no more than say 1.3 times the NPV of loan life cash flows, it can be seen that borrowers can suffer a limited drop in cash flow and lenders can still have their debt repaid. However, RBL structures go one step further. Some specific risks and the risk control measures used are detailed below.

7.1 Reservoir risk

The most significant risk faced by lenders when looking at RBL facilities is that of reservoir risk – that is, that the quantity of hydrocarbons actually produced by the RBL assets is below that forecast in the model. If there is no production then the debt can never be repaid as the asset will produce no positive cash flow and consequently have no value. Before any lending, lenders will undertake a significant amount of subsurface due diligence using either own internal bank engineers or external consultants. The lenders will review the borrower's own data (eg, well logs or subsurface simulation models), as well as the independent engineering report provided to the company. If any further information is required the bank engineer may discuss specifics directly with the independent engineer or may ask that the report scope be increased to include it.

RBL manages individual reservoir risk through the technical assumptions included in the banking model. Financings for single asset or assets with little or no production history (ie, including all development assets) will generally be assigned P90 reserves – that is, a 90% probability that these reserves will be exceeded under the Society of Petroleum Engineers (SPE) definitions. Although even this conservative production profile may be further reduced should there be specific doubts or concerns.

Multiple asset financings benefit from reservoir diversification, where production under-performance in one field may be offset by better than expected performance from another. It has therefore become more common for international RBL to credit diversified portfolios with P50 reserves, that is, a 50% probability that these reserves will be exceeded under the SPE definitions. Asset portfolios must be truly diversified and a maximum individual field NPV contribution covenant may be documented to control this. Ultimately, the lenders will have the final say on what reserves will be given value in the model, but the above are reasonable guidelines in the current market.

The semi-annual redetermination process is a key reservoir risk management tool, in that it allows lenders regularly to adjust the available amount depending on actual reservoir performance and changing views of the independent engineer. Lenders generally also have the option to call for an interim redetermination if it is felt that the reserves downgrade is significant enough. This gives lenders the potential to accelerate repayments, hopefully protecting remaining security value and avoiding repayment problems in later years.

7.2 Commodity price

Where an asset's hydrocarbon production is marketed and sold on an established spot market or sold with reference to a known benchmark (eg, Brent crude, WTI or Henry Hub) there is an inherent exposure to adverse movements in commodity price. Crude oil prices have historically been very volatile, with world prices falling to record lows in 1998 and 2009. Between 2008 and 2009, Brent crude dropped from $147/bbl to $38/bbl. How does RBL deal with this volatility? What is a sensible commodity price to use when modelling future cash flows?

Lenders begin with a commodity price deck that is generally reviewed and approved by its internal management on at least a quarterly basis. The price deck is not a lender's view of what it believes the commodity price will be at some point in the future, rather it is a price deck at which the lender believes is appropriate for lending senior debt (noting earlier comments regarding no upside for lenders). Each lender will generate its own price deck. However, it is common to see a general consensus view from the leading oil and gas banks with little differences between their internally generated price decks. The way that RBL is structured and syndicated among many lenders ensures that this consensus price deck is achieved and communicated around the market. An RBL with a price deck too high might find that no lenders are willing to participate and so fail to close, while a lender with a price deck too low will find that it is uncompetitive. So although internally generated, a price deck must acknowledge current market conditions.

The semi-annual redetermination process also allows for the price deck to be reviewed regularly on an individual facility basis. Contrary to popular belief, lenders are generally loth to modify the price deck too swiftly in response to market volatility. Dropping a price deck too quickly could cause a large repayment to be triggered that a borrower is unprepared for, which could increase the likelihood of default. Lenders therefore tend to make only gradual adjustments to the price deck. In general the price deck is set at a level below the forward curve that allows for short-term market volatility to be absorbed with little ill effect, but is updated regularly to reflect longer-term trends so that the RBL leverage is appropriate in the long run.

Commodity price exposure can be eliminated if a borrower has a long-term off-take agreement with a clear pricing mechanism not linked to market prices, although lender satisfaction with the off-taker's creditworthiness is necessary.

The risk management benefit of commodity price hedging through the use of derivatives is widely used in conjunction with RBL. Borrowers can use swaps, collars, put options or three-ways to manage their exposure to adverse movements in commodity prices. A borrower can hedge a proportion of production to support a capital expenditure programme by ensuring that sufficient sales proceeds will be available to meet the expenditure plan. For lenders, hedging will reduce the risk of the facility to short-term volatility in commodity prices. As the hedging undertaken by the borrower is included in the lending model and is generally undertaken at a level above the price deck, hedging will also increase availability. This is particularly useful when a borrower wishes to maximise debt availability (eg, when funding an acquisition). The RBL will generally document all hedging undertaken with lenders as ranking equally with the debt. This incentivises the borrower to hedge with the lenders, as opposed to other unsecured hedge providers.

However, hedging must be used with caution and lenders would not wish to see a borrower overhedge its production as a combination of lower than expected production alongside increases in commodity prices can give rise to large margin calls that a borrower may be unable to meet. This is particularly applicable to development assets, where a delay in first production can give rise to hedging problems. For this reason lenders will agree an appropriate hedging policy with the borrower prior to financial close. In particular, lenders will allow future production from development assets to be hedged using only put options, if at all, as these carry no credit risk in the event of a production delay.

7.3 Development risk

Assets under development carry increased risks over existing producing assets. Development risk is the generic term for construction risk, technical risk, cost overrun risk, delay risk and all the other risks associated with bringing a new asset into production.

In general, lenders are wary of any new or untried technology and tend to prefer established technologies that have a clear and demonstrable track record. Complex projects may require the appointment of a third-party consultant to provide an independent verification of the technological risk and cost and schedule achievability. The consultant is often retained during the development phase of the asset to report back to the lenders on the asset's progress towards completion and first production.

Lenders may use increased cost contingencies, as well as extended development periods, as a base case in the lending model in order to build in additional conservatism. Higher FLCR and LLCR covenants are also commonly employed to lower leverage. Sufficient liquidity (from debt and equity) to meet the full development costs is a key principle when structuring an RBL facility for development assets. Lenders carry out sensitivity analysis to assess the magnitude of potential cost increases and/or delays. Borrowers will be required to place additional equity funds into a secured escrow account for cost overruns, which are then released post-completion if unused. If desired, lenders may also occasionally structure an additional RBL tranche to be used specifically to part-fund cost overruns.

RBL structured and priced for a portfolio of producing assets will often include a covenant that limits the maximum NPV contribution for assets under development, as the introduction of a large development asset could skew risks within the portfolio such that lenders are exposed to more development risk than was originally conceived.

7.4 Other risks

In order to minimise exposure to foreign exchange rates it is common for RBL to be denominated in the same currency as the received revenues. Even though a significant proportion of the development costs may be in a different currency, the RBL should always be denominated in the revenue currency. If foreign exchange rate hedging is to be implemented, it is always better to hedge in the short term of the development period rather than over the tenor of the facility for the revenues. Similarly, operating costs may require payment in currencies other than that in which the facility is denominated. However, as revenues should always exceed the operating costs by some margin, it is better to hedge the operating costs instead of the revenues.

Interest rate risk is another aspect of financing that can be managed or mitigated through hedging. Although it is not always easy to predict the actual drawn level of the facility due to the revolving nature of the RBL, so an imperfect hedge could result. For larger borrowers with a predictable level of borrowing the sizing of the hedge is somewhat easier.

A lender's view of operator risk is a difficult balance; if a borrower is an operator then it has control over its destiny but may lack some of the capabilities to bring the asset to a successful conclusion. If, however, the borrower has only a non-operated interest in an asset being led by a major E&P company then it may have limited scope for input. There is no ideal and each asset should be considered on a case by case basis.

E&P companies now participate in a global industry and lenders are asked to provide funding accordingly. Noting that some countries are off limits due to international sanctions or political unrest, lenders will seek to satisfy a borrower's financing needs where they can. In a cross-border financing with assets in multiple jurisdictions, lenders must consider the country risk for each asset and also the relative contribution that each asset brings to the facility.

Appropriate structures and pricing mechanisms can then be implemented that ensure that lenders are compensated for the commensurate risk that they are taking and structures utilised that best protect the security value in the portfolio.

8. The lender universe

International RBL provides E&P companies with the opportunity to access a deep liquidity pool that is predominantly based in Europe. Financial institutions spread across the United Kingdom, France, Germany, Norway, the United States and Japan are all known, generally through their European offices, as active players in this market. This bank-funded liquidity differs from other sources of funding such as equity or the debt capital markets, and the diversification of funding sources is a major attraction for these companies as the equity and debt markets have a history of closing for considerable periods. Fortunately, the RBL market has maintained a strong history of remaining open, although borrower selectivity and the value of established relationships have played a significant role. All lenders will generally participate in RBL for larger borrowers that have established production. The lender universe for first-time borrowers and those with mainly development assets is markedly smaller; often being restricted to the lead oil and gas banks that have a strong in-house technical capability.

The RBL market also benefits from the active participation of the International Finance Corporation and the World Bank, as well as the selective participation of export credit agencies (ECAs) that are keen to promote their indigenous service industries. ECAs can participate directly in RBL or provide a measure of risk mitigation to lenders through guarantees (covered facilities).

Emerging from the most recent financial crisis in Europe, there is speculation as to the longer-term appetite of banks and other financial institutions for on-balance sheet liabilities such as corporate debt. However, RBL has established an excellent track record of limited defaults and engenders a close relationship between borrower and lender that leads to significant opportunities for ancillary business for the lenders (eg, hedging, cash management, advisory and equity brokerage). As the industry's search for reserves widens and the standing of E&P independents in the industry grows, it is likely that RBL will continue to be attractive to these companies for the foreseeable future.

9. Other funding sources

An E&P company's first source of funding is generally equity. This may come from the public markets or from private equity investors. If a start-up E&P company only has exploration assets it is likely that equity will be available only to fund a drilling programme, which is entirely appropriate. The limited chance of success inherent in exploration drilling is inconsistent with the repayment obligations associated with debt. Once an E&P company makes a commercial discovery, other avenues of funding present themselves. As mentioned previously, RBL providers generally cannot fund development until the asset is fully appraised and government development consent is granted. Therefore mezzanine providers can often provide an alternative to straight equity to bridge the gap between discovery and development. A few lenders have the capability of offering pre-development facilities (PDFs) that can be used to fund late-appraisal/near-term development assets prior to RBL development financing. PDFs are generally short tenor (one to two years) bullet repayment mezzanine facilities. However, PDF availability is limited and very borrower and asset specific. Few alternatives to RBL are available to E&P companies undertaking their first development, or few that come close on an overall cost basis. The majority of funding alternatives or those that are complementary to an RBL become available to these companies only once production is established.

The equity capital markets can source funds through convertibles and other similar structured notes where there is a demonstrable opportunity for capital growth and provided that the borrower is listed on a recognised exchange. Larger borrowers with well-established production can access the high-yield debt capital markets. However, there are currently only a handful of examples of this other than domestic US producers. The tenors available to bond issuers are attractive at five to eight years, but the bullet repayment nature of a corporate bond, unlike an amortising RBL, does not match the characteristic declining value of producing reserves. However, it is common to see them used in the United States to provide a base level of unsecured debt subordinated beneath a revolving RBL that is not generally fully drawn. The process of obtaining a rating can be protracted and expensive, and the likely success of such an issuance often depends entirely on the market appetite at the time.

Borrowers with established production that are seeking the benefits of an RBL, but wish to avoid regular availability redeterminations can be considered for a corporate RBL facility. These are senior secured revolving credit facilities from lenders similar to standard RBL facilities, but notably using a reserves valuation metric rather than FLCR and LLCR covenants to set the maximum availability limit. A reserves valuation metric of $5 to $10 per barrel of audited 2P reserves has historically been used, depending on asset economics and jurisdiction. This avoids the need for regular redeterminations involving a complex financing model. In addition, corporate RBL facilities tend to be bullet repayment structures rather than amortising. The flip side to this more flexible structure is that corporate RBL facility tenors are usually shorter; generally two to three years in length. Overall, more leverage is likely to be obtained from a standard RBL facility (particularly with the benefit of commodity price hedging) than a corporate one, but at the cost to the borrower of increased information undertakings, amortisation of the facility amount and semi-annual availability redeterminations.

10. Advice for potential borrowers

It is difficult to be generic when discussing RBL structures and transactions, as each one is bespoke and tailored to the characteristics of the assets being financed and the profile of the borrower involved. Even more so when there is a portfolio of assets – the combinations and permutations of degree of development risk, country risk and capital expenditure profile are too numerous to discuss individually. However, this section seeks to offer an overview of the process, describing the interaction between borrower and lenders that will lead to a successful transaction. It also sets out the alternatives a borrower has in terms of syndication strategy.

10.1 Be prepared

Figure 6. Summary of information needs

- Reserves report from an approved consultant (scope agreed with the Technical Bank)
- Draft field development plan (or similar, if applicable)
- Production history (if any)
- Details of planned contracting strategy and timing
- Capital expenditure budgets including contingency and committed expenditure
- Details of all planned development & commercial agreements
- Ring fenced attributable tax losses
- Security documentation
- 'Know your customer' undertakings

Lenders need to undertake a significant amount of technical, commercial and legal due diligence before committing to an RBL, so it is important that the potential borrower gathers as much information up front as possible. Information is required for the bank engineer to take a view on the technical assumptions (eg, reserve reports, production history and development plans). Commercial agreements, cost forecasts and financial information are also required to generate the lending model. A summary of lenders' information needs is set out in Figure 6 for reference. Not all this information may be available initially, however, it is important to be aware that it will be required before full credit approval by the lenders and certainly by financial close.

When selecting an appropriate lender with whom to begin discussions, borrowers should consider the lender's:

- existing or historic banking relationships;
- experience and credentials for similar transactions;

- structuring and syndication capabilities;
- in-house technical knowledge; and
- ability to perform administrative roles.

Leveraging existing banking relationships is particularly important when a borrower is seeking its first financing. Development finance-focused RBL will generally appeal only to a limited number of banks; if a borrower can expand that number through its existing banking relationships, this can be a positive factor in gathering commitments.

It may make sense to work with more than one lender at this early stage, to generate a sense of competition, to gauge market appetite or to gather as many financing ideas as possible. Early engagement with several lenders may actually form part of the planned syndication strategy, which will be discussed in more detail later.

A general outline of the various steps in the process of putting an RBL in place using a clubbed syndication is given in Figure 7. Although the process is shown to be sequential, many of the activities will actually run in parallel (eg, documentation is often undertaken at same time as the club banks seek credit approval).

Figure 7. Outline flow diagram for a club transaction

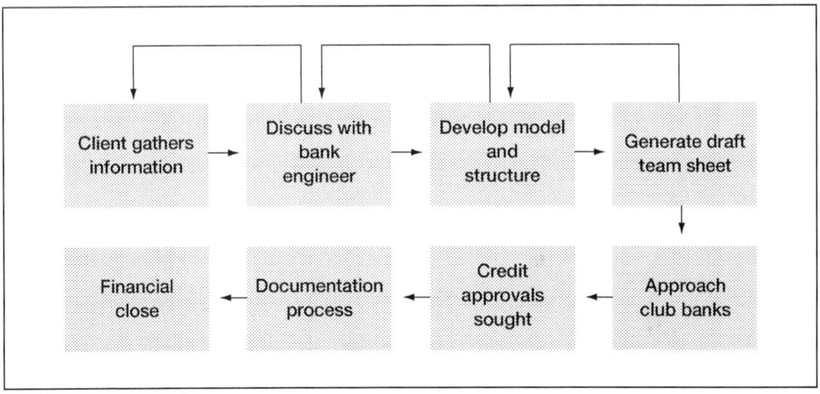

At the outset there would normally be much discussion and feedback between the borrower, the bank engineer and the modeller, all coordinated by the bank's origination team. The target outcome is a lending model that reflects the technical and economic assumptions that the bank finds acceptable within a RBL structure that achieves the borrower's aims. Those aims could range from maximising flexibility or availability, to minimising financing costs. The borrower should be explicit on what its key drivers are when considering financing structures, so that an appropriate structure can be developed.

At this point, sensitivities may be run on the lending model, which may lead to asset-specific structures (eg, development assets may require an equity escrow account to meet potential cost overruns). All the structuring ideas and requirements that are developed at this stage are then formalised in an indicative term sheet. The term sheet can be traditionally short or long-form, where the former just gives a brief outline of the structure, pricing and covenants and the latter goes into significantly more detail. At this stage the term sheet may be reviewed by two sets of legal counsel, one acting on behalf of the borrower and another for the lenders. This provides the basis for lenders to seek credit approval from their respective management teams.

Once credit approval is received or at least is well underway, the term sheet will be used by the lenders' counsel to construct the formal facility documentation. One significant point to highlight here is that the borrower will be expected to pay the associated fees for all external consultants and even the lenders' counsel. Having in place a well-negotiated term sheet before the lawyers become involved will help to keep costs to a minimum. Although the borrower will be consulted in the selection of legal counsel and approval sought for all external consultants used by the lenders, the final choice will always require the satisfaction of the lenders.

Once the documentation is completed to the satisfaction of all parties and any conditions precedent to signing completed, the RBL can be signed and reach financial close. There may be further conditions to be satisfied before the first drawdown can take place, but at this point all lenders are committed.

10.2 Syndication strategy

The above process has detailed the steps for a club transaction, whereby a group or club of lenders each sign up to the RBL at the same time. There may be one or more lead banks in the club that have played a major role in the structuring and documentation of the facility, but at signing each bank only commits to fund its share of the total facility amount. This form of syndication differs from a fully underwritten facility in that the lenders do not undertake to underwrite a larger commitment than their intended final hold with a view to a coordinated primary syndication. Clubbed transactions are particularly common in uncertain markets, where no lender or group of lenders is willing to take the risk of a failure to sell down to their final hold level in primary syndication. Another circumstance when a clubbed transaction may be preferable for a borrower is when it wishes to maintain some competitive tension for a facility that is expected to be receive a lot of syndication support. Underwriters expect some compensation for the risk of a failed syndication; a clubbed transaction avoids this premium and should work out cheaper overall for the borrower.

Clubbed transactions can be bank-led or self-arranged. In a bank-led financing, one or more lead banks will structure and document the RBL and then present the 'cooked' deal to the lending market, providing advice to the borrower on the appropriate structure, pricing and even identifying suitable lenders to join the syndicate. The lead banks are then appropriately compensated at financial close for their increased involvement in putting the RBL together. However, experienced borrowers with established lending syndicates looking to minimise costs may decide to self-arrange. In this way, no individual bank takes the lead and competitive tension is kept high. In the latter stages it is normal for one bank to lead the documentation process on behalf of all lenders.

The choice of syndication strategy must be made giving due consideration to the experience of the borrower, the purpose of the RBL and the appetite in the lending market at the time. If a borrower requires certainty that a particular level of commitments will be received (eg, for the funding of an acquisition), then it may decide that the additional cost of an underwritten deal is worthwhile, also noting that underwritten deals with fewer lenders tend to fund faster than club transactions with many more lenders involved. However, lenders will still look for market flex clauses and the like, that enable them to modify structure and pricing, to ensure that they have the best opportunity for a successful primary syndication. Conversely, a borrower may wish to access as much commitment as possible within a certain pricing range and so be willing to accept fewer commitments initially should some lenders require more than is offered.

10.3 Pricing

This chapter deliberately offers no guidance on pricing. The pricing of an RBL facility, in terms of upfront fees, underwriting fees, margin and commitment fees, is market-led and borrower dependent. Where liquidity is scarce, either due to tight market conditions or to limited appetite for particular assets, then pricing will naturally be higher than when circumstances are more favourable or assets more desirable. However, overall, RBL pricing is advantageous for borrowers when compared to the alternatives. The highly structured and covenanted nature of the financing, alongside a comprehensive security package, means that it is also an attractive proposition for many lenders and is generally priced accordingly.

10.4 Timing

An ideal timeline for the successful completion of a syndicated RBL transaction from start to finish is in the order of 10 to 12 weeks. Smaller facilities requiring fewer lenders can take less time as there will be fewer parties at the negotiating table. Borrowers with established lending syndicates can also refinance relatively quickly as the lenders and their credit committees are already familiar with the borrower's name and assets, meaning that generally only an update is needed.

Large facilities with multiple assets across several jurisdictions or complex developments will generally take longer, sometimes significantly, as the quantity of information and depth of analysis required to make a lending decision will naturally take additional time. Any efforts that a borrower can make to provide the required information in a timely and efficient manner will be beneficial.

11. Conclusion

For more than 30 years E&P companies have looked to the RBL product as a key element of their capital structure; enabling them to fund developments, finance acquisitions or just to release equity trapped in producing assets to be recycled in the business. The above description of the structure, risks and implementation of RBL financings has, hopefully, provided some perspective on how they work, who is involved and what is required to put a facility together. As the upstream sector in Brazil continues to develop and even more E&P independents are drawn to the hydrocarbons yet to be produced there, the appetite among borrowers and lenders for RBL for assets in Brazil and elsewhere in the Latin American region is expected to grow accordingly. The RBL product has a bright future in South America.

The views expressed in this chapter are those of the author and do not necessarily express the views of Bank of America Corporation and/or any of its affiliates.

Law and jurisdiction

Ludmilla Corkey
Luis Cláudio Furtado Faria
Marcelo Viveiros de Moura
Pinheiro Neto Advogados

1. Introduction

As mentioned in other chapters, the Brazilian legal system is based on the codified Roman civil law. As a general rule, the lower courts are not obliged to follow the decisions of the higher courts, as they are in common law countries. Former judicial decisions are therefore not the principal guidance in ruling on a case.

The Constitution is the foundation of the legal system and grants parties in administrative or judicial litigation the rights to due process, adversarial proceedings and full defence. Under the Constitution, everyone is equal before the law. This precept is deeply enshrined in civil procedure laws, and means that judges must accord equal treatment to litigants, whether they are Brazilian or not.

The Civil Procedure Code (Law 5,869/1973) contains the main rules for civil court disputes. The only restriction on the filing of a suit for foreign litigants is in Article 835 of this code. This states that foreign companies without domicile and assets in Brazil must post bond to secure court costs and the fees of the other litigant's attorney. This restriction is not because of the foreign status of the company, but rather the fact that the litigant has neither domicile nor assets in Brazil by which to meet any costs that might ensue from an adverse decision. The foreign company does not need to post bond in enforcement proceedings and counterclaims.

The principal source of Brazilian civil law is the Civil Code (Law 10,406/2002). This maintained most of the rules of its predecessor (Law 3,071/1916), but reduced the strength of some principles, such as individualism and, consequently, the extensive freedom to contract. It replaced these with others such as objective good faith and the social role of contracts. In addition to the Civil Code there is also a substantial body of civil legislation to regulate specific matters, including the oil and gas sector.

Whenever legislation is silent, the courts must look to other sources to resolve disputes. These are classified as indirect or mediate, and include legal writings and case law, as well as custom, analogy and general principles of law and equity.

The Law of Introduction to the Civil Code (Decree 4,657/1942) is composed of 19 articles that deal with the basic principles of law.

Article 5 states that "when applying the law, the judge shall take into consideration the social purposes to which the law is directed, as well as the demands of public welfare". This provision must be applied in accordance with Article 127 of the Civil Procedure Code. This establishes that judges may only decide in equity when permissible by law, so emphasising the submission of judges to statutory law.

Hence, judges must seek to adjudicate on cases submitted to them, but cannot rely on their personal criteria of justice over the application of objective law and other applicable principles.

Furthermore, the Brazilian legal system allows that the law that governs an agreement may come from the laws of any country. However, there is disagreement among Brazilian jurists as to the scope of that provision. The most appropriate doctrinal understanding seems to be that choice is allowed, as long as the foreign law does not infringe Brazilian sovereignty, public policy or good morals.

There are some cases where Brazilian law is mandatory, such as:

- family issues;
- bankruptcy;
- nationality; and
- inheritance rights.

Certain underlying procedures must also be observed whenever obligations are to be executed in Brazil, with due regard for the foreign provision on extrinsic requirements. These provisions are a matter of public policy and the choice of law will not be effective.

Some Brazilian laws are subordinate to others, depending on their source and the importance and extent of their application. The Constitution pre-empts all other forms of legislation. After this come the supplementary laws, which contain the detailed constitutional rules and, after them, the ordinary laws that constitute the vast bulk of all Brazilian legislation (such as the codes).

Delegated laws and provisional measures have the same status as ordinary laws. The former are enacted by the president, under special delegation from Parliament. The latter are issued by the head of the federal executive, using his or her legislative powers and under specific circumstances provided for in the Constitution.

The following sections provide a more detailed explanation about the laws applicable to the Brazilian oil industry and the mechanisms by which disputes are settled.

2. Governing law and dispute resolution

2.1 Court jurisdiction

Jurisdiction is exercised by the various bodies of the judiciary. For convenience, a number of specialist courts deal with particular areas of the law. These include the labour courts, the electoral courts and the military courts. Issues relating to the Brazilian state come within the sphere of the federal courts, while the ordinary state courts have jurisdiction over matters outside the jurisdiction of the specialist or federal courts.

Furthermore, the Civil Procedure Code establishes territorial criteria as a general rule for defining jurisdiction. Actions involving movable property must be brought in the courts of the place where the defendant is domiciled. Actions involving rights over immovable property must be brought in the courts of the place where the property is located.

According to the Law of Introduction to the Civil Code and the Civil Procedure Code, Brazilian courts have jurisdiction when:

- the defendant, whatever its nationality, is domiciled in Brazil;
- the obligation is to be performed in Brazil; or
- the action results from an event or action that took place in Brazil.

This jurisdiction, however, is considered non-exclusive or concurrent.

Brazilian courts have exclusive jurisdiction on issues relating to real estate located in Brazil. Furthermore, they have exclusive jurisdiction on actions relating to international contracts entered into by Brazilian federal, state and municipal government entities. So if the dispute may come under exclusive jurisdiction, the parties may not choose a foreign jurisdiction for its resolution.

However, if the jurisdiction is non-exclusive or concurrent, the parties may choose a foreign jurisdiction. Although the choice of jurisdiction is acceptable under Brazilian law, some court decisions state that the Brazilian party has the right of process in Brazil, regardless of whether the parties have agreed otherwise. This is especially the case when the main object of the contract is to be performed in Brazil. The election of a foreign jurisdiction does not therefore remove the parties' right to file a suit in Brazil, or the right of a Brazilian judge to settle the dispute.

The Constitution draws a distinction between ordinary and special jurisdiction. Special jurisdiction is accorded to the military court, electoral court, labour court and state military courts. Ordinary jurisdiction is exercised by federal and state courts, which are empowered to adjudicate any matters not reserved for the specialist courts.

In this scenario, federal courts can hear the following:

- cases brought by or against the federal government, independent agencies (eg, the National Agency of Petroleum, Natural Gas and Biofuels (ANP)), or government-owned companies;
- litigation between foreign countries or international organisms and the municipalities or persons based in Brazil;
- disputes based on international treaties; and
- cases relating to crimes against the federal government.

The state courts have residual jurisdiction.

Finally, as is detailed below, a lower court decision may be appealed to higher instances. As a result, the lower instance jurisdiction is that exercised by a single judge. They will usually hear and adjudicate upon a case from its outset. The higher-instance jurisdiction, however, is exercised by bodies with the authority to hear appeals against lower court judges.

(a) Structure of the judiciary

As mentioned above, the judiciary is divided into federal – specialist or common – and state courts. Each has different jurisdiction. As a general rule, disputes are tried at the state courts unless one of the parties is a federal authority or entity.

The judiciary is structured in seven parts:

- Supreme Court;

- Superior Court of Justice;
- regional federal courts and federal justices;
- labour courts and judges;
- electoral courts and judges;
- military courts and judges; and
- state and federal district courts and judges.

The right of appeal to a second instance is ensured by the Constitution in federal and state courts. In specific cases, parties can also appeal to a higher instance, represented by the Supreme Court and the Superior Court of Justice. These are responsible, respectively, for matters of a constitutional and legal nature already tried at the second-instance courts.

The normal procedure is for a lawsuit to be brought before a first-instance court and adjudicated by a single judge. Their decision may then be appealed to the respective higher courts, and reviewed by a body of judges.

A first-instance decision handed down by a single state judge may therefore be reviewed by a court of justice in that same state, whereas a first-instance decision rendered by a federal judge may be reviewed by the regional federal court with jurisdiction over the corresponding circuit.

There is a further exceptional appeal to the higher courts of the country, the Supreme Court and the Superior Court of Justice. These are separate from and above the courts. They come into action only after all appeals to ordinary court instances have been exhausted or, in exceptional cases, when the dispute involves the interpretation of federal laws, and not mere factual issues or matters involving state or municipal laws.

There is a current trend towards bringing the Brazilian legal system closer to some features of common law. These include valorising the precedent to be followed by single judges and courts of appeal. Recent changes in the Civil Procedure Code determine that decisions and general statements rendered by the Supreme Court and the Superior Court of Justice may take on the status of a precedent, and must be respected and followed by lower courts in similar cases.

Before filing a lawsuit or a defence, it is therefore not only necessary to understand national statutory law, but also advisable to know how the higher courts are interpreting and applying the law to the matter in question.

2.2 Recognised types of dispute resolution

The most common method of dispute resolution in Brazil for general business (but not oil and gas operations) remains court proceedings. The Brazilian culture for settling controversies in this way was based on court proceedings and Article 5 of the Constitution, which rules that "no law may exclude from review by the Judiciary Branch any injury or threat to a right".

However, a judicial crisis led to the gradual development of alternative dispute resolution procedures. The number of claims rose to an overwhelming level, with more than 70 million lawsuits in course before the Brazilian courts (one for every three people). The Superior Court of Justice currently has around 250,000 pending cases every year. A lawsuit may last 10 years before a final solution is reached by the Brazilian courts.

All those factors created a scenario with:

- an excessive amount of cases;
- overloaded courts; and
- extremely lengthy proceedings.

The problems were compounded by Brazil's fast economic growth, which increased the demand for efficient mechanisms of dispute resolution.

To this end, the Arbitration Law (Law 9,307) was enacted in 1996 to provide the parties with the option of arbitration proceedings for settling their disputes. There has since been an increase in the number of companies that choose to settle contractual disputes through arbitration.

Mediation has also been developed as an alternative means for settling disputes. Several draft bills have been presented to Parliament that seek to regulate mediation as an alternative method of dispute resolution. However, none has yet been effectively enacted.

For example, a draft bill was suggested on September 24 2001 that created two different types of mediation. These were "pre-court mediation", voluntarily chosen by the parties before court proceedings began; and "in-court mediation", chosen by the parties during court proceedings. Before this came Draft Bill 4,827/1998, presented at the Congress on November 10 1998. This also sought to encourage mediation in dispute resolution.

Brazil is seeking alternative solutions to state jurisdiction, and the ideal of more efficient and adjustable dispute resolution methods is rapidly becoming a reality. A brief description of the current dispute resolution methods follows.

(a) *Conciliation and mediation*

A current trend towards encouraging alternative methods of dispute resolution, such as conciliation, mediation and arbitration, can be identified. These may be preferable to civil litigation. The study of conflict resolution is always being renewed, since relationships and disputes in society are constantly changing.

Some of the theories that explain the development of alternatives to traditional civil litigation relate to their informal and flexible procedure, confidentiality, faster solutions, greater involvement of parties and more suitable and efficient solutions to disputes.

Although early settlement through conciliation and mediation is a valuable solution to the problem of overburdened courts, in Brazil the culture of litigation is still very present. This makes the introduction of these alternative methods a slow process that needs to be progressively strengthened.

Brazilian statutory law normally treats conciliation not as an independent way to solve a conflict, but as one stage within the civil litigation process. It may be an early stage, but still takes place after the claim has been brought to the judiciary. Under the Civil Procedure Code – Articles 331, and 447 to 449[1] – conciliation hearings are designed as a previous stage to discovery and judgment hearings throughout ordinary proceedings. The same approach is applied to summary proceedings, in which conciliation attempts are regulated by Article 277.[2]

Article 125 of the Civil Procedure Code also imposes a general obligation on judges to attempt conciliation between litigants whenever possible. This may be attempted at any point in the proceedings and in any court instance. It is not restricted to pre-trial, discovery and judgment hearings. Nonetheless, in practical terms, judges often use conciliation just once, at the beginning of proceedings, when expressly required.

In general terms, and despite occasional attempts to encourage conciliation as an alternative to civil litigation before the beginning of court proceedings, conciliation under the Brazilian system is still seen as an early phase of a claim that has already been brought to the state courts.

Mediation can be briefly explained as a way of reaching a peaceful solution through approaches and structures appropriate to the characteristics of the case. It consists in the use of a third-party mediator who will help the opposing parties to achieve a suitable solution to their conflict. Mediation is a procedure that seeks a harmonious solution. It does not imply a formal structure; on the contrary, it is supposedly built around the peculiarities of the dispute and the will of the parties.

Mediation is therefore a private, simple, flexible and informal procedure. The parties can choose not only the mediator, but also what information will be disclosed to the other party, the degree of confidentiality, the location of the meetings, the duration of the process and even whether to follow up a settlement, as it is not binding.[3]

Nevertheless, there is currently no mediation law in Brazil, and mediation will always depend upon an express provision in agreements between parties. Most important agreements provide for multi-tiered clauses (mediation and arbitration), but enforcing a mediation clause will depend on the parties' intention to start mediation proceedings before arbitration.

Draft Bill 94/2003 sought to enforce mediation as a mandatory stage, prior to judicial proceedings. This model has met with success in countries such as Argentina, but jurists and practioners are sceptical about its approval in Brazil.

---

1 "**Art. 331.** Whenever none of the situations described in the previous sections occur, and the claim deals with transactional rights, the judge will designate a preliminary hearing, within 30 days, to which parties will be notified to attend, or be represented by an attorney or an agent of the company entitled to conciliate.

§ **1o** Once a settlement is reached, it shall be put in writing and ratified by the judge."

"**Article 447.** When the litigation deals with equity rights of a private nature, the judge shall, ex-officio, determine that the parties attend the preliminary discovery and judgment hearing.

Sole Paragraph. In family-related cases, conciliation will also apply, in the events and for the purposes where the law authorizes settlement."

"**Article 448.** Before initiating discovery procedures, the judge shall attempt conciliation between the parties. If a settlement is reached, the judge shall determine that it be put in writing."

"**Article 449.** The conciliation instrument, signed by the parties and ratified by the judge, shall have the same effect as a decision."

2 "**Article 277.** The judge shall schedule a conciliation hearing, within 30 days, summoning the defendant at least 10 days before, adverting about paragraph 2 of this article, imposing the presence of the parties.

§ **1º** The settlement shall be put in writing and ratified by an award, and the judge can be aided by the conciliator

3 Fuller, Lon F *Mediation – Its forms and functions*. HeinOnline – 44 S cal L Rev 307 1970–71, p 308

The number of mediations presently taking place in Brazil is not representative, and they are normally conducted by arbitration institutions that maintain a centre for mediation.

Although access to the judiciary is a fundamental right guaranteed by the Constitution, it is notable that Brazil is also following, albeit slowly, the trend towards focusing on the rights of society at large over the rights of the individual. So if the interest of society rests with granting individuals their right to resort to the state courts, it also lies in preventing free-riding and bad-faith litigation as well as discouraging legitimate but avoidable litigation.

However, this coming together of alternative methods and state court litigation should be cautious and gradual. It should keep in mind the peculiarities of each legal system and the specifics of the dispute when assessing the value of an alternative dispute resolution method or litigation procedure. A hasty reponse may damage potential benefits such as freedom of choice and commercial spontaneity.

In any case, a healthy combination of alternative methods with litigation seems an inevitable and necessary model of dispute resolution in the current global context.

(b) *Litigation*

As mentioned above, the most common method of dispute resolution in Brazil remains court proceedings. Alternative methods of dispute resolution are possible only if the dispute revolves around a contract in which the parties have expressly agreed, such as happens when parties decide in advance to go to arbitration should a problem arise.

Brazilian civil procedure is governed by several principles. These include:

- equal treatment of parties;
- adverse proceedings and ample defence – that is, the litigants must be able to express themselves on each and every procedural act, and the defendant must be given ample opportunity to defend;
- rational conviction of the judge – that is, the judge must rule based on the facts brought before him or her, all of which must be considered under judicious and rational criteria;
- disclosure of grounds for a court decision;
- right of appeal; and
- publicity.

Court proceedings in Brazil are divided into three different steps: cognitive, enforcement and precautionary (or injunction). The type of claim will determine the course of action that best suits the plaintiff's interests. Choosing the proper action for collecting credits is extremely important in Brazilian civil procedure because it refers to the interest in the subject matter of the suit, which is traditionally associated with the appropriateness of the action chosen. The following is an outline of the most common proceedings.

Proceedings	Description
Cognitive proceedings	These are designed to determine from the available facts which litigant should prevail. Cognitive proceedings are, in turn, subdivided into three types of actions: declaratory, condemnatory and constitutive. Through a declaratory action, the plaintiff seeks a judicial declaration of his or her rights but no specific relief beyond that declaration. Through a condemnatory action, the plaintiff seeks specific relief, such as damages, from the defendant. And through a constitutive action, the plaintiff seeks to create, modify or extinguish a legal status or relationship. This may be a suit for divorce or the termination of a contract.
Enforcement proceedings	Enforcement is the fastest procedural means by which to recover credits in Brazil. It enables the plaintiff to seek execution of: • negotiable instruments, such as bills of exchange and promissory notes; • obligations to pay a certain sum or to deliver fungible goods; • mortgage debts; • judicial awards of fees, costs, expert witness fees; and • tax debts. Enforcement is often brought as a summary proceeding for collecting liquid and certain debts without the need for a previous cognitive judgement. The intention of enforcement proceedings is to seize assets belonging to the debtor to satisfy the creditor's claim. Its success depends on the existence of attachable assets, and on the willingness of the debtor neither to raise opposition nor create difficulties to its processing.

table continued on next page

As should be clear from this summary, the recovery of debts in Brazil depends upon the type of action the creditor may bring against the debtor. Whenever possible, all negotiations should be reflected in documents that meet the legal requirements to create an enforcement instrument that can support an enforcement action.

They must include a clear and detailed description of the obligations assumed by the parties, indicating their amount or a method for calculating their amount, the due date, the payment venue and any interest, default charges or other necessary information, so that if the debtor defaults, the credit becomes liquidated and may be judicially collected.

Proceedings	Description
Precautionary proceedings (injunctions)	Injunctions are designed to aid or protect the outcome of cognitive and enforcement proceedings. They cover ancillary proceedings and provisional remedies that are incidental to a cognitive or enforcement proceeding. A successful provisional proceeding usually results in the attachment of the defendant's property or an order requiring that he or she post a bond. Injunctions can be divided into four categories: • techniques for assuring the production and protection of evidence; • devices to preserve the status quo between parties or to preserve property; • measures to protect persons; and • measures to protect the court's jurisdiction. In addition to these injunctions, Brazilian courts have general powers to authorise or prohibit practices or acts and to issue provisional measures they deem necessary to avoid future damages.

The standard civil proceeding of a state or federal court begins with the filing of the complaint in the lower civil courts. This states:

- the judge or court to which it is directed;
- a description of the litigants;
- the facts and legal grounds for the claim;
- the claim and its specifications;
- the value of the matter under dispute;
- the evidence that the plaintiff intends to bring forth; and
- a formal request for service of summons on the defendant.

The complaint should also be accompanied by any documents necessary to substantiate its claims.

The defendant has the right to file an answer. Once summoned (by mail, court clerk or public notice), the defendant has 15 days to present a defence. The defendant may submit various types of defence during this period, including a plea of lack of jurisdiction if they do not agree with the criteria adopted by the plaintiff for choosing the place to file the suit. These matters must be decided before any others. The defendant may also file a counterclaim if the claims have a connected subject.

Following the defence, the plaintiff may reply. The defendant will probably also be entitled to a rejoinder. The plaintiff also has 15 days in which to defend against a counterclaim, and a further reply and rejoinder may also follow.

The judge might establish a conciliatory hearing. If this is successful, the proceeding is finished. If the parties decide not to conciliate, the case will proceed to a phase of production of evidence (ie, filing of extra documents, depositions of witness and production of expert testimony).

After the production of evidence and with all the necessary elements in hand, the judge will finally decide the case. This decision, as explained before, may be subject to appeal. The first instance phase may last from one to five years, depending on the scope and length of the evidence production phase.

Based on Article 300 of the Civil Procedure Code, the defendant must raise all its arguments of defence at the first opportunity. It must make a full exposition of its version of the facts and considerations of the law; otherwise the claimant's allegations will be considered true. If a counterclaim is to be filed, it must be done simultaneously with the defence.

The party that initiates proceedings must bear the costs of initiation. Similarly, the party that files an appeal must pay the costs of that appeal. Each court has a different method for calculating its costs, but it is usually a percentage of the amount under dispute (between 1% and 5%). After the final decision, the defeated party reimburses the winning party for all court costs, including up to 20% of the disputed amount as fees for the winning party's attorney.

According to Article 835 of the Civil Procedure Code, foreign claimants must pay initial costs and post a bond of up to 20% of the amount under dispute. This aims to guarantee future payment of costs and the other party's attorney's fees should the foreign claimant lose.

Brazilian courts have very specific rules on how defendants should be summoned in court proceedings. These have further implications on the recognition of a foreign court decision in Brazil. Summons in a Brazilian court case must be made by means of a letter delivered by a court official or by registered post. A copy of the complaint must be attached in both cases.

Summons to parties resident outside Brazil have to be made through a diplomatic letter rogatory. A lawyer's fax and/or letter, for example, is insufficient. Summons of a Brazilian party in a legal action initiated at a foreign court must also be made through diplomatic channels. Such documents must be translated into Portuguese by an official translator and sent to Brazil through both countries' embassies. In Brazil, the service is supervised by a Brazilian court and carried out by a court official.

Full disclosure is not allowed in Brazilian civil proceedings. However, parties may request the disclosure of documents from the court. In this case they should specify in detail the document and its purpose, indicating the facts that relate to the document and the circumstances, and the grounds on which the party bases its belief that the document exists and is in the possession of the other party.

Evidence may consist of personal deposition by the litigants, the oral testimony of witnesses, expert examination and the filing of documents. Under Brazilian civil procedure, the burden of proof generally rests with the plaintiff, concerning the facts relating to its rights; and with the defendant, as to the existence of any facts that might impair, modify or extinguish the plaintiff's rights. However, certain legislation (eg, the Brazilian Consumer Code) provides exceptions to this rule.

The judge will not allow any party not to disclose evidence if:

- the party has the legal obligation to disclose;

- the party made reference to a document as part of its evidence; or
- the content of the document is common to both parties.

After evidence has been submitted, the judge shall grant a decision. In a suit for damages, for instance, the award is given on the basis of the actual losses sustained by the plaintiff and what they have reasonably failed to earn as a result of the defendant's conduct. The Brazilian courts do not normally award punitive damages like those of the US legal system. As a general rule, the damages should be commensurate with the extent of the injury.

When a decision is published, the defeated party typically has 15 days to appeal. Afterwards, the winning party is notified to present its counterarguments within the same period. If an appeal is filed in a proper and timely manner, it is distributed to the court of appeal. An appeal is generally distributed to one of the second-instance judgment panels, which usually comprise five judges. Appeals are heard by a body of three judges, one of whom is designated the reporting judge and who will prepare a report on the case.

In principle, an appeal prevents the creditor from enforcing the first-instance decision. As a rule, enforcement may be initiated only once the court of appeal has confirmed the first-instance decision against the debtor. However, this enforcement is provisional until the decision in the creditor's favour is finally judged. For this reason, the judgment creditor may be required to post bond to secure the indemnity payable to the judgment debtor for losses arising from the provisional enforcement should the decision be reversed by the court of appeal.

Depending on the matter and on the circumstances of judgment in the second-instance court, the interested party may also file a special appeal to the Superior Court of Justice and/or an extraordinary appeal to the Supreme Court. As explained above, the admissibility of such appeals is subject to formal review.

Legal fees are agreed between an attorney and his or her client; in the absence of such an agreement, they are determined by court order. In either case, fees are paid by whoever has retained the corresponding legal services. Attorneys sponsoring litigation cases in court are also entitled to loss-of-suit fees. These are payable by the defeated litigant to the winning party's attorney.

Loss-of-suit fees are set by the judge in each case. As a rule, they range between 10% and 20% of the award. If the award entails a nominal or non-ascertainable value, or if there is no sentencing involved, the fees are set by the judge after equitable consideration. If loss of suit is reciprocal, attorneys' fees are payable in a reciprocal and proportionate manner.

It is not possible to estimate how long it will take for a final judgment to be rendered. As a rough estimate, lower court decisions take at least three years to be handed down. Second-instance decisions are usually rendered within three years. These estimates may vary depending on the complexity of the controversy and the subject of the claim. Expert examinations and procedural obstacles raised by the defendant may also delay the final judgment.

Finally, Brazil also has a class actions legal system. Class actions may be filed by the federal or state public prosecutor's office, the federal government, the states, municipalities, certain public entities and civil associations legally organised one year before the case is filed. Class actions can deal with consumer, environmental or economic issues, or any other community or collective rights. If no public entity is involved and the case is not filed by a federal prosecutor, Brazilian state courts have jurisdiction over these actions. In any case, the public prosecutor's office will always act as legal custodian, no matter what the subject.

There are no certification proceedings for class actions filed by civil associations in Brazil. The only requirement is one year's prior organisation and thematic pertinence between the social purpose of the association and the subject of the case filed. For cases dealing with consumer issues filed by civil associations, the judge may even waive the one-year prior organisation requirement.

(c) *Arbitration*

Although litigation continues to be important in Brazil, the use of arbitration has been increased in recent years as a valid and efficient way of dealing with disputes, especially in the oil and gas sector.

The Brazilian legal system has always been conservative and quite bureaucratic in adopting arbitration. However, this scenario changed in 1996 with the enactment of the Arbitration Law, which created specific means for enforcing arbitration clauses and awards, and established the general features of arbitration in the country. Five years later the Supreme Court recognised the constitutionality of the Arbitration Law. The positive growth of arbitration in Brazil was further boosted by the country's ratification of the New York Convention, in 2002.[4]

Since then, arbitration in Brazil has developed quickly and strongly, and is becoming one of the most important methods for dispute resolution in the country. The oil and gas industries have long favoured arbitration for settling disputes.

One of the main reasons for this steady development is the unquestionable support of the Brazilian courts, in particular the Superior Court of Justice in Brasilia, which is responsible for deciding the last appeals on court cases and for recognising foreign arbitration awards for future enforcement.

Brazil is therefore considered a convenient place for arbitration which provides foreign and Brazilian parties with a reliable, binding and faster method for dispute resolution than the courts. This is especially the case for complex contracts and transactions in which there is a need for a deeper and more specialised examination of the matter under discussion.

---

4 Brazil had already ratified certain bi- or multi-lateral treaties on arbitration. Within the sphere of MERCOSUR, three are noteworthy:

- In 1992, Brazil signed the Lãs Leñas Protocol with Argentina, Paraguay and Uruguay, providing for international judicial co-operation among the MERCOSUR countries and, among other matters, regulating recognition and enforcement of foreign arbitral awards;
- In 1994, Brazil signed the Buenos Aires Protocol, also with Argentina, Paraguay and Uruguay, which provides for the parties' free will to choose the competent jurisdiction to settle conflicts arising from international agreements and authorises the parties to elect arbitration as a method for resolution of their disputes; and
- In 1996, the same year in which the Brazilian Arbitration Law was enacted, Brazil ratified the Inter-American Convention on International Commercial Arbitration (Panama Convention) of January 30 1975.

Although there are some exceptions, the Brazilian judiciary has not failed to grant emergency conservation measures, whether to assure the institution and opening of an arbitration tribunal or, after arbitration has begun, to guarantee the effectiveness of the award.

In general terms, the judiciary has also guaranteed the enforcement of awards rendered in Brazil and abroad, and has tended to trust the effectiveness of the arbitration clause and enforceability of awards issued by arbitration tribunals. This trend will boost the number of arbitration procedures involving Brazilian companies in the near future.

The following is a brief overview of the main aspects of the Arbitration Law.

Arbitration clause: Under the Arbitration Law, both arbitration clause and arbitration agreement are binding. An arbitration clause, when clearly defined and inserted in an agreement, is binding and enforceable. The great innovation of the law lies in its Article 7, which provides that "when there is an arbitration clause and also resistance against instituting arbitration, the interested party may petition for service of process on the other party to appear in court in order to sign the arbitration agreement, the judge to schedule a special hearing for such purpose". The action will therefore be for compulsory or specific performance of the arbitration clause.

Procedure: The Arbitration Law states that the arbitration procedure must comply with that agreed upon in the arbitration agreement. This may refer to the rules of an arbitration institution or specialised entity. If no provision is made regarding the arbitration procedure, the arbitrators will regulate it.

The Arbitration Law also allows the parties to adopt, under an arbitration clause and/or in an arbitration agreement, the rules of an institutional arbitration body or specialised entity, whether Brazilian or foreign. They may also choose for arbitration itself to be administered by that entity, without affect the place of arbitration. The parties are further allowed to choose the place of arbitration – which may be in Brazil or abroad – as well as the language in which arbitration will be conducted.

In this way it is possible for the parties, whether they are Brazilian or not, to resolve their disputes in accordance with the rules of any specialised arbitration body. However, during the arbitration proceedings the principles of due process, equality of treatment and the arbitrator's impartiality must be observed.

Although the parties may choose an international entity for arbitration, there are excellent arbitration bodies in Brazil.

Evidence: The availability of discovery and disclosure proceedings depends on the rules governing the arbitration. However, the parties are free to agree on such a pre-hearing discovery/disclosure if the rules in place do not provide for one.

Confidentiality: The confidentiality of arbitration proceedings is not a given. If the parties want a private and confidential arbitration, the arbitration agreement must set out a specific provision ruling on this.

Language: The parties are free to choose the language in which the arbitration is conducted, as well as the nationality of the arbitrators.

Arbitrators: The parties are able to choose a qualified person with full knowledge of the type of contract under discussion. This differs from the judiciary, where disputes are decided by a judge who is often unfamiliar with highly complex transactions. It is also important to point out that the arbitration tribunal will devote a substantial amount of time to reaching the best solution for both parties. This does not occur at court, where the judge has to cope with a heavy workload and might not concentrate on one single case.

It is also worth mentioning that there is no restriction on the number of arbitrators who may be chosen. The same is true of the method of selection of arbitrators. The parties are therefore free to determine the number and method for selection of arbitrator as they wish.

Arbitrability: There are some areas of law in Brazil in which, based on the requirements indicated in Article 1 of the Arbitration Law,[5] arbitration cannot be used. These include family-related disputes, some environmental law disputes and compliance with competition requirements etc.[6] Questions still remain over the use of arbitration in labour matters (although the law allows the resolution of disputes arising from strike rights, as well as the participation of employees in the sharing of profits and revenues), consumer protection, bankruptcy-related cases and other instances.

Court intervention: Local courts may intervene in the arbitration procedure in the following cases:

- should one of the parties wish to seek injunction relief in court;
- should one of the parties challenge the commencement of the arbitration, in which case the interested party may seek a court order to compel the challenging party to take part of the arbitration; and
- should the arbitrators seek a court order to compel witnesses to attend the hearing.

The parties may also request a court order to annul the arbitration award, provided that they can provide evidence, for example, that the arbitration agreement is null under Brazilian law or the award was made by an arbitrator who is not recognised by law.

Local courts will frustrate arbitration only if one of the parties seeks a court order to declare the arbitration award null and void. This will happen if:

---

5 Article 1: The eligible parties to a contract may refer any dispute as to defeasible equity rights to arbitration.

6 "Nonarbitrable matters (incompetency, matters involving a nondisposable right, violation of good moral principles and public order) must be examined ex officio by a regular judge or upon the request of an interested party at any time or at any court level, since the negative and positive effects of the arbitration agreement most certainly do not apply to these." (Antunes da Costa, Nilton César, *Efeitos Processuais da Convenção de Arbitragem*, Ed. Servanda, São Paulo: 2006, pg. 141).

- the arbitration agreement is found null and void;
- the arbitrator does not have the power to serve as an arbitrator;
- the legal requirements set out in the Article 26 of the Arbitration Law are not observed;
- the award is rendered beyond the boundaries of the arbitration agreement;
- the award does not settle all the issues to be arbitrated; or
- the award infringes the principles of due process and ample defence.

Award and enforcement: The arbitration awards made in Brazil are as effective as a decision from the courts and are similarly enforceable. The defeated party may not resort to the judicial courts to reverse the decision.

Foreign judgemnts are treated differently: The Constitution, the Civil Procedure Code, the Arbitration Law and the internal regulations of the Superior Court of Justice all require that foreign judgements to be enforced in Brazil be ratified by the Superior Court of Justice. The place of arbitration is particularly relevant in this context, since Article 10 of the Arbitration Law states that the arbitration agreement must give "the place where the award will be rendered"; and Article 34 establishes that "a foreign arbitral award is one rendered outside of the Brazilian territory".

Experience shows that requests to have foreign judgments recognised take an average of two years to be granted. In view of this, it may be better to choose Brazil as the place of arbitration when at least one of the parties is Brazilian and its assets are situated there. Awards rendered in Brazil are considered domestic and do not need further recognition from the superior court of justice.

Article 23 of the Arbitration Law rules that the award may be handed down within the term established by the parties. If no term has been pre-established, the award may be rendered within 180 days from the beginning of the arbitration proceedings. The parties may extend this term at any time during the proceedings.

State entities. Finally, the ability of public administration bodies to contract may be limited by the so-called principle of strict lawfulness. This is contained in Article 37 of the Constitution. According to this, public bodies may contract only as expressly permitted by the law. There is still controversy in this area, but it seems that the Brazilian courts have adopted the understanding that state-owned companies may bring disputes to arbitration, provided that these disputes derive from commercial activities and are not related to non-disposable rights.

The view in Brazil today is that arbitration is an effective and expeditious way to settle litigation, as opposed to the lengthy Brazilian court process. Such disputes usually require highly specialised knowledge and a fast resolution.

The growth of new oil and gas projects across Brazil thanks to ambitious energy programmes is provoking a substantial increase in demand for arbitration.

2.3 Requirements of the Petroleum Law

The exploration and production of hydrocarbons are regulated by both the Petroleum Law and the new Pre-Salt Law (Law 1,2351/2011). In addition to extensive regulation, these activities are specifically regulated by the relevant granting instruments – that is, concession agreements. These are formalised under the concession regime established by the Petroleum Law and, more recently, the Pre-Salt Law, which established the production sharing agreement regime.

Considering the significant sums involved and the need to avoid interruptions to activities or delaying operations, the oil and gas industry has tried to minimise conflicts as much as possible. When a dispute is unavoidable, parties usually seek the fastest way to solve it, with the least impact on their activities.

For these reasons, arbitration clauses are currently adopted throughout the worldwide oil and gas industry. A wide range of topics is subject to arbitration in the oil and gas sector, including:

- disputes arising from concession agreements, licenses, service contracts and so on;
- disputes between members of joint operation agreements; and
- conflicts arising in the course of agreements related to the downstream oil sector (including sales, transportation, lifting, service rendering and other agreements).

The Petroleum Law established that concession agreements must include rules on dispute resolution, including the use of international arbitration:

The concession contract must accurately reflect terms set forth within the respective invitation to bid and within the approved proposal. Essential stipulations shall include: … rules for settling disputes related to the contract and its performance, including reconciliation and international arbitration.[7]

The Petroleum Law also provides that the ANP's internal rules should establish the proceeding applicable to dispute resolution between economic agents and consumers, with an emphasis on reconciliation and arbitration. This is established in Article 20 of the Petroleum Law:

The bylaws of the ANP will govern the proceedings and will be used to settle disputes between economic agents and between these and users and consumers, with emphasis on reconciliation and arbitration.

Since the enactment of the Petroleum Law, all concession agreements include an arbitration clause. Arbitration therefore leads other permissible methods, such as expert determination and conciliation, as the main dispute resolution mechanism under the concession regime. The most recent concession agreement, dated 2008, established the following:

Applicable Law

3.1 This Agreement will be executed, governed and construed in accordance with Brazilian law, which will be strictly enforced by the Concessionaire in the exercise of its rights and performing its obligations.

7 Petroleum Law, Article 43.

Conciliation

3.2 The Parties shall make every effort to resolve any dispute or controversy arising from this Agreement or related to it in an amicable way. They may also, provided that unanimously agreed in writing, resort to an international expert, who shall provide a reasoned opinion, which may lead to settlement of the dispute or controversy.

3.3 After execution of an agreement for intervention of an international expert in accordance with paragraph 31.2, recourse to arbitration, as provided in paragraph 31.5, may only be exercised after this expert has issued a reasoned opinion.

Suspension of Activities

3.4 In the event of dispute or controversy, ANP shall decide whether activities involved in the dispute or controversy shall be stayed during the decision procedure, using as a criteria for its decision the necessity to avoid risks to personnel or material of any kind, particularly with regard to the Operations.

'Ad hoc' arbitration

31.5 If at any time a Party considers that there are no conditions for an amicable solution for dispute or controversy as referred to in paragraph 31.2, the dispute or controversy shall be submitted to ad hoc arbitration, using as parameter the rules of the Court of Arbitration of the International Chamber of Commerce and in accordance with the following rules:

(A) The choice of arbitrators will follow the proceeding established in the Rules of the Court of Arbitration of the International Chamber of Commerce.

(B) The dispute shall be settled by a three-arbitrator's panel. Each Party shall choose one arbitrator. The two arbitrators shall appoint the third arbitrator, who shall serve as president.

(C) The City of Rio de Janeiro, Brazil shall be the place of arbitration and delivery of the award.

(D) The language to be used in the arbitration proceeding shall be Portuguese. The Parties may, however, present statements or documents in another language if the arbitrators so authorise.

(E) On the merits, the arbitrators shall decide the dispute under Brazilian laws.

(F) The award shall be final and binding upon the parties.

(G) If there is a need for precautionary measures, whether preparatory or incidental, the Party concerned may request them directly to courts, based on the applicable legislation.

Jurisdiction

31.6 For the purposes of Law 9307/96, on issues related to non-disposable rights, the Parties hereby elect the Federal Court – Judicial Section of Rio de Janeiro, Brazil as the only competent authority, expressly waiving any other courts, however privileged they may be."[8]

8 Free translation of 31st Concession Agreement referring to the 10th round, according to the draft made available at www.anp.gov.br.

As with previous bidding rounds, the agreement is governed by Brazilian law. This follows from Article 9 of the Law of Introduction to the Civil Code, which requires agreements to be subject to the place in which they are made. Concession agreements settled in Brazil are therefore subject to Brazilian law.

The clause stipulates that in the event of a conflict, the parties will try to settle through conciliation. It also establishes that the parties may agree in writing to submit their disputes to an international expert, who will provide a reasoned opinion. It is important to note that this step is not mandatory or essential to initiate an arbitration. Parties may then initiate arbitration proceedings even without having attempting to conciliate. However, if the parties do decide to involve an international expert, arbitration can be established only once that expert's opinion has been submitted.

Sub-item 31.5 of the clause quoted above provides for *ad hoc* arbitration as a resolution mechanism. Disputes in this case will be decided by a three-arbitrator panel; each party will choose one arbitrator, and these two will appoint a third arbitrator, who will serve as president. The arbitration will take place in Rio de Janeiro and will be conducted in Portuguese. Brazilian law will apply. Finally, the arbitration clause stresses that the award will be final and binding.

Although the last item of the clause authorises the parties to request urgent or interim measures directly from the courts, arbitrators are generally able to grant such orders once tribunal has been installed. Therefore, courts will be able to entertain such requests only in specific cases, where it is impossible to request the arbitrators to do so, or when such a request may be ineffective (eg, when arbitrators does not have enough power to order attachment or seizure).

It is important to stress that, in line with previous concession agreements, Clause 31.6 provides that the courts in Rio de Janeiro have jurisdiction over disputes regarding non-disposable rights. This provision is in accordance with the Arbitration Law, which stipulates that only "disposable patrimonial rights" may be subject to arbitration proceedings. This comprises rights that can be "renounced", "transferred" or "assigned"; that is, characteristics not inherent to the public interest.

In fact, and regardless of the above clause, the Administrative Law establishes that public interests are not disposable, so the use of arbitration in cases involving such rights is not permissible.

The interpretation of this legal provision has given rise to extensive debate among legal specialists concerning the legality of those provisions that support arbitration in the Petroleum Law and concession agreements, since these involve natural resources and public interests.

Considering that the concession agreements deal with oil and gas resources, with the federal union, through the ANP, as a party to the contract, authorising arbitration has triggered a controversy. This is based on the fact that the arbitrability of certain public concerns and the capacity of public entities to enter into arbitration clauses is disputed under the Arbitration Law.

Different opinions have emerged. Some scholars support the arbitrability of the rights under the concession agreements, stating that it would be necessary to distinguish only whether the dispute refers to non-disposable rights (ie, public interests) or merely to private rights.

On the other hand, others state that using arbitration in concession agreements is impossible due to the public nature of the rights involved, and because of the presence of the federal union, through the ANP. This opinion is a formal interpretation of the provisions made in Article 1 of the Arbitration Law.

A third group of specialists argue that arbitration is possible only when a previous law has authorised its use in a specific situation. Without this legal provision, the public entity is forbidden from entering into an arbitration agreement, since as a rule, the public interest is involved.

Despite this controversy, the Brazilian oil sector has seen 10 bidding rounds since the creation of the concession regime in 1997 and, as a general rule, all of the concession agreements have established arbitration as the main mechanism for dispute resolution.

The more recent production sharing agreement regime has only confirmed the possibility of using arbitration. Article 29 of the Pre-Salt Law determines that agreements will contain rules for dispute resolution proceedings, and these may include conciliation and arbitration:

The following clauses are considered essential clauses in the Production Sharing Agreement:

... the rules regarding the dispute resolution proceedings, which may establish the use of conciliation and arbitration.

This recent legal provision confirms that arbitration has been considered, at least from the legislative point of view, as a valid mechanism for the oil and gas sector. This may prove an interesting option, taking into account the potential advantages of such a method. However, it remains to be seen how the courts will decide on the validity of arbitration clauses in specific cases.

Finally, it is worth mentioning that there are specific cases where a dispute may fall outside the concession agreement and, therefore, may not be subject to the arbitration clause. For example, the relationship between oil companies combining efforts in a bid round lies beyond the regulated sphere. Companies most commonly enter into a joint bidding agreement, and are free to choose both the applicable law and dispute resolution proceedings to regulate their rights and obligations.

It is therefore necessary to consider carefully which rights or contractual relations are at issue in order to identify the applicable dispute resolution methods – arbitration or the courts.

3. Conclusion

The most common type of dispute resolution proceedings remains litigation. However, the development of so-called alternative methods, such as conciliation, mediation and arbitration, must also be noted. Arbitration in Brazil has developed quickly and is becoming one of the most important methods for dispute resolution in the corporate sphere.

Both the Petroleum Law and the new Pre-Salt Law determine that the concession agreements and production sharing agreements must contain rules for resolving disputes, which may include conciliation and arbitration. In fact, all concession agreements have favoured arbitration for resolving disputes involving disposable rights. The Brazilian courts are thus given jurisdiction to settle disputes with regard to non-disposable rights and precautionary measures, when they cannot be granted by the arbitration tribunal.

Nevertheless, the oil and gas industries have favoured arbitration for settling disputes. Among the benefits of this are:

- swiftness of proceedings;
- confidentiality; and
- the possibility of choosing specialist arbitrators with specific knowledge of the industry.

This last benefit is one of the most attractive to the industry.

The new challenges of the pre-salt regime and the rapid growth of the oil industry in Brazil invite companies and professionals to follow closely the development of the industry's dispute resolution mechanisms.

About the authors

Décio Pio Borges de Castro
Senior associate, Pinheiro Neto Advogados
dpioborges@pn.com.br

Décio Pio Borges de Castro graduated with an LLB from the Catholic University of Rio de Janeiro (PUC) (2003) and with an MBA in corporate finance from *Fundação Getúlio Vargas* (FGV) (2009). He is a senior associate of the corporate/banking practice of Pinheiro Neto's Rio de Janeiro office, where he works mainly on mergers and acquisitions, project finance and capital markets transactions. Mr Borges de Castro has advised several Brazilian and foreign companies, financial institutions and international economic groups on M&A transactions, private equity investments and divestitures, project finance, corporate finance and capital markets deals. He has also advised foreign clients on exchange, insurance and oil and gas regulation.

Jorge Tuffi Pasin Dib Cassab
Junior associate, Pinheiro Neto Advogados
jtcassab@pn.com.br

Jorge Tuffi Pasin Dib Cassab holds an LLB from the São Paulo Catholic University (2011).

His experience comprises litigation and consultation on environmental law, with an emphasis on the energy sector, and litigation in public civil actions.

Luiz Claudio Campos
Partner, Ernst & Young Terco
luiz-claudio.campos@br.ey.com

Luiz Claudio Campos is the partner in charge of the project finance group of Ernst & Young in Brazil, with a focus on energy, transport and infrastructure clients. He has an economics degree and an MBA, and has specialised in private finance initiative (PFI)/public-private partnership (PPP) projects and other project-financed transactions for over 15 years while based in Rio de Janeiro and São Paulo.

In particular, Mr Campos has led Ernst & Young teams throughout Brazil and Latin America on a number of leading PFI/PPP transactions in a variety of sectors, including multibillion-real oil refinery projects and airport concession projects in Brazil. In addition, he is the leading partner of the transaction advisory services team in Ernst & Young's oil and gas centre, located in Rio de Janeiro.

Ludmilla Corkey
Senior associate, Pinheiro Neto Advogados
lcorkey@pn.com.br

Ludmilla Corkey is a senior associate at Pinheiro Neto Advogados. Before joining Pinheiro Neto's oil and gas practice, she worked for integrated oil companies for over 10 years, advising on regulatory matters, business development projects, M&A transactions, infrastructure projects and oil and gas marketing. Ms Corkey received her BA and MPhil from the Catholic University of Rio de Janeiro, her LLB from Candido Mendes University and her LLM from Columbia University School of Law in New York. Ms Corkey began her career in the Rio de Janeiro office of El Paso Corporation. She also worked in Statoil's offices in Rio and in Oslo.

Elina Cunha
Counsel, Pinheiro Neto Advogados
ecunha@pn.com.br

Elina Cunha is a counsel in the litigation department of Pinheiro Neto law firm in Rio de Janeiro. She practises in the litigation field, with a focus on administrative, environmental and construction law (consultation, negotiation of contracts and judicial/arbitration litigation). She holds an LLB from the Rio de Janeiro State University (1996), with a postgraduate degree in environmental law from the COPPE Engineering School of the Federal University of Rio de Janeiro (2008).

She has been practising in the private sector for more than 16 years. Before joining Pinheiro Neto Advogados in 2000, she worked in the legal department of Construtora Norberto Odebrecht (1995-2000), where she served as direct adviser to the managing officer for the North/Central-Western Region (1998-2000).

Andrew Duncan
Director, Bank of America Merrill Lynch
andrew.duncan@baml.com

Andrew Duncan joined Bank of America Merrill Lynch in September 2010 and is currently a director in the energy and metals finance team within the corporate banking division. Mr Duncan has over eight years of oil and gas finance experience, having worked for The Royal Bank of Scotland and Halifax Bank of Scotland providing structured financings to exploration and production independents for producing and development assets. Prior to banking, Mr Duncan spent 10 years in industry as a chartered mechanical engineer, where he designed topsides facilities for UK North Sea platforms as well as designing fluidised catalytic cracking units for multiple refineries in Europe. Mr Duncan has a BEng (Hons) in mechanical engineering from Nottingham University and an MBA from London Business School, and is a chartered member of the Institute of Mechanical Engineers.

José Virgilio Lopes Enei
Partner, Machado, Meyer, Sendacz & Opice Advogados
jvirgilio@machadomeyer.com.br

Virgilio Enei is the co-head of the infrastructure and energy department of Machado Meyer law firm, headquartered in Sao Paulo, Brazil. He has practised for more than 15 years at Machado Meyer, and has developed extensive experience in M&A, project finance and other transactional matters in sectors such as oil and gas, electricity, renewables and transportation.

Mr Enei obtained law degrees and an MBA in Brazil and an LLM in the United States. He is also admitted to practise in New York, where he worked as a foreign associate for Dewey Ballantine LLP from 2000 to 2001. Mr Enei has been consecutively named as a leading attorney in the fields of projects and energy by *Chambers Global, International Financial Law Review* and other major publications.

Andrea Falcão
Lawyer
abfb@globo.com

Andrea Falcão is a recognised lawyer with more than 20 years' practice. She recently left her position as a partner in the oil and gas practice of Vieira, Rezende, Barbosa e Guerreiro Advogados to lead the legal department of a leading services company in the oil industry.

Ms Falcão combines deep technical knowledge of the upstream segment of the oil industry with solid legal experience. She is known for her familiarity with typical instruments and agreements pertaining to international oil law, such as unitisation and joint operating agreements and charter agreements involving maritime rigs and floating production storage and offloading facilities.

Ms Falcão holds a bachelor's degree in law from *Universidade Cândido Mendes* in Rio de Janeiro. She also holds an executive postgraduate degree in oil from the COPPE Engineering School of the Federal University of Rio de Janeiro. She is a member of the Brazilian Petroleum Institute and of the Association of International Petroleum Negotiators.

Luis Cláudio Furtado Faria
Senior associate, Pinheiro Neto Advogados
lcfaria@pn.com.br

Luis Cláudio Furtado Faria is a senior associate at Pinheiro Neto Advogados. He joined the firm in 2000 in the dispute resolution and litigation team. His practice focuses on administrative and judicial litigation, national and international arbitration. Mr Faria received an LLB from *Universidade do Estado do Rio de Janeiro* (2003). In 2008 he received a master's in civil law from the same university. Mr Faria also received an LLM in international commercial law from Queen Mary University of London (2010). In 2011 he was a foreign associate at Herbert Smith LLP and Reed Smith LLP, both in London. He also practised at the Secretariat of the International Court of Arbitration of the International Chamber of Commerce, Paris (2011).

Felipe Rodrigues Caldas Feres
Associate, Campos Mello Advogados
felipe.feres@dlapiper.com

Felipe Rodrigues Caldas Feres is an associate in Campos Mello Advogados' energy and corporate practices, currently seconded to DLA Piper LLP's New York office.

His focus is on energy project development and financing in the oil and gas (upstream and downstream) and related maritime sector, as well as in power and renewables. He also has considerable experience in mergers and acquisitions in several economic sectors.

Other key areas of practice include foreign investments in Brazil, general corporate and civil law, regulatory law and overall infrastructure development and financing.

Mr Caldas Feres holds an LLM from the University of Chicago Law School (2010), a postgraduate degree in corporate and capital markets law from the Getúlio Vargas Foundation (2008) and a BA in Law from the Pontifical Catholic University of Rio de Janeiro (2006).

Camila Galvão Anderi Silva
Partner, Machado, Meyer, Sendacz e Opice Advogados
canderi@machadomeyer.com.br

Camila Galvão Anderi Silva is a partner in the tax practice at Machado, Meyer, Sendacz e Opice Advogados in Brazil. She has a postgraduate degree in tax law (*Faculdade de Direito da Pontifícia Universidade Católica de São Paulo*, Brazil) and advises on taxation and administrative litigation. She has extensive knowledge of the taxation of imports and supply chains.

Ms Silva has advised several foreign companies on the structuring of activities in Brazil and works directly with foreign investors involved in the manufacture or commercialisation of products.

She has also been involved in several relevant projects, tax issues and administrative proceedings involving energy and oil and gas companies, acquiring important insight into the operational aspects and the main tax discussions arising from such activities.

Werner Grau Neto
Partner, Pinheiro Neto Advogados
wgrau@pn.com.br

Werner Grau Neto is a partner in the sustainability and climate change team at Pinheiro Neto Advogados in São Paulo. He holds a law degree and has specialised in environmental law. He also has a master's in international law from the University of São Paulo and a PhD in tax law from the same institution.

He has coordinated the Environment and Energy Group and the Carbon Market and Climate Change Group at the International Chamber of Commerce, where he is a member of the Environment Legal Group. Furthermore, he has been deeply engaged in a number of committees, such as the Environmental Law Committee of the Brazil-Germany Chamber of Commerce and Industry.

He has also been a consultant at the Inter-American Development Bank, the German Technical Cooperation Agency and the World Bank. He is the current chairman of the executive board at the Nature Conservancy in Brazil.

Maria Christina M Gueorguiev
Senior associate, Pinheiro Neto Advogados
mgueorguiev@pn.com.br

Maria Christina Gueorguiev graduated from the University of São Paulo School of Law, and holds a specialist degree in environmental management from the State University of Campinas and an LLM from University College London.

She has practised in the private sector for more than 10 years, and her experience involves a variety of legal matters across the environmental area, including climate change and sustainability.

Ms Gueorguiev has participated in several infrastructure projects, involving highways, oil and gas and power plants. Her experience also encompasses environmental M&A due diligence, advice to financial institutions on environmental matters, negotiations with public authorities and litigation in public civil actions. She has participated actively in the discussion and drafting of environmental laws and regulations, and lectures on environmental law at national events.

Luiz Antonio Lemos
Partner, Campos Mello Advogados
luizantonio.lemos@camposmello.adv.br

Luiz Antonio Lemos is a partner in Campos Mello Advogados' energy and corporate practices, based in Rio de Janeiro. He has extensive experience in the areas of infrastructure, oil and gas, power, biofuels, corporate, mergers and acquisitions, project finance and foreign investment.

His clients include Brazilian and international companies in many sectors, such as aerospace and defence, basic and advanced materials, energy and water, infrastructure and shipping offshore and transportation.

He worked for more than 14 years in the litigation and corporate areas in the legal department of Brazilian oil and gas multinational Petrobras, including a period as general counsel for Gaspetro, a subsidiary which undertakes gas-related activities. During his time at the company, he was involved in many projects, such as the Brazil-Bolivia Gas Pipeline project.

Mr Lemos holds a postgraduate degree in corporate law.

Luis Antonio Menezes
Senior associate, Campos Mello Advogados
luis.menezes@camposmello.adv.br

Luis Antonio Menezes da Silva is a senior associate in Campos Mello Advogados' energy and corporate practices, based in Rio de Janeiro. He practises across different areas of law, with a special emphasis on infrastructure, oil and gas, corporate and foreign investment and project finance.

Mr Menezes da Silva has extensive experience in corporate matters – in both upstream and downstream sectors – as well as other types of contract and project. He previously worked in the legal department of Petrobras Gás (Gaspetro), assisting on all legal aspects of the development of natural gas pipeline projects and the incorporation of natural gas state distributors.

Mr Menezes da Silva holds postgraduate degrees in corporate law and oil and gas.

Leonardo Miranda
Partner, Machado, Meyer, Sendacz & Opice Advogados
lmiranda@machadomeyer.com.br

Leonardo Miranda is a partner in the infrastructure department of Machado Meyer law firm, based in Rio de Janeiro. He practises M&A, project finance, contracts and regulatory law, with a focus on the natural resources industry.

Mr Miranda obtained law degrees and an MBA in Brazil and an LLM in the United Kingdom. He worked as a foreign associate for Allen & Overy LLP from 2004 to 2005. He has been named as a leading attorney in the field of natural resources by *Chambers Global* and is a member of the Association of International Petroleum Negotiators.

Eduardo Pereira
Corporate director, Petra Energia
egp@petraenergia.com.br

Eduardo Pereira has been active in the oil and gas industry for over five years, and is an expert on joint operating agreements. His experience in this area – both academic and practical – is extensive. Dr Pereira is corporate director of Petra Energia and chief legal officer and vice president of Petra BV. He has played a key role in assisting Petra Energia in becoming Brazil's leading onshore oil and gas company. He concluded his doctoral thesis on oil and gas joint ventures at the University of Aberdeen. Currently he is also a research fellow at the Oxford Institute for Energy Studies.

Daniela Ribeiro Davila
Partner, Vieira, Rezende, Barbosa e Guerreiro Advogados
dribeiro@vrbg.com.br

Daniela Ribeiro Davila coordinates the oil and gas/shipping-offshore practices at Vieira, Rezende, Barbosa e Guerreiro Advogados.

A pioneer in Brazilian petroleum law, and with extensive experience in the exploration and production and offshore industries, she advises ship owners on construction and charter agreements, and equipment and service providers on offshore contracts, as well as advising on the financing of offshore projects in general.

Ms Davila graduated in law from *Pontifícia Universidade Católica do Rio de Janeiro*. She has an MBA in economics and corporate law from the FGV Postgraduate School of Economics, and an MBA in petroleum business from the COPPE Engineering School of the Federal University of Rio de Janeiro. She is a member of the Brazilian Petroleum Institute and the Association of International Petroleum Negotiators.

Chambers Global and Latin America, *Latin Lawyer* and *Who's Who* have listed Ms Davila as a leading oil and gas practitioner in Brazil.

Marcelo Romanelli
Associate, Campos Mello Advogados
Marcelo.romanelli@camposmello.adv.br

Marcelo Romanelli de Oliveira is an associate in Campos Mello Advogados' energy and corporate practices, based in Rio de Janeiro. He practises across different areas of law, with a special emphasis on commercial contracts, corporate, energy sector infrastructure projects, oil and gas, power (hydro, thermo, wind and solar), regulatory and tax.

Before joining the firm, he was a tax consultant in Deloitte's oil and gas team in Rio de Janeiro, and then in the energy, infrastructure and utilities team in London.

Mr de Oliveira holds an LLM in petroleum

taxation and finance from the University of Dundee (United Kingdom).

Fernando Tonanni
Partner, Machado, Meyer, Sendacz e Opice Advogados
fernandotonanni@machadomeyer.com.br

Fernando Tonanni is a partner in the tax practice at Machado, Meyer, Sendacz e Opice Advogados, Brazil. He holds a postgraduate degree in tax law (*Faculdade de Direito da Pontifícia Universidade Católica de São Paulo*, Brazil), and an LLM in international tax law (University of Leiden, Netherlands). Mr Tonanni is a member of the Brazilian Bar Association, the *Associação Brasileira de Direito Financeiro*, the International Fiscal Association and the International Bar Association. He is also the coordinator of *Revista de Direito Tributario Internacional*, a Brazilian international tax law magazine.

Mr Tonanni's main area of expertise is direct taxation, with a focus on M&A, corporate restructurings, tax treaties, transfer pricing and taxation of financial investments. He has extensive experience in structuring foreign investments in the Brazilian infrastructure sector, such as in the energy, mining and oil and gas industries.

Marcelo Viveiros de Moura
Partner, Pinheiro Neto Advogados
mvmoura@pn.com.br

Marcelo Viveiros de Moura graduated with an LLB from the University of Rio de Janeiro Law School (UERJ – 1988) and with an LLM from the University of Cambridge (Hughes Hall, 1993). He is a partner in the corporate area of Pinheiro Neto's Rio de Janeiro office, having also worked as visiting associate at the London offices of Slaughter and May (1992). Mr Viveiros de Moura specialises in corporate law, with a focus on mergers and acquisitions and corporate restructuring; regulatory law in the oil and gas, capital markets and insurance areas; project and corporate finance; and government procurements and contracts. He is a professor of corporate law at the *Fundação Getúlio Vargas* Faculty of Law. He has served as chairman of the British-Brazilian Chamber of Commerce (2007-2009) and is currently a member of the board of the chamber.